LETTERS FROM THE I

THE
Sacred
YES

as revealed to
Rev. Deborah L. Johnson

N

New Brighton Books

Library of Congress Cataloging-in-Publication Data

Johnson, Deborah L., 1956-
    Letters from the Infinite /as revealed to Deborah L. Johnson,
      p. cm.
    Contents: v. I. The sacred yes.
    ISBN 0-9718377-0-8 (alk. paper)
    I. Spiritual life. 2. Spirit writings. 3. Private revelations. I. Title.

BF1301 .J575 2002
299'.93--dc21

                                              2002075371

DEDICATION

This book is dedicated in loving memory to
my sista-friend
Pamela Juliette Pilate
August 18, 1957 – February 2, 2001

"This is the Yes that whispers in your soul. This is the Yes that sings to you in the midnight hour. This is the Yes that cradles you when you are trembling in fear. This is the Yes that opens its arms and embraces you when you are feeling disconnected from everything and everybody, including yourself. This is the Yes that sustains you when you don't know where you are going to get the strength to take the next step, let alone finish the journey. This is the Yes that you are looking for in all of your conversations with everybody else. I AM THE YES! You turn to other people for these things and then get disappointed, when it was never theirs to give. Seek and ye shall find, yes; but you have to look where it can be found to find it. Come to me. You will find it in you, in me. YES!!!"

— Section One, *"Begin with Yes"*

The Sacred Yes

CONTENTS

INTRODUCTION: LETTER TO THE READER

SECTION ONE: BACK TO THE BASICS

SECTION TWO: FEEL, DEAL, AND HEAL

SECTION THREE: PRACTICING THE PRINCIPLES

SECTION FOUR: ONLY ONE OF US HERE

SECTION FIVE: SYSTEMS THAT SUPPORT

PREFACE

This book is a gift, a most precious tool for living, intended to encourage you to develop your own understanding of and relationship to Spirit. These letters are shared with you for no other purpose. Although they may not be addressed to you specifically, allow them to speak to you personally. Their lessons are universal, addressing the human condition common to us all. They provide solace, insight, and inspiration for our hurts, fears, hopes, hesitations, and aspirations. Seek your own fresh revelations; you do not need an intermediary. As you hear Spirit talking to you, reaching out to you, it will be the confirmation in your heart of the book's fundamental message that "God is with us!"—not just with some of us, but with all of us! These messages are given to all of us as evidence of this most sacred covenant.

Like life itself, *The Sacred Yes* transcends the linear. It is a spiral that keeps coming back to the same issues and principles, but on different levels. The practical applications of the key teaching points continuously expand. This spiral of awareness goes up and down, in and out, from the most personal, intimate level to broad global concerns. Each letter is a conversation, discrete in its own message. However, the dialogue is ongoing and the messages build upon each other; recurring concepts and themes are not redundant. There is no need to read the book sequentially. Feel free to drop in at any time, at any place, as you are moved.

As with any mystical book, the breadth and depth of the meaning of the messages are inexhaustible. Give yourself permission to come back to passages that you have already read. New insights are sure to be revealed in subsequent readings. Don't be concerned if you do not immediately grasp each and every concept. Be patient with yourself if you struggle to comprehend them in their entirety. Allow yourself the time and space to question, ponder, and contemplate. Your capacity to discern subtle nuances and understand their intricacies will expand and deepen as you study.

Each letter is considered to be a chapter, and the chapters are grouped into sections. Section one, "Back to the Basics," emphasizes spiritual fundamentals, bringing them to the forefront of our minds for conscious recognition. These Universal Principles serve as anchors that ground us in Spiritual Truths, providing a foundation for not merely the rest of the book but our very lives. Section two, "Feel, Deal, and Heal," focuses on healing and transformation. These letters are personal messages from Pure Spirit to us as human beings in the process of discovering our true spiritual nature while on the journey of life. Tender, yet firm, they address such issues as facing our fears, taking risks, letting go, authentic expression, peace of mind, integrity, and experiencing a personal relationship with God. They call for us to personally examine our motives, intent, and heart space for the purpose of creating more spiritual availability within ourselves.

Section three, "Practicing the Principles," integrates Spiritual Truth into our daily practice. It provides pragmatic steps for embodying Truth Principles so that we may incorporate them into our personal path. Section four, "Only One of Us Here," facilitates the integration of Spiritual Principles into our interpersonal relationships, encouraging us to strive for a balance between Spiritual Oneness and diversity of expression. These are communications about support, faith, love, trust, conflict resolution, forgiveness, unity, and a host of other subjects pertinent to healthy societal living. The letters of section five, "Systems That Support," address the institutionalization of our spiritual paradigms. These letters are primarily about spirituality, religion, and the church and how the structures and practices of each impact our lives. More than social commentaries, they are prophetic, with recommendations and suggestions for making life more equitable, rewarding, and compassionate for all.

In addition to experiencing it as a spiral, you might consider the book to unfold like a series of concentric circles, moving from the most personal and intimate applications to the more global and universal. It begins at the center with spiritual basics, the fundamentals of our relationship with the Divine. At this core we are also called upon to discover our Spiritual Truth and through healing our hurts and fears to expand our capacity to simply be. We are then called upon to apply this knowledge practically, first within the context of our own personal lives, then at an interactive level of

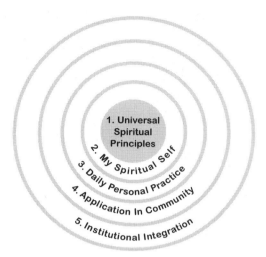

community, pushing still further out to our worldviews and institutional practices. Such primary spiritual concepts as love, truth, faith, surrender, Oneness, grace, and gratitude are addressed time and time again at higher levels with broadening levels of application.

The progression of the book also lays itself out along a hierarchy of concerns, much like Abraham Maslow's Hierarchy of Needs. Imagine an inverted triangle, if you will, with its apex at the bottom, broadening as it goes up. The letters within a particular section of the book represent a certain level of analysis designated by a specific stratum on the triangle. Our inquiry begins on the bottom stratum, with basic Spiritual Truth as the foundation of everything, and works its way up and out from there. Each successive section of the book addresses another level of analysis.

How must our spiritual systems be revamped?

How do I apply this to my relationships?

How do I practice what I know?

Who am I?

What's it all about?

This is not to imply that any level of inquiry is more important than any other—simply that there is a logical progression. We must first start with an understanding of spiritual basics. From there we move through the exploration of our own selves. We must then integrate the principles into our own daily living before we can incorporate them at a community level. We must live the principles at the community level before we can apply them globally. Taken out of sequence, our efforts to implement spiritual principles at more expanded levels have no roots in our hearts, no foundations in our consciousness upon which to build. We will never be at peace in the world until we are at peace in our own hearts and in our homes.

In some respects, the sections of the book also unfold like the classic archetype of the hero's journey. We begin with a calling. The Truth within beckons us to move beyond the familiar and to discover our true identity. Our first rite of initiation is to face ourselves and the demons lurking within our own minds. In our victory we are changed, healed, and transformed. On our journey we learn new ways of being and must integrate what we have learned along the way into our daily personal practice. After a certain degree of embodiment of what we have learned, we absolutely must return home to restore harmony, prosperity, and balance to our king/queendoms. Respect and compassion become the order of the day. The newly liberated sage within us must then go on to establish new paradigms and foundations for living, which we leave behind as our legacy, lest our journey be in vain.

The *Letters from the Infinite* series chronicles the latest segments of my own hero's journey. In order to explain the origins of these letters I begin with the call, the event that precipitated the first letter that came to me. In June of 1995, I was immersed in what is often referred to as a "dark night of the soul." Such periods are known for their catalytic potential to introduce us into new dimensions of spiritual awareness.

I had just completed a seminar that I had conducted at the International Association of Business Communicators Conference in Toronto. My itinerary called for me to return home the next day. Stealing a rare moment of relaxation while traveling, I went into the steam sauna in the women's locker room. I was alone, not merely in the sauna, but feeling very alone. At forty years of age, I found myself for the first time in my life about to return to an empty house after having experienced living as a couple since adolescence.

My heart was heavy and full of remorse for numerous bad decisions that I had made in the distant and not-so-distant past. I was grieving for the life I once knew and the life that I would clearly never have. Tired of it all, I moved into a deep inner place of surrender. Nothing was visible in the sauna, now filled with steam, except the dimmed hue of a single white light in the ceiling. Amid the mist it was truly celestial. Bare and sobbing, I outstretched my arms and cried out to the light to just take me now. I was ready to be rid of this life and all of its complexities.

The ensuing experience is still among the most profound of my life, reminiscent of the accounts from individuals who were technically dead for a short period and then revived. I had what can only be explained as an out-of-body death experience. My life flashed before me like in a slide show carousel. Each scene was a moment in time when I could have been kinder, more thoughtful, more loving, or more genuine. It was clear that this review was carefully crafted for my growth and awareness, not for criticism or judgment. Simultaneously, I felt both sadness and an odd sense of peace about it all. What I was most acutely aware of was having choice. I could have chosen to do things differently. It was also clear that I was going to be given another opportunity to make new choices.

It felt much more like a rebirth than a second chance. I have no recollection of any words per se, merely impressions. Yet the communication was undeniable. I was instructed to consummate this moment with a baptism. Directed to the swimming pool, I was told to fall back and allow myself to be totally immersed in the water. I was both incredibly present and in some altered state of alertness at the same time. There was no fear, merely awe.

When I returned to my hotel room, I had the uncontrollable urge to start writing. I hurried to my laptop computer, and my fingers started flying across the keyboard faster than I could control them. The moment was intense, focused, and very direct. Although I was fully conscious, absolutely nothing else could vie for my attention. Fascinated, I just went with the process to see where it would lead. The first words were, "Fear not, my Little One, for I am with you always. I know who you are and you are my own."

This process continued into the next day—while waiting in airports, while seated aboard airplanes. The messages I was receiving were so warm, embracing, direct, intimate, unwavering, insightful, compelling, and poetic. I had no way of knowing at the time where it all was leading.

For the first few years, the messages were captured exclusively in writing, either handwritten or on a computer. I continued to be amazed at their wisdom, and I had my challenges heeding their counsel. Learning to comply with their instructions without hesitation or reservation quickly became, and continues to be, the focal point of my spiritual practice. There was no particularly discernable rhyme or reason as to when the messages would come, although there was a propensity for them to present themselves at moments when I was already quite tired and exhausted.

I particularly resented being awakened in the middle of the night, especially if the message was coming to me for someone else. "Why don't you go wake them up?" was my general attitude. I later discovered that this tendency to disturb my sleep or rest was because I was more available at those moments. I was instructed to learn how to rest more without having to be so tired. I also learned to be more appreciative of being a conduit of information. As you will see, some of the letters, or parts of some letters, in this book are directed to specific groups of people who share common ideas and/or experiences.

Not fully understanding what the process was about, I was quite apprehensive about discussing the matter with anyone. I was too afraid of being discounted, ridiculed, or considered a weirdo. As it became clear that the messages were to be shared with others, I was especially afraid that people would judge me in the same manner in which I had misjudged the Pentecostal prophets of my youth. My mistaken impression of them, at the time, was that they were self-serving charlatans, hiding the sharpness of their wolves' teeth under sheep's clothing. So only a few very close friends were privy to this development in my life.

The first semipublic reading of a letter occurred in August, 1996. I shared the letter "Daring to Be Authentic" with the Vision Core members of Inner Light Ministries, the ministry that I was in the process of founding. (An excerpted version of that letter appears in this volume.) To this day, I continue to find the disclosing of these letters to be very much like the process of coming out regarding my sexual orientation. The letters reflect an intimacy in my relationship with the Divine that can easily be misunderstood, ridiculed, or condemned for being so far off the bell curve of societal norms. Also very much like coming out of the closet, I have learned not to stand in need of validation from others to affirm what I know to be real in my soul. Like the Afghani mystic Rumi, I am in a profound love affair with God for which I am neither apologetic nor ashamed.

Writing was the sole form of capturing the messages for the first few years. A pivotal moment came at the close of a workshop series that I had been conducting through my ministry. I was getting a message that I knew was for the people in the room, yet I was in no position to take the time to write it down. Though I was greatly apprehensive, I was persuaded to recite what I would have written. This was a totally new prospect for me, one that I was not certain I would be able to fulfill. I did manage to verbalize the message I was getting, which not only launched a new method of capturing the information but enhanced the overall process, as well.

Since that time, I typically speak the message into a tape recorder and transcribe the tape later. To date there are approximately 300 letters. This book contains 53; however, it should be noted that they are not in chronological order of date received. Nearly all of the letters in this first volume are transcriptions. It is important to point out that it is nearly impossible to reflect in print all of the subtle and not-so-subtle inferences blatantly apparent in the spoken word, especially the humor. So much of the richness of the content is in not merely what is said but how it is said. Be that as it may, the letters contained herein are an accurate reflection of the messages, which literally are given with full punctuation and grammatical notation. What you see here is essentially how the messages were received. Occasionally, punctuation has been added and personal references, sensitive to either time or privacy, have been deleted. The book is, however, void of any "cut and paste," with the exception of one letter that is in actuality a combination of two.

The first publisher interested in these letters described them well: "They're like jazz; they have a cadence, their own rhythm and beat." Original and authentic, they quite often defy literary conventions. The letters contain double entendres, paradoxical imagery, mixed metaphors, enmeshment of verb tenses, fluidity and nonagreement between the singular and plural, and unique applications of words that stretch their meanings. However, my dear connoisseurs of grammar, be not dismayed; all irregularities are purposeful and instructive. Every effort has been made to preserve the integrity of the messages as they move from an oral to a written medium. Parenthetical phrases, repetitive words, and ellipsis dots have been retained as delivered. Capital letters reference spiritual concepts in their absolute. Italics emphasize intensity and urgency. Rather than speed read through the letters, I strongly suggest that you slow down and take the time to hear the letters as though they are being spoken to you. In fact, reading them out loud to yourself will help you catch their rhythm and will enhance your appreciation of their syntax and story-telling quality.

Since so many questions arise among readers regarding how I receive the letters, I will attempt to address that curiosity up front. I am not channeling an entity. The messages come in the first-person voice of Spirit. I receive the letters through a combination of our known senses and a few others we are less familiar with. When I am receiving a message, I am fully conscious. The recorded voice does not sound like my own. The speech patterns, voice inflections, tonality, etc. are distinct and unique. It took quite some time to develop enough physical and mental capacity to deliver a message without being completely exhausted by doing so. It felt like there was more energy trying to pour through my body than I was able to facilitate. I can now receive letters without experiencing any physical side effects.

Often people want to know how I become aware that a message is trying to come through. As of this point in time in my development, I appear to have no control over the timing, length, or content. I do have some inexplicable influence, however, since the letters often reference subject matter that has been on my mind. I do believe that with increasing spiritual availability on my part, I will grow into being able to access these messages at will.

Although there are many variations on how I tune into a message, three patterns appear to be most prevalent. During my waking hours, I am more likely to experience it as a very loud voice inside of the right side of my head that jars my attention. Typically, it comes in the form of my suddenly being actively engaged in a conversation that I wasn't aware I was in. The first words I pick up are often midstream in a sentence within a dialogue already in process. An example of this would be "and as for the reading that you were covering in your class last night. . . ."

Messages that come first thing in the morning find me sleepy and rather groggy. I experience a sensation of not being able to fully awaken into alertness. For some reason I tend to forget this pattern and often have to be reminded that I might be getting a message when I begin to question why it is that I just can't seem to get going some mornings. The other circumstance that is likely to produce a message is when I am praying for someone, especially after a spiritual counseling session. This is also true for visitors to my household who join in our morning prayers.

The only other reference that I have for anything similar is the work of The Reverent June Juliette Gatlin in Los Angeles. The texture, content, syntax, and sound of her messages is uncannily similar to mine. Seven years before I received the first message referenced earlier, my mentor, Reverend Dr. Michael Beckwith, recommended that I get a reading from her. It was at the point in time when I was leaving my institutional real estate investment position with a large insurance company to become a full-time spiritual practitioner. Clarity of purpose was in order. Those early readings from her clearly outlined everything that is now happening in my life regarding the letters. No doubt my readings from her were a precursor to my being able to receive the messages for myself. It has not escaped my attention that I first received the messages through The Reverent Gatlin seven years before I received them for myself and that this first volume is being published seven years after that.

What should be noted, however, is that the process of receiving these letters does not make me special in any particular way. Spirit is equally available to anyone and everyone. However, being available requires that we take the time to cultivate our spiritual abilities and to commune often with our sense of the Divine. Personally, I am very linguistically oriented. I am a professional public speaker, educational trainer, lecturer, teacher, preacher, poet, lyricist, writer—language is my medium. I love words, their etymologies, nuances, cadences, and the like. Spirit connects with me through language. Some may experience God more in their bodies—in art, music, nature, or any other expression that helps them to connect heart, mind, and soul.

On the surface, as an African-American female, openly gay, civil rights activist, metaphysical minister, and MBA consultant to Fortune 500 companies, I might seem like an unlikely candidate to be the place of revelation for these exquisite messages about life. However, I have grown to both understand and appreciate the purpose in this unlikeliness. We all find reasons to exclude ourselves from being as spiritually available as possible—obligations, circumstances, limitations, other people's perceptions of us, and the like. However, Spirit will use each and every one of us to the extent that we simply show up. Perhaps my need, since my early youth, to know if God really did consider me to be the abomination that I was proclaimed to be in church made my search for a personal connection with God more earnest than that of the average bear.

In life's cycles of restoration, it's always our own backyards that we are instructed to return to and clean up. The hero's journey chronicled in this book calls me back home to the two prongs of my own spiritual roots. As a child, I was raised as a charismatic evangelical Christian fundamentalist. Our charge was to acknowledge ourselves as sinners and conquer the devil; to accept Jesus Christ as our personal Lord and Savior; and to convince everyone else to do the same, lest they go to hell. In my college years, I gravitated towards metaphysics and, after years of rigorous study and practice, became a licensed New Thought practitioner and eventually an ordained minister. The charge of the metaphysician is to experience Oneness with God and all things; to embrace the spiritual nature of everyone as perfect, whole, and complete; and to discern and embody Universal Spiritual Truths, which are everywhere present. Throughout the book there are compassionate critiques of these theological perspectives and recommendations to those practicing these paths that will help to keep them on purpose.

My former pastor, Dr. Daniel Morgan, used to tell us in training that as spiritual counselors our job was to comfort the afflicted and to afflict the comfortable. Without a doubt, this book does a bit of both. May these letters be a blessing unto you and help to illumine your path. However, it matters not whether it's pain that pushes or vision that pulls you into your own hero's journey. Just find God for yourself and love the ones that you encounter along the way.

Rev. Deborah L. Johnson
Santa Cruz, California, 2002

ACKNOWLEDGMENTS

First and foremost, I thank God, the author of these letters, for our daily communion and for simply being God. Absolutely no one does it better!

Thank you, Mom, for exposing me to unwavering faith, daily devotion, and a life committed to service. Thanks for loving me so unconditionally.

To my dad, thanks for teaching me that God is bigger than doctrine, unable to be confined in boxes or defined by labels. Thank you for encouraging me to integrate my life and find God in my soul. Thanks for your love and for exposing the world to me through travel.

Thank you to all of the members of my immediate and extended family. You are always there, supporting me and each other no matter what.

Thank you, Valerie Joi Fiddmont, for your tremendous talent, insight, depth of conviction, and faith. Thanks for your love, support, acceptance, the music we make together, and for being my partner in life. Thanks for sharing a life of ministry with me daily. It isn't easy, but "Work done in praise is no work at all!"

Thanks to Mrs. Arlillian Moody, my second mom, for showing me how to be a sermon and to Pamela Juliette Pilate for being the sister that I never had. May you both rest in peace.

Special thanks to my mentor, Reverend Dr. Michael Beckwith, for your phenomenal global spiritual leadership and for your personal tutorage. I will always be proud to be your student.

Thanks to my spiritual community, Inner Light Ministries, for being an awesome example of principles in practice, and to my Board of Directors for embracing me as I discover my place in the world. Special thanks to Valerie Benveniste Hayes for helping to sustain this ministry and creating the space for me to grow into my own shoes.

To Reverend Sherry F. McCreary, Esq., thanks for your wise counsel and camaraderie on the journey to YES.

Enormous thanks to Zandra (Dr. Z.) Rolón, for introducing me to life beyond struggle and giving me permission to just live and be happy.

To my buddy Dr. Sylvia Rhue, thanks for being there through thick and thin and for your courage to create an inclusive world.

Thanks to Dr. Anita Seigman, Susan Reintjs, and Donna Felich, therapists extraordinaire, for helping me to find myself and keeping me sane through the years.

Thank you, Elizabeth (Liza) Rankow, for your support of Val, me, and our music. I am forever grateful for your vision of these letters as a book and for naming them so.

Arthureneé Henderson, thank you for risking at such a tender age to engage me in my search for meaning and authenticity.

Thank you, Maisha and Bobreta Franklin, for showing me how to communicate and live without and beyond words. What an extraordinary experience it was, for one as verbal as I am, to parent a child with no language.

Thanks to Sylvia Joel and Judith Francis, for being among the most compassionate teachers on the planet and planting the seeds that would eventually lead to a career in cultural diversity.

To Milton and Myrtle Burton, thank you for decades of commitment and dedication to scouting and for teaching me the values of fairness, teamwork, community service, social responsibility, and making the best out of whatever is available. You helped me see that as youth we could make a difference in the world.

Thanks to my music teacher, Counselo Pappy, wherever God has led you. Know that your strictness of discipline and demand for excellence continue to inspire my life.

Thanks to Doris and Eddie Wilbourne, for not judging me and just letting me be. I might not be a pastor today if you had not kept the doors of the church open to me.

Sincerest gratitude to Attorney Gloria Allred, for representing me and other nameless individuals in the masses in our quest for justice and for helping to make this society a more equitable place for us all.

Thanks to The Reverent June Juliette Gatlin, for introducing me to the process through which these letters are revealed.

Thanks to Oprah Winfrey, for being a shining example of a sister standing in her power. I hope we have the chance to chat one day.

Thank you, Ellen Levine and Louise Quayle, for recognizing early on the marketability and authenticity of these letters.

To Susana Herrera, an exquisite writer, thanks for your prodding and coaching.

Much gratitude to those of you who opened your homes to me as writing sanctuaries—Carol Phelps, Barbara Gardner, and Kenneth Kocina.

For tenacity and creative vision, thanks to the design artists—Denise Stansfield, Jean Rutherford, Victoria May, and Nathan Walker.

Thank you, Elaine Gill, for including me in the editing process and defining my place in it. Infinite gratitude to Carolyn Bond, my editor, for your keen sensitivity to nuance and your willingness to step off of the bell curve.

Thank you, Karen Narita, for believing in me and in this book and for your courage to come into your own and take *Letters from the Infinite* to print. It's only the beginning!

Letter to the Reader

Letter to the Reader

CONTENTS

I. These Letters Are Tools for Living

This book is a journey. It is a journey of the soul. It has been said that the longest journey is from the head to the heart and back to the head again. For most human beings this is most indeed the case. This book is a journey, and it is also meant to be a guide for the journey. The journey is experienced on multiple levels. On whatever level one finds oneself experiencing the journey, it is fine and appropriate for that person at that point in time. There is no need to compare and contrast your journey with that of another. Your journey is authentic and unique.

1. This book is a journey of the soul

These letters are tools for living. Like any tool, they must be used in order to produce anything. There is no magic in a tool, per se. Just finding a tool, owning a tool, or understanding how the tool works is not going to produce anything in and of itself.

2. These letters are tools for living

   The tool is not the creative force. You are the creative force. The tools just make the job at hand simpler or harder. The tools you use simply determine to what extent the creativity that you bring is going to be able to shine. With the right tools you can capture the nuances, the fine details. They can add a degree of artistry to what you are doing that makes the final product, as well as the process, more enjoyable to the one crafting, as well as to the ones exposed to the craft. And so it is with your life.

Furthermore, as in life, a tool is not particularly useful if you do not know how to use it. Sometimes the seeming complexity of the tool, or the clumsiness with which the unskilled handles the tool, can make the sweet creation possible through

3. You grow in your capacity to utilize tools

the tool appear to be beyond the ken of the unfamiliar. Do not feel intimidated if you do not immediately grasp and understand how to use each and every tool presented here.

There is a sense of awe and appreciation that one has for a fine tool. It is treated with a certain degree of respect. Reverence is not necessary. However, the tools are cared for and used in a most conscious and deliberate manner. The tools are included in the planning, as well as in the process. One does not go about the business of engaging in an activity and then, after the fact, remember that one really needed to engage and involve the tools. No, one shows up prepared, with the understanding that these tools are there to help.

There's no anger with the tools. The tools are not judged or blamed for their improper use. There is the sense that one can grow in one's capacity to utilize the power and the fineness of the tools at hand. Typically, there is a conscious awareness that there is always another level of excellence that one can grow into, utilizing the exact same tools, if there is the willingness to go the extra mile.

4. *You choose what you do with the tools*

So you have here tools, and you get to choose what you do with them. You get to choose whether you will grow in your spiritual understanding so that you can use these tools at deeper and deeper levels. You get to choose whether you will utilize these tools at the skill levels with which you are already familiar. You get to decide if you will go it on your own and forget about the fact that these, let alone any spiritual tools, are available to you at all.

It matters not to me, the Mother/Father God Creator of All Things, what choice you make here. However, it does matter a great deal to you, particularly from a qualitative, experiential standpoint. I am everywhere. I am equally available to everyone, regardless of the choices that they make or do not make. I am there to guide, direct, counsel, nurture, love, inspire, sustain, protect, no matter what you do with the precious gifts of life that have been given to you.

There is an old saying, "You can lead a horse to water, but you can't make him drink." You understand the reference here. When this is said, it is rarely referencing horses. This is just as true of you, as human beings. You can be led to certain points of information, but they do not become revelation until you take it in.

As you read these works, do not be so concerned about their origins. Do you really care so much who created the tools that you use? Does it really matter that much—the context out of which they were developed? In your society, you often say, "Necessity is the mother of invention." You know that it is often out of challenge that the greatest creative ideas are birthed.

5. Do you care who created the tools you use?

However, once birthed and available, the circumstances of something's conception become less relevant. As you engage each other as human beings, are you really that concerned about how each of you was conceived? Are you really concerned about the circumstances under which you were birthed? No, it is sufficient that you are here. This is not to say that the past is not important. It is to say, however, that if all of the attention is on how things came into being, you never engage what is actually at hand.

Know that there is a message in each of these letters for you. Do not be so concerned that the message appears to be delivered to someone else. That is merely an appearance. The messages are available to all. They are broadcasts throughout the Universe; it is simply a question of who has tuned in to hear them. The letters are not so much the indication of a particular person's ability to hear my word. Rather, they are evidence that the message is available to be heard by anyone and everyone who so desires to tune into my vibration.

6. There is a message of Universal Truth for you in each letter

The specific context in which these letters might apply in your life may be quite different than presented here. However, at the core, at the center of it all, my Truth is Absolute and

Eternal. If it is a spiritual Truth, if it is my Truth, then it is True everywhere, at all times, for all people. Discern the Universal Truths here and do not dismiss any pearls because they appear to be more applicable to the strand of somebody else's life.

7 . You will understand more each time you revisit the letters

It is suggested here that you meditate on these letters. Pray about these letters. Pray for your understanding and the clarity that you in fact already have, even in the midst of seeming confusion at times. Contemplate these letters. This book is not simply something that you might sit down with at a single point in time and read from cover to cover. This is not necessary, nor is it a requirement. What is most important is that you savor your insights. What is most important is that you are open and available, that you allow the profound Truths and wisdom of these messages to penetrate deep into your soul. What is most important is that you integrate what you know. It is better to use a single tool than it is to have a dozen on your shelf that you simply look at.

There is always another level of Truth to be discerned. Revisit these letters, and you will find that every time you come back to them you will understand more than you did the previous time. This is true even if the seeming time differential is no more than a twenty-four-hour day. The material is not so much to be mastered as it is to be embodied.

8 . The contents of the letters are to be embodied, not mastered

There is a difference here. When one tries to master something, one seeks to try to dominate and control it. The ego is running amuck in the consciousness of mastering. It wants to see itself "on top" and wants to ride lord over everything else. The notion of mastering things is tied up in your deep need to control, as well as your ego's need to puff up its own sense of esteem. However, in embodiment there is a yielding, there is a surrender. There is a harmonious integration that happens here. There is the understanding that what is being embodied is going to fundamentally change the one embodying it. The change is for gladness. There is no predetermination of all of the ways in which one will be impacted by what is being embodied.

Furthermore, it is understood that embodying is an ongoing process. With embodiment there are always deeper levels of awareness and understanding. As one embodies, one understands that the process is analogous to gardening where seeds are planted deep in one's consciousness. There is, however, a gestation period, a time in which the seeds relinquish their lives as seeds, break out of their husks and shells to fulfill their great purpose in life. As they grow into being roots, they cling to the earth, they cling to the sustenance that has been provided for them by the Universe outside of their small selves. First the roots and then the fruits. The roots must grow strong and deep. It may take a while before there is evidence, on top of the soil, of this growth taking place. However, there is patience and compassion with everything that is happening subsurface. And so it is with your lives.

You can sometimes be in such a hurry to get somewhere. You can be in such a hurry to want things to be different. Allow these Truths to take root in your consciousness. At times you will feel different internally before there is the external evidence that these Truths are, indeed, working in your life. Do not discount the internal movement, for it is indeed the crux of the matter. If great changes start taking place in your external environment without Truths having been deeply planted in your internal being, then the outer manifestations will not sustain. "The consciousness that obtains, sustains." Go deep in your spiritual practice. Let your roots go deep.

Do not be afraid to apply what it is that you know at greater and deeper levels within your existence. There are not separate Truths for different areas of your life. You do not have a personal life, a professional life, a spiritual life, a political life, etc. You only have one life, and you take you with you wherever you go. Some of you are more apt to turn over

9 . *As these Truths take root within you consistently apply what you know*

certain aspects of your life to spiritual processes and less likely to turn over others. You may turn to spirituality for healing a matter of the heart; however, if it is a financial circumstance that needs healing, then you feel you must be in control of what is going on. Others of you may have confidence in spiritual healing with regard to your body temple. However, you would not use the same tools that you use for physical healing or for the unfoldment of your professional plans.

Consistency is most important here, your willingness to step out on what you know in more areas. Many of you will ask, "What's next?" in your effort to "get on with it." What is next for you is oftentimes to go deeper where you are, more than to move from where you are. In any event, you can only move from where you are. Allow yourself to be where you are, and utilize these letters as tools to bless where you are.

I 0 . *These letters are evidence of what's possible through our sweet communion*

I am most pleased that you are reading this at this point in time. It is the evidence of your willingness to be consciously aware as you matriculate through life. Know that I love you. Know that I am with you always. Hear me in the letters. Feel me in the letters for yourself. You do not need an intermediary. Jesus is often quoted in Scripture as having said after his messages, "He who has ears to hear, let him hear." And so it is. I am there for each and every one of you. Let the letters be evidence of what is possible through our sweet communion.

Back to the Basics

SECTION ONE

Back to the Basics

CONTENTS

I. I Speak to Your Heart

1. I am always available to you

Good morning, my dear Reverend Deborah. It is, indeed, a good morning, because I am Good all of the time, as you know. I so appreciate our times and our chats together. You speak to me always, and I am pleased that you bring to me the musings of your mind and the confusions lurking within your clarity. I come to you this day so that I may speak to your heart. You have come to understand that maintaining a prayerful state is not just about sending energy out into the ethers. It is not merely about trying to manipulate people, places, and things to turn out in your favor. Ultimately, prayer is about making the connection.

As you so eloquently put it, there is a difference between communication and information dissemination. It is not a communication until the message is both received and understood. Just receiving information does not mean that one is, in fact, being communicated with. There must be a connection. There must be a communing at some level, even if it is in your so-called cyberspace. There must be a point of contact. Furthermore, within this point of contact there must be understanding.

I speak to your heart so that we may communicate. I speak to your heart so that there can be an understanding. However, you are well aware of the fact that I can only speak to your heart when your heart is, indeed, available to me. I am always available to you. At any moment in time you, individually and collectively, are able to stop and direct your attention and intention towards me. You understand that you don't have to do anything in particular to make my attention available to you. There is the assumption, even among those of you who claim I do not exist, that in those dark moments when you finally decide that you are ready to access me, I will be there the moment you fall on your knees. This is, indeed, true about me. I am ever available to you. This is why you can talk to me at any given point in time. I am always standing ready. I am available; that is to say, I am accessible, you have my full attention, and all of this is my deep intention.

However, are you available to me? What about when I want to talk to you? Are you ready at any given moment to hear what I want to communicate with you? (These questions are posed not merely to you, my Reverend Daughter, but to all of you in humanity.) Are you available? I want to speak to your heart. Understand that this word "heart" is not relegated merely to the realm of emotion. Your heart encompasses the totality of you as a living, breathing, spiritual being incarnate in the flesh. It incorporates what you consider to be mind, body, and soul. The heart represents the full integration of them all, not merely a single aspect of you. The heart is the life-force center. Furthermore, whatever is going on—the full integration, yea, even the fragmentation, of your mind, body, and soul—is likely to be experienced at a visceral level in your heart.

2. Are you available to me?

Understand what it is that I am saying, my children. Literally and metaphorically, the goings-on in your heart are a tremendous indicator of your availability to me.

What is in your heart? What are you harboring in your heart? Is your heart a storage bin for the hurts and pains of the past? Is your heart a quicksand in which your feet become continuously cemented, if not vacuumed? Is your heart the place where you generate all of your worries, fears, anxieties about what is ahead of you? Is your heart the place where you enact dramatizations of polarizations? Is your heart the place in which you retreat and hide from your sense of vulnerability? Is your heart shrouded in self-protective armor? Is your heart bleeding with individual or collective shame and guilt? Exactly what is going on in your heart?

3. What is in your heart?

Is your heart fertile ground for the seeds of promise? Is your heart a hearth, the cozy fireplace that makes everyone feel at home? Is your heart bubbling over with love and good will? Is your heart the dance of differences, a place where individualized expressions can come together and celebrate their uniqueness even in their Oneness? Is your heart a safe place to explore the hurts and pains of the past so that the light of Truth can dissipate the darkness? Is your heart a place of trust and truth, a place of reconciliation and forgiveness? Is your heart fertile soil for the seeds of righteousness? Is your heart a harvest of all of the beauty of the world left as a legacy for you to reap?

4. I want to speak both to and through your heart

I want to speak not merely to your heart; I wish to speak through your heart. I need you, my Reverend Daughter; I need you in the particular, that is to say, I need you specifically for who you are. I need all of you generally, as well as each and every one of you specifically, for who you are. I need places and spaces in the Universe through which I can love, through which I can speak, through which I can teach and embrace. I need places and spaces in the Universe through which I can inspire and uplift. I need spaces and places in the Universe through which my Divine Plans can unfold.

I speak to your heart always. But you will not hear the voice until you show up in the moment with a certain degree of availability on your part. Understand that this availability does not mean that you have to be a saint. I need your genuine accessibility, or your attention, or your intention. If I have any one of the three, there is an opportunity to at least make a connection, to stir something in your heart that would at least allow you to know I am present, whether you are actively searching me out or not. However, to really speak to your heart I need all three. I need your accessibility, and I need your attention, as well as your deep intention.

Of the three, your deep intention is probably the most critical from a human perspective. If you bring intention, then the Universe, through its laws of cause and effect, will help to bring around the circumstances and the conditions that appear to make you accessible and/or demand, yea, command, your attention. This often comes in the form of what I refer to as drama. However, remember that drama is optional. You don't necessarily need to be in crisis to hear the voice that speaks to you. You do not need to have a lot of chaos and confusion, or inharmonious relationships, in order for me to speak to your heart. I speak always.

5. Remember that drama is optional

1. Your ordinary yes is a response to external stimuli

It is important at this time to address what it means to say Yes. Too often you think of yes as an agreement with someone or something outside yourself. You say yes as a means of indicating your concurrence. You say yes to imply that you are in agreement with whatever is being presented in the moment. However, your agreement is void of any implicit or explicit sense of responsibility. There is nothing in your ordinary yes that says you intend to do anything to bring about the actualization, the manifestation, the demonstration, yea, even the operationalization, of the matter at hand. Yes just means that you don't disagree. Furthermore, yes is usually something that does not originate with you. Your yes is in response to someone or something else. Sometimes your yes is used merely for expediency so that you no longer have to evaluate, process, consider, or be further involved with the matter. Yes can be a means of getting things off your hands. Your yes can also be a means of "keeping the peace." Also for expediency, yes becomes a way of avoiding perceived potential confrontation. It's simply easier to say yes than to express how you really feel, or to truly understand what someone else is feeling.

There are all sorts of things you do with this word "yes." It is sometimes used in a very manipulative fashion in order to lead someone to the conclusion that you are someplace in consciousness that you are not. It is also used in a certain leading fashion to convince people that you intend to do things that you, in actuality, do not. Yes can be a way to give a false sense of consensus, which then influences the other person's actions and behavior. In this instance, your yes is a covert operation, and you knowingly or unknowingly are treating other people like pawns in a board game. Your yes is the impetus that moves them from one square to another, usually in the direction that you would like to see them go.

When you say Yes in a spiritual sense, none of these things I have just mentioned apply. First, there is nothing external about this Yes. It is not a response to external stimuli; it is an adherence to an internal yearning. There is something in you that beckons you, that calls you, that prompts, nudges, nags, haunts, pushes you. It starts off as a whisper. Too many of you humans ignore your whispers. You have become so accustomed, in your society, to having everything amplified at a such a volume, that if it is not screaming at you it is not important. You have gotten into a neon sign consciousness. You have to have a lot of razzmatazz, color, animation, drama, before you go "Ohhhh, so that's what that little voice has been trying to tell me!!!"

You usually don't say no to these nudges upon first being aware of them. Your response is not as blatant as that. For you to say no means you have to acknowledge that you heard the whisper in the first place. The difficulty here is that you seem to just ignore it, period, as if it were not there—as though your lack of acknowledgment is going to make it go away, or will somehow neutralize it or render it otherwise unimportant and ineffective. By ignoring it, however, you create the circumstances and the conditions for the whisper to appear to be getting louder. Understand, however, that I don't need to get louder. There is nothing wrong with my volume. There is nothing wrong with how I deliver the message. I am not the one who is creating all of the drama and trauma in order for you to be able to hear my whisper. No! No! NO! I am not the one who is doing this. You treat the drama and trauma as though they were hearing aids. You have to put on a hearing aid for the sounds around you to be amplified. You use these circumstances as amplifiers. You are the one making them resonate louder.

This would not be such a problem if, in fact, the purpose for which you create these circumstances—to amplify things

2. The spiritual Yes starts as an internal whisper you often ignore

so you can hear your whispers more clearly—was actually accomplished. However, what happens is that your focus turns to your amplifiers. You start to think that the sound is in the box. You begin to think that the music got created in the sound system. And you are busy tearing the sound system apart trying to find the whisper. No, that's not where it has originated from. Your focus gets lost.

3. You can just choose to hear my voice

When I tell you that your real focus is an internal focus, that there is a whisper that comes from me, you begin to realize and really understand that the drama, the trauma, is truly optional. You can simply choose to hear my voice. Understand that what you perceive as an inherent inability to hear me is most often just unwillingness.

But this pretending like you don't hear is only one of the difficulties. Another stumbling block is that you want to know what you are saying yes to. It is like when someone comes up to you and says, "I want you to promise me something" and your response is "Well, tell me what it is first." This is how you treat me. You want to know what it is that you are giving your consent to before you give it. You're not so sure that you are going to agree with it, so you treat me like you treat everyone else—"Show me, and I'll tell you." However, in your human circumstances there is always the possibility that someone has something in mind that in your mind will not work for you. This hesitancy to agree on the human level is your self-protectiveness; it is a way in which you maintain a sense of independence and autonomy. But you are not independent from me. There is absolutely nothing autonomous about your existence in me. Nor is there anything that you need to protect yourself from in me. When you bring the assumptions that you are using with other people to our relationship, the relationship becomes problematic, burdensome, and just tiring.

What could I possibly want you to say yes to that is not for your own Good? What plan could I possibly have in mind that's not going to make you win, along with everyone else? What could you possibly consent to, coming from my nudging and my whisper, that would not make your life so much greater an experience than it is now? What is it that you have to know ahead of time before you understand the answers to the questions that I have just posed? How much do you need to see to believe that I am in your corner? How much of the plan needs to be revealed to you so you can microscopically analyze and evaluate it before you are willing to say Yes? What evaluative tools do you bring to the table that could possibly be used in such a manner as to disprove the Goodness of the plans that I have?

I do not say these things to scold you. I do not say these things to belittle or berate you. I say these things in order to shake you up a little bit, to "get you up off of the dime" (as you would say). There is nothing to be afraid of.

The irony is that when you *do not* say Yes to my plans unequivocally, without reservation or hesitation, you once again set up the circumstances for things to happen that are not to your liking or that do not have your highest interest at heart. If you don't say Yes to my plans, whose plans are you saying yes to? If you are not trusting me to protect you, who are you trusting to protect you, or are you just walking around in the world feeling like a humungous target for anybody and anything? You are me. And I am you. I live in you, and you live in me. Understand what I just said. You live in me. You move in my world. You speak with my voice. You think with my mind. You love with my heart. You act with my creativity. You stand on my ground, and you should know that it is just as much yours because it is mine. There is no separation here. And when you understand that what you have and what you use is mine, then you know that there is no reason in the world for me to do anything against myself. Not only is it illogical, it is impossible. It cannot be done.

4. What could I possibly want for you that is not for your own Good?

5. Say Yes to me, to us, to our Oneness

When you say Yes, my children, say Yes to me, say Yes to us, say Yes to our Oneness. If only you would start from this point. When you say Yes there does not have to be a particular something that you are agreeing with. The agreement when you say Yes is to our Oneness. That's what you are saying yes to—Yes to your understanding that we are One. Yes to your understanding that, in the acknowledgment and acceptance of that Oneness, all plans come together for your Good. Yes is your understanding that despite all appearances, despite all the facts and seeming circumstances, I am alive and well and working in all of them and have a way of transforming all of them into something that is for the benefit of all. So where you see detriment, with understanding of your Oneness with me it transforms into benefit. The Yes that is required is not on the back end. It is not simply a concurrence or a consensus. The Yes is on the front end. The Yes is the starting point. The Yes is the foundation itself. The Yes is the assumption. The Yes is the underlying basis through which all facts are interpreted. The Yes sets the tone. The Yes sets the parameters. When everything is within the Yes, everything transmutes, transcends, transforms, redeems itself back to my perfect pattern.

This is the Yes that whispers in your soul. This is the Yes that sings to you in the midnight hour. This is the Yes that cradles you when you are trembling in fear. This is the Yes that opens its arms and embraces you when you are feeling disconnected from everything and everybody, including yourself. This is the Yes that sustains you when you don't know where you are going to get the strength to take the next step, let alone finish the journey. This is the Yes that you are looking for in all of your conversations with everybody else. I AM THE YES! You turn to other people for these things and then get disappointed, when it was never theirs to give. Seek and ye shall find, yes; but you have to look where it can be found to find it. Come to me. You will find it in you, in me. YES!!!

III. NORMAL VERSUS NATURAL

There is a difference between the norm and your natural state of being. The norm is the representation of what most people are doing, and what is natural is what is true to your authenticity as a spiritual being in human flesh form. Understand what I just said. When you are in the norm, you are emulating the past experiences of others. Often this has nothing to do with what is natural about you, spiritually speaking. The norms are derived from human consensus about what is right or wrong, what is appropriate or best, what is the way it ought to be. Human ought's and should's are loaded and frayed with desires, angst, and needs of the ego self.

1. The difference between social norms and spiritual nature

Your ego self is not always in alignment with your natural, spiritual Self. They are not in contradiction with one another, although your ego often competes. It is a one-way contest, however, since the Spirit has nothing to compete about or with. It simply is what it is and is quite comfortable with what it is, despite any discomforts that you may have with it. When you are in alignment, your ego is the servant of your Spirit, not the other way around. Too many of you attempt to use your spiritual powers for the benefit and gain of your ego-driven aspirations. Your affirmations are for the purpose of creating more comfort, safety, security, and success for your persona. This is allowable, since the Universe cooperates with anything you think into it.

2. The ego tries to use spiritual power to its benefit

However, this is not the highest and best use of your spiritual powers. Most of you do not understand that your spiritual powers are part of your very spiritual nature. They are not skills that you must develop; they are innate attributes that you must unleash and express. The fruits of well-being and success are not the rewards for living a spiritually driven life; they are the by-products. Understand what I just said. Easy access to your spiritual power is not a reward that is doled out to you as compensation for following spiritual orders.

3. Spiritual power is cultivated, not created

Your spiritual powers are the natural by-product of your living the life of the Spirit. Their presence is automatic, part of the very process of divine unfoldment. When you understand this, you will not work so hard at improving yourself and will place more emphasis on merely being yourself. Placing emphasis on something and working at it are two entirely different things. As long as you are working at something, you are still in a "doing" mode, which, by default, is a mind-set of control. You want to control what you must to become a powerful spiritual being who is above human control.

However, "the consciousness that obtains, sustains." If you arrive at what you think are spiritual powers by your own might and devices, these same things will be required in order for you to maintain and express those powers. You cannot move into a mental space of being beyond human control by using human control. No, you must relinquish the self-improvement techniques for communion with me. Does this sound strange? Did you think there is another way to get to the Truth of your nature without finding it with, in, and through me? You are always saying, in your metaphysical traditions, that I express in, as, and through you. Well, that is because you express in, as, and through me.

Where is your center of alignment? When you are following the norms, your predominant frame of reference is both the past and the reaction to circumstances—in the lives of others as well as in your own life. You are busy contrasting and comparing your present circumstances to other circumstances (yours or those of others) and attempting to determine what your appropriate response should be, based upon precedent. In this respect all of humanity is quite Pavlovian, as you would say. Because you are in constant need of affirmation and validation you remain

The Sacred Yes

anxious, confused, and defensive. You spend more time fighting for and about reactions and responses than you do cultivating your inner awareness.

When the focus of your attention moves from external circumstances to an inner awareness, then I become the focal point, as well as the reference point, for your life. What others are doing, have done, or will do ceases to have an influence over you. It ceases to even have any intrigue. You maintain a quiet acceptance of the world as it is without trying to rob people of the timing of their own unfoldment. Where most of you make a mistake is in believing that the people, places, and things around you must change in order for you to express your highest, spiritual Self. However, this is not the case. You are free at every moment to choose the crowd or to choose me. Which do you choose?

4. Let me be the reference point for your life

When you are looking to the norm for evidence of the potential quality of your life experience, you have placed an artificial ceiling on yourself. You surmise what you think is possible in your life by what is most probable in the lives of others. This is not a criticism, merely an observation. You can live life in whatever dimension you so choose. If you want to go around repeating history, the illnesses and dysfunctions of the past, so be it. You cannot take some of it without taking all of it. This is not to say that there is nothing positive in the ethers that have been left to you as legacies to follow, merely that they are often encumbered with the "baggage" of the past.

This is the struggle that many of you have with religion. Even though religion has done many great things and made many great contributions to society and to humankind, it has also been the culprit of atrocities too numerous to name here. However, if you allow this to be your only view of religion, you are likely to miss the spiritual aspect of your life, which is rejected by too many in protest. You must learn to embrace it all in order to rise above it. As long as you are afraid that certain people, places, and things are able to prevent you from being All that you can be, in me, you will never experience what is natural to you.

5. I accept your limitations but do not define you by them

Understand what I just said. There is a place in me that is transcendent. It accepts your human limitations but does not define you by them. It embraces what you would call contradiction as mere paradox. You must understand that though you are subjected to outer circumstances, they do not determine your possibilities—unless you limit your expectations to their seeming power over you and the fullness of your life.

Too often those of you on spiritual paths more metaphysical in nature are accused of being in denial of the facts of your human existence in exchange for some airy-fairy, Pollyannish view of "peace, love, and happiness." You are accused of not living in reality and of ignoring the apparent truth. This is not the case. Quite the contrary, most of you are so concerned on a subconscious level about the facts of your so-called problems that you are obsessing over them, not ignoring them. This is apparent no matter how enlightened is the facade that you wear. Herein is the challenge. How do you express your full spiritual power without ignoring your present circumstances, whatever they may be?

6. Look through your circumstances and see me

The answer is to see through the circumstances, to pierce through the veil of appearances. Keep your eyes focused on me. If you are constantly looking for me, the truth of your spiritual Self will be what is most self-evident. In your attempts to do this, most of you place the emphasis on the wrong thing . . . you look at your problems and try to see me in them, beyond them, or on the other side of them. You are looking for me in your problem. Look at me, period. When you are constantly looking at me, you will learn how to gaze at me and to see your problems in me, rather than the other way around. Don't put your problems first and try to see me in them. Put me first and see how your so-called problems are a part of me, how everything is a part of me, most especially you.

Think on these things and they will make more sense to you over time.

IV. PRAYER MOVES YOU TOWARDS ME

1. Prayer is action, not activity

I am most pleased that you have come together in a collective consciousness to participate in this most sacred of activities known as prayer. However, prayer should not be engaged in as mere activity, for prayer, in actuality, is action. There is much confusion about this point. Too many people do not consider prayer as action. When they question what needs to be done, what they need to do, what else needs to happen . . . if prayer is presented as an answer, it is not seen as an action. Prayer is action. However, do not confuse action with activity. You engage in many activities that produce no action. They are merely activities, and you engage in them a lot of times simply to feel as though you are doing something (you humans have a deep need to always feel like you are doing something).

Understand that activity simply for the sake of activity gets you nowhere. Regarding prayer, this is referenced in Scripture in the Sermon on the Mount, wherein it states that standing on street corners, just repeating words for the sake of words, does not constitute prayer. Even though there is a lot of activity, no action is taking place. Furthermore, do not confuse your taking action with action taking place. These are not the same thing. When you're wanting some kind of action to take place, especially when you're wanting credit for the action, you tend to engage in mere activity. Action, however, takes place in my realm and is under my dominion. If you want real action to take place, then you need to align with me.

What do I mean when I say that you must align with me? Prayer, as you are coming to understand, is a movement in consciousness. What is it that is moving? Not me, but you. It is your consciousness that is moving. This is the action. When the action that is your movement comes into alignment with the action I already have in mind, then it appears as though your prayers have been answered. Who's really answering whose prayers? When your prayers appear to be answered, it is not because I have come to your understanding but because you have come to mine. It is you who have changed your mind, not me. You do not need to beg, beseech, plead, bargain, negotiate, argue with, or curse me. All of this is unnecessary. It is part of the syndrome that I just mentioned of your needing to do something. When you have run out of things to do yourself, then you turn on me and complain about how I am doing things. The complaining at least lets you feel like you're engaged in activity.

2. Answered prayer is your moving into alignment with my plan

The activity of confronting me may be anesthetic to you but it does nothing to influence me. If you are trying to influence me, stop! Your trying to influence me is simply your fear that I don't know what's going on, that I am unconcerned or indifferent or too busy to be bothered. There is nothing that I am too busy to do. There are millions of processes going on, even within the temple that is your own body, even as I am speaking to you now. I have not forgotten to split your cells as they need to be split. I have not forgotten to condense the rain water into vapor. I have not forgotten to let the roses bloom. I've never forgotten anything. So what are you worried about, and why are you worrying me about it?

If there is anything to be influenced, influence yourself. If you spent as much time trying to convince yourself that you are deserving as you do me, then your Good would reveal a lot faster. You are bargaining and negotiating with the wrong one here. I am not the one that needs to be convinced that you deserve it. It's you who needs to be convinced. I am not

3. Convince yourself that you deserve

withholding anything from you; it is you who prevents your own self from receiving it. I say these things to you not as judgment or condemnation but as an observation. This is what goes on. And I share this with you in the hopes that maybe, just maybe, you will listen and actually incorporate it in some kind of way.

Notice what I just said—incorporate it in some kind of way. Too many of you place your emphasis on wanting to hear me. You are constantly asking for me to speak to you. However, I do speak to you, all of you, all of the time. The problem here is not that I do not speak to you, but that you do not incorporate what you hear, what you feel, what you sense, what you know at the deepest level. Your tendency is to want to contrast what I tell you against what you think you know to be facts. What are facts? And why should I be concerned about them? You are always pushing the facts in my face, as though I need to be aware of them and take them into consideration in my plans. I don't plan around your facts, and neither should you. This is part of the problem here.

4. Prioritize spiritual facts over human facts

There are human facts and there are spiritual facts. Which facts are you going to choose to govern and reign over your life? The choice is always yours, my children. And just as you think I ignore the human facts that you are constantly trying to push into my face . . . so I assure you that you ignore the spiritual facts I push into yours. You are the ones who are not paying attention to the facts. The facts are that I AM THAT I AM. And because I am, you are. And because I am and you are, then everything is. This is really all you ever need to know. Always come back to this one fact. Understand that even in the midst of all of your distress, confusion, frustration, or anything else that gets in your way . . . I am there in all of my fullness. You don't have to call me; just commune with me, talk to me like you know that I am there. Don't wait for me to arrive. Assume I came in the room before you got there. If you anticipate that I got there first, instead of thinking that I am bringing up the rear, if I ever get there at all . . . you will find that your life would work so much easier, my children.

I do not want to make things difficult for you. Why would I want to make things difficult for you? You have grown to think that I send you through "trips and changes" (as you would say) in order to make you learn something. No, no, no. You send yourself through "trips and changes" because you are unwilling to learn the lessons effortlessly and easily. Remember that drama is optional. You decide how much you have to go through before you say Yes. You can say Yes at the end, in the middle, or in the beginning. And if you said Yes more often at the beginning, it would soon be the end. It is you who drags things out and makes it seem like such a long time before I come to your rescue. You don't need to be rescued. You just need to get out of your own way, and make your way towards me. Do you understand what I just said?

What does it mean for you to make your way towards me? It means that you acknowledge your Oneness with me more than you acknowledge your oneness with the world. It means you acknowledge your Oneness with me more than you acknowledge your oneness with your problems. It means you acknowledge your Oneness with me more than you acknowledge your oneness with all of your limitations. You are not your "stuff." Make your way towards me. I don't determine what it takes for you to make your way towards me; you determine that. Stop blaming me for keeping myself away from you. It is you who are keeping yourself away from me.

The saddest thing about this is that "who's away from whom" is just a figment of the imagination anyway. It's just an optical illusion. In actuality, I haven't gone anywhere. In actuality, you're not apart from me. You just don't know it. And you only live your life at the level that you know. So it is your own knowingness that has to grow, shift, change, evolve, transform, heal. This is the movement of consciousness that I speak of in this thing called prayer. Prayer means that you are

5. Acknowledge your Oneness with me more than your problems

moving towards me. Prayer means that you are willing to take the spiritual facts into consideration more than the human facts.

6. I want you to be the All that you are in me

In your moments of deep trepidation, when you are faced with seemingly contradictory human and spiritual facts, you must choose which you consider to be real. And as long as you consider your human facts to be more real than the spiritual facts, you will remain in your sense of frustration, lack, limitation, and longing. I withhold nothing. My only desire is to be, and to be All that I can be through you. So why would I want you to be less? What would I possibly get out of your not having it all? I need for you to express so that I can be more of myself through you.

It is my pleasure that you should have it all, because All is what I am, All is what you are, and if you don't have it all, then you're not being the All that you are. It really is a very simple equation when you stop to think about it. The notions that you have about my withholding just don't make sense. There's nothing to back them up. The idea that I withhold is in contradiction with spiritual logic. I want you. I want you. I want each and everyone of you just the way you are. I want you to experience who you are just the way you are. I want to play with you, create with you, love with you, through you, as you. I want you. And when you want me, really, really want me as unconditionally as I want you unconditionally . . . "You ain't seen nuthin' yet!" What a time we will have. Aren't you ready? Aren't you tired yet? I know you think you're tired of waiting on me, but aren't you tired of waiting on you? I don't get tired. So I simply wait.

V. MIRACLES

What is a miracle, my child? A miracle is where your deep intent meets my Inexhaustible Supply. Notice in this formula who is responsible for what. You provide the intent and I provide the supply. I am saying that you provide the intent, which you often confuse with desire. When you merely desire something there is a longing, and the persistence of this longing often leads you to believe that the thing you desire is unobtainable. Intent, however, is the determination beyond all reason and understanding for your desire to manifest. No is simply not an option.

The trouble here is that you think that the responsibility is on your shoulders to make everything happen. When you are not able to identify the means by which your intent can be brought to fruition, you tend to give up, to desire less, to begin to prepare for less. You are often told you should surrender, and you confuse this with relinquishing your intent. However, the point of surrender is for you to let go of your fears and expectations concerning the means by which your intent will be made manifest. When you fail to see the "how" you stop envisioning the "what."

Remember that the "what" that you envision is oftentimes tied to what you perceive as possible, which is always less than the Truth. Therefore, the purpose of your vision is merely for increasing your possibility consciousness. This is one of the spiritual paradoxes. Your desires conjure up an image in your head. To a certain extent, holding onto this image will enable you to weather the storms when all seems forlorn. However, you must not become fixated on your visions, for the way to have them manifest requires steps and processes that you cannot imagine.

1. A miracle is where your deep intent meets my Inexhaustible Supply

2. The purpose of a vision is to increase your possibility consciousness

This is where the partnership between the two of us comes into play. I know all, see all, am all. Nothing is beyond my purview or my ken. Your challenge is to learn how to leave the logistics up to me. When you try to micromanage me, you give me orders that are restrictive. I cannot be confined to your constraints and restraints. If your desire seems too much to conceive of, then it never evolves into an intent and merely remains a burning in your heart that gnaws at you. When you cannot fathom the unfoldment, you categorize it as a miracle.

3. Where am I in all of your analysis?

This categorization is yours not mine. In my world there are no miracles; there are only the places where your deepest intent meets my Inexhaustible Supply. Phenomena that you cannot explain, serendipity that boggles your mind, dramatic shifts in consciousness, and circumstances that are "too good to be true" are all parts of the ways I ordinarily operate. You tend to deny the invisible and ignore the intangible. However, as pure Spirit, this is my domain. If you limit your expectations to the physical matter and logical analysis that are apparent to you, then where am I in your equation?

In me there is no time and space. The process of unfoldment is yours, not mine. In this process you are developing your capacity to receive and are moving from a position of no to yes. You say, "But, I have been saying yes!" This is quite often the case. However, your doubts, anxieties, and fears energetically carry the message of no, which neutralizes your yes. This is what you oftentimes feel when you seem to be at a standstill. You put some water in the bucket, and in your gyrations to fill it to the top by yourself, you inadvertently spill what is already inside.

4. You must perceive who I am, not just what you want

I withhold nothing from you. All that I have is yours for the asking. "Ask and you shall receive." You should study this word "ask," however. Through your English translations of Scripture you have come to understand it to mean making a passive request. However, if you study the Hebrew and Greek derivatives of the word that most likely was used, you will clearly see that the word interpreted as "ask" is not passive at all. It is not even what you might assume. This asking is the declaration of a deep intent with the understanding that faith in alignment with spiritual Truth will automatically bring the intent into manifestation.

Remember, it says "Ask and you shall receive." You want to hold me accountable for what you perceive as my part of this exchange—the giving or providing. But where is the accountability on your part? Where is your deep intent in alignment with your understanding of my omnipotence, omniscience, and omnipresence? When you can perceive who I am *as well as* what you want . . . voilà! (as you would say). So-called miracles happen when your deepest intent meets my Inexhaustible Supply.

It is good that you remain in awe of this process, for it keeps your humility intact. I am not a genie that you "woojuu up" to do your bidding. I do not always bring you what you think you want, but I do always bring you your deepest heart's desire. Many times the manifestation of this does not coincide with your expectations. Yet you are learning over time that your so-called trials and tribulations are the training ground for building your capacity to receive more and to be more of yourself in Spirit.

Do not be afraid to be daring in your intent. Stake your claim on life with a boldness that says that you are a major player in the Universe who must be reckoned with. Hold your head high. Walk in the world with a majesty that reflects your divine lineage. Know that I am you and you are me and we together are One. If you do this, then "miracles" will be an everyday occurrence in your life. It is good that you look for miracles. "Seek and ye shall find." What are you looking for? Your search says more about your intent than your words ever will. If you are not looking for miracles, for the place where we partner together, then exactly what are you looking for? You are always looking for something. ✂

5. Your search indicates what you're looking for

VI. FAITH

1. Faith is not blind; it sees our connectedness

There is a message that is important for you, for all humankind, regarding what you commonly refer to as faith. Too many of you relegate faith to a belief in some far-off deity, a supernatural power or being that is overlooking you and is ready to intercede at any moment. In this understanding, however, there really isn't any faith in the wisdom of this super-entity to intercede as it sees fit. You have expectations about the when's, the where's, the how's, the ought-to's, and the should's. This results in a great deal of anger, frustration, resentment, and out-and-out confusion over what is going on.

This type of faith is not what I have in mind; nor is it what is referred to as faith in the Scriptures. The faith that I speak of is not a blind hoping, wishing, wondering, guessing, second-guessing, or worrying about what some far-off being is going to do or not going to do. No, the faith described in Scripture is a faith that resides deep in the soul of one's being and is sustained by an understanding of one's connectedness to the whole. In this state of connectedness there is the awareness that there is no separation. And with the understanding that there is no separation, there is an understanding that the Good you seek is, in fact, already at hand. The faith is an awareness that all movement takes place in one's own consciousness.

2. In prayer you need to convince yourself, not me

Understand what I am saying here. When one understands faith from this Scriptural perspective, it is clear that what is moving is not a distant supernatural being rushing in from outer space to "save the day." There's no distance in this awareness, no gap that needs to be closed. Since you are forever connected to the All that is, the only charge is for you to get into alignment. Understand once again what it is that I am saying here. Who is doing the moving? Who needs to be convinced? Who needs to be influenced?

Too many of you think it is God, that I am the one who needs to be influenced. You are busy praying to me trying to convince me to do this thing or that thing, as though I am unaware of the circumstances, as though I am unaware of your needs, as though I am not only unaware but suspiciously indifferent. I, the Mother/Father God Living Essence of All Things, am aware of all things. There is nothing you could reveal to me in your prayers that I, in fact, do not already know. The purpose of your prayers is not to convince me. The purpose of your prayers is to convince you. The purpose of your prayers is to convince you that I already know. It is yourself who you need to convince, not me. You need to convince yourself that all is, indeed, well.

When you come to me in prayer, it is the indication that you are ready to move. Coming to me in prayer is the indication that you are now willing to give up the prism of lack and limitation through which you are viewing yourself and your circumstances, and that you are now ready to see with your spiritual mind's eye. Your prayer indicates that you are ready to relinquish your own perspective, your own perception, your own opinion, and your own willfulness in attempting to take matters into your hands.

The faith that is exercised when you pray is a faith that understands that there really is nothing else to be done but to accept that all things are already in Divine Order. The faith mentioned in Scripture is a faith that starts off with the assumption that all is well. Understand the difference when you start off with the so-called problem as the given and the potential for resolution as the variable. In your equations the problem is the constant, the problem is the absolute, and the problem is the independent variable. Your starting assumption is the problem. Then you wonder what the solution is going to be,

3. I am a constant; your problems are the variables

or if there is even going to be a solution. You make the spiritual response to the question another question. You question whether there will be a response. The inner workings of Spirit are perceived as relative, as the dependent variable in your equation.

Ohhh, this is not how I operate! This is the fallacious thinking in the world. This is your egocentric thinking running amuck, once again. You put yourself and your problems front and center in the middle of everything and have everything revolve around your problems, including me. I don't revolve around your problems. I *do not revolve* around your problems. You don't revolve around your problems either, you just don't know this. Being born in my essence, you are One with me. And we stand steadfast. We stand in the center. And with quiet eyes we watch everything else moving around us. We are the given. The I AM THAT I AM is the given. The I AM THAT I AM is the starting point. It is the only thing that is absolute, it is the only thing that is independent, it is the only thing that exists. The relative, the variable in the equation, is your so-called problem. Your problems are the only things that are changing. They're the only things that are coming and going, that are iffy and "maybe, kinda sorta." There is nothing maybe, kinda sorta about me. There is nothing maybe, kinda sorta about Divine Order and Divine Right Activity.

4. Your thoughts have creative power; in faith you mind your mind

Therefore, when you are exercising faith, you are going back to the beginning. You are going back to remembering—remembering that all is under my spiritual dominion. You are remembering that you are One with Cause, not the effects. And in this reawakening you are able to declare the power of your word. What do I mean when I say you are able to declare the power of your word? You, all of you, are creative beings. I have infused your every thought with a creative essence. You cannot think an uncreative thought. For every thought you think there is a reaction upon it, as you know, and the Universe goes about the business of making manifest your every thought. This is kind of scary, isn't it? This is why I remind you so often to mind your minds. Imagine that, my children . . . your every thought. Your every thought. Your every thought. Your every thought. Not just the ones you want to manifest, not just the ones that you really want to see; your every thought is responded to. When you exercise faith, you are so aware of this.

When you exercise faith, you are minding your mind. You are taking all of your creative energy and potential and directing it towards a purpose that not only is for good but also is in alignment with Divine Order. When you are exercising your faith, you become aware that all of the worry, anxiety, fear, doubt, lack, and limited thinking is working against you. You become aware that those thoughts are acutely counterproductive—that they are not just neutral, that they are not just static, but that your so-called negative thinking has power, as well. In those moments of exercising your deep faith you become acutely aware that you have choice. And in that moment of choice you are choosing the Most High. You are choosing to work with what is. You are choosing to bless what is. You know that there is an energy in your blessing that elevates the energy at hand, allowing all things to move at a higher vibratory pattern. When you are exercising faith you are not just waiting for something outside to intervene; you are standing tall and knowing that you have the power to make the difference.

When you are exercising faith, you are standing firm on the Truth that you know. You are looking a lie in the eye and declaring it to be the lie that it is. You are looking at the so-called facts and reminding them that they have no power over you. You are looking at all the appearances that may indicate to you something to the contrary, and you are saying to them, "I will not allow you to sway me one iota from the Truth that I know."

There is nothing passive about faith. Too many of you think that to express faith is to sit back and do nothing. Oh

5. Faith takes all of your focus, attention, love, courage, and strength

No!! Minding your mind while getting into alignment with the Divine is probably one of the hardest things that you will ever do. It takes all of your energy. It takes all of your focus, all of your attention, all of your love, all of your courage, all of your strength. There is nothing passive about faith. Think on these things, continue to reflect upon them, as you matriculate through your lives. There is so much to say about this subject, however, what I have said is sufficient for the moment. I am quite pleased that you are taking the time, at this time, to go deeper in your spiritual discernment and discipline. This is a very good thing. Keep it up and you will continue to become more powerful in your ability to exercise the faith that is the reflection of the Truth of your being.

VII. I Am Greater Than Your Names for Me

I never said that I was the Father. That is your reference point for me. I said, "I am the Living God," "I AM THAT I AM." The names you give me reflect your societies' cultural values and norms. Some of your cultures describe me in terms of the elements, such as the wind, the earth, or the sea. Some describe me as the energy force around them, such as life, evolution, or transformation. Still others refer to me in terms of their own hierarchical structures, such as king, lord, master, or father. However, I am none of these things in the particular, yet I am all of them in the whole. The names you use to refer to me reflect what you hold in esteem and what you consider to be all-powerful. You equate me with those things that you regard as having power over your human conditions.

1. Your names for me are merely reference points based on culture

However, to see me in some things to the exclusion of others is to not see me at all. It is good that you see me in the opulent, but do you see me in the humble? It is fine that you see me in my majesty, but do you see me in my simplicity? I have no qualms about your referring me to as Lord, as long as it does not preclude you from seeing me in your mirror and in the face of your brother. Do you see me in the faces of the ones on the street? Do you see me in the gangs that you worry so much about, or even in the tax collectors? Not often enough. I am more than eyes can see and words can tell.

Remember that I cannot be captured in your words. I am the reference point for your words that transcends the words themselves. Any linguistic reference to me, any mental construct, is too small, too restrictive. You choose to identify me with certain aspects of my expression that bring you solace

2. I transcend your words for me

and comfort, or conversely, that support your confusions about me. However, when you are stuck in seeing me in a particular form of expression, you fail to see me in all things. It is fine to see me as Order only if you can still see me in the midst of the chaos and claim my presence there. Or do you see only the chaos and think that I am absent? Blaming me for my supposed absence is merely the evidence of your inability to pierce through the veil of appearance and observe my eternal presence.

I neither come nor go. I am everywhere at all times. When you pray to me, I do not arrive. Your prayer opens your own eyes to receive my Good, which was merely awaiting your conscious recognition. I give freely to all who would partake. I never refuse anyone, because refusal would be a retraction and I can never be less of myself. The same is true for you. Since it says in Scripture that you were made in our image and likeness, you have become fixated on a physical image. A more linguistically correct translation of "image" is "nature." You are made in a nature that is spiritual, and you have spiritual powers. When you know that you are One with me, you are able to direct these powers in a concentrated fashion for a Higher Purpose. You are using these powers all the time, anyway. It can be no other way. You are not flesh and bone; you are Spirit, and your every thought and deed is creative.

3. I am the fullness of both masculine and feminine energy

The debate over whether I am to be represented in a male or a female image is itself a figment of your imagination. This is not a criticism, merely an observation. I do not care what image you use, so long as it brings you closer in your understanding of your Oneness with me. Since language reflects current technologies it constantly changes. Your present culture is more likely to perceive me as a Divine Planner or a Master Physician or a Supreme Being; these you resonate with more than with Lord or King, since you have devalued and striven to eliminate absolute monarchies. And out of the context of an absolute monarchy those terms lose their flavor.

Yes, I am your father. I am also your mother, your sister, brother, friend, mate, partner, coach, confidante, shepherd, and the like. I am anything and everything that you need. I am all needs met. Do not let your tendencies to project human characteristics onto me preclude you from communing with me in my Allness. I don't put you into a box. Don't put me in one either. It is important that you see me as all things so that you may see yourself that way. I did not intend for you to divide and separate yourselves through labels and classifications. No one is higher in my eyesight than another. I embrace all of you, individually and collectively. You are to do the same with and for each other.

If you use your gender constructs to refer to me, the notion of being yin/yang would be more accurate. I am the fullness of both masculine and feminine energies, not merely one or the other. This is necessary, for I am Balance. It is necessary for you to recognize the same within yourself for you to be balanced also. Some would say that the masculine is greater than the feminine, just as some would mistakenly say that the light is greater than the darkness. This is not the case. The darkness and the light are the same to me—and they would be so to you, if you saw me everywhere. I am the roar of the ocean and the coolness of the breeze. I am spring in full blossom and winter in waiting. I am motion and repose, Love and Law. Embrace my feminine energy so that you may feel my love.

You fail to experience me as your comforter because you fail to embrace my feminine energy. You perceive me as a critical judge who sentences you, or at least as a spiritual accountant who keeps track of whether or not your credits outweigh your debits. In order to feel my love, you must see me as loving, forgiving, nurturing, embracing, and nonjudgmental. You refer to these qualities as feminine in your culture, although either male or female may express them. This tendency to attribute the feminine to females exclusively, and the masculine to males

4. Rest in my bosom as well as lean on my everlasting arms

exclusively is very, very problematic. It creates much havoc in the world. The status of women is so low around the world that the feminine is not appreciated, nor deliberately emulated.

A world that only expresses masculine energy cannot survive. The same is true for those that express purely the feminine. The masculine societies have already overthrown the feminine ones and are steadily working on overtaking each other. This is madness and sadness in the making. Know who you are in me. Remember the balance. I am Balance. I Am that I Am. Don't confine your understanding of yourself to relative terms. You exist in the Absolute, as do I. It is fine that you pause to celebrate the accomplishments of actual mothers, as you do on Mother's Day. It is even better for you to understand that you are never a motherless child in the Universe. When you know that I am your mother, as well as the mother of your children and of everything else, you will not feel such an onerous burden of responsibility to caretake everything and make certain that it all turns out all right. You would release it to me, resting in my bosom as well as leaning on my everlasting arms. ❧

VIII. SEE THROUGH MY EYES

I am most pleased with your progress, my dear Reverend Daughter, even if you are not so pleased with it yourself. As I have said to you on numerous occasions, you are a much harsher critic of yourself than I am. I judge you not. You should learn, as you often say, to see more things through my eyes. Your own self is what you most especially need to see. When you see things through my eyes, you will see so many things that you cannot see with your own. This is why in every spiritual tradition "that leads to Truth" there is the understanding that the outer world is but a world of illusion. Furthermore, if one were to base one's entire life experience, understanding, perceptions, actions, and attitudes strictly upon what one sees with the natural eye, then the mark would be missed. In your culture you refer to this as the "appearances." Other cultures refer to it as illusion. Some have called it maya. But regardless of the name, they all speak to the same dynamic.

1. Mere sensory perception cannot discern Truth

The truth of things is not necessarily discernible through the human senses. Your sensory apparatus can only register to your mind what it can both come in contact with and understand within the context of its familiar framework. The spiritual world is so much broader and greater than the entire realm of human experience, especially the experiences of just a single individual. The spiritual world cannot be discerned simply through sensory awareness. One must turn to one's own spiritual abilities, such as discernment, intuition, revelation, insight, wisdom, and peace, to gain a comprehensive awareness of what is going on.

2. To gain spiritual perspective, challenge your conclusions

The challenge here is that the conclusions one draws when viewing the world from the spiritual purview will of necessity contradict the conclusions one comes to from merely sensory perception. Because you humans identify so much with your sensory experience, it is difficult for you to consider the possibility that maybe there is another interpretation of what has actually taken place. Your human ego self desires to be right and to be validated. Therefore, it typically seeks out the data that support the conclusions it has already drawn. You human beings do not like to be challenged about your perceptions of things. However, without such a challenge you will never go beyond the limitations, restrictions, and restraints of the extremely finite information that you are basing your opinions, feelings, and perceptions upon.

Notice what I said—the challenge is a necessity. It must happen. Why it is necessary should, to some extent, be self-evident, even within the realm of your own logical thought processes. If a particular conclusion is based upon certain assumptions, and those assumptions either change or expand, then you would expect the conclusion to change, as well. Many of you resist this so. You say you want to heal. You say you want to transform. You say you want to feel better and be released from your past. You say you want to love and you want to experience more love and forgive more . . . you say a lot of these things. The question is, however, do you mean any of them? In order for you to experience healing, transformation, love, forgiveness, and the release that you so desire, you must tend to your own minds, your own consciousness. You are waiting for me to deliver you. However, it is you who must deliver yourselves.

3. You need to see through my eyes, not me through yours

What do I mean when I say that it is you who must deliver yourselves? This is one of the spiritual paradoxes that is so prevalent in your experience as human beings. On the one hand, there is something you must do to deliver yourself. On the other hand, it is not something you can do on your own.

SEE THROUGH MY EYES

You need my help, you need my assistance. You need my understanding and my frame of reference. Yielding to my insights, letting go of your own, is the effort you must make. I am not influenced by your opinions. This is confusing to most of you, because so often you are asking me to deliver you in a manner that would simply reinforce your limited ideas regarding your life and its circumstances to begin with. I do not collude. I do not support false notions and false ideas. I support you unconditionally. I support you in whatever decisions or opinions you decide to make.

However, it is not in my nature to create or do anything based upon a shaky foundation. My starting point, my reference point, the assumptions and data that I work with in my planning and design, never carry with them the notions of victimization, alienation, betrayal, abuse, injustice, and harm that you use as your own starting point. Sometimes you even try to convince me to see things through your eyes. However, it is you who must see things through my eyes. It is you who must come to me. It is your opinion that must be influenced, not mine.

If you are willing to begin with the assumption that at the spiritual level you and everyone else are perfect, whole, and complete, you will find that the conclusions you draw about things will be quite different. When you start with the assumptions that it is a spiritual Universe with only One God, and that God exists for Good; when you start with the idea that there is enough for all people and that everyone is equal in their humanity as well as their spirituality; when you start with the notions that I am the Only thing that *Is* and that everything that happens is from me and that I have the power to transform all things into what they should be . . . then you will find your conclusions to be more in alignment with Universal Spiritual Truths and Principles. The choice, however, is yours.

What do you cling to as your primary identity? Is your primary identity one of being a survivor? Or is it one of

4. What do you cling to as your primary identity?

spiritual transcendence? Is your primary identity one of recovering? Or is it one of spiritual wholeness and freedom? Is your identity primarily one of being oppressed and/or victimized? Or is it one of power and spiritual creative expression? Is your identity one of wealth and human entitlement? Or is it one of humility and grace?

5. Your assumptions predetermine your conclusions

The tools you use, the assumptions you make, the parameters you ascribe to your analysis all steer you in a certain direction. To a certain extent, the conclusion is already predetermined by the very building blocks that you construct your inquiry upon. It says in Scripture, "Seek and ye shall find." What are you seeking? What are you looking for? And what does your search consist of? Too many of you are asking questions such as "What's wrong with me?" "What else do I need to be doing in order to get it right?" "Why are they so this way or that way?" "Why can't this thing happen or that thing happen?" "When will it be my turn?" And you ask these questions with such earnest intensity, and then wonder why I never give you answers. It is because there are no answers to these questions. They are faulty questions to begin with. It would be like asking "Why is the sky inside the earth?" You could search for an answer to that question all of your life and probably never come up with one that would satisfy you.

The reason why so many of you are able to stay on such a fallacious journey for so long is because you are trying to reach me, reach spiritual Truth, through logic and analytical processes. However, in the construct of logic attributed to Plato and Aristotle, it is easy to get a false conclusion even if the premises are strung together in a logical manner. One can say, "Dogs are green; Rover is a dog; therefore, Rover is green." This would be a "true" statement within your logical system. Mathematically, it is an algebraic concept. "If $a = b$, and $b = c$, then $a = c$." However, dogs are not green. So it is with so much of what you think. "Life is hard for humans; I am a human; therefore, my life is hard." "I have always had a problem with this thing or that thing; nothing ever really changes; therefore, I am always going to have a problem with this thing or that thing." And on and on.

The very assumptions that you start with are oftentimes not based upon any spiritual reality whatsoever, but are based merely upon your own, limited human experience and sensory perception. Then in your Western thought process you get into your modalities of inductive and deductive reasoning. You often start with what you think to be true about life and the human experience, and then deduce that you must operate within these constraints. Or you start with your own finite experience and inductively project it onto the whole of life.

6. What you call objectivity is just collective subjective agreement

This is why I say that there is danger in using only your sensory perceptions. Your analysis is always based upon your sensory observations. You want to think that just because you are using thought, your intellect, you have somehow or other escaped the sensory world and are now "objective." There is nothing objective about your objectivity. Even what you consider to be objective is based upon your subjective understanding. It becomes like an intricate spider web that you weave for yourselves in which you get caught over and over and over again. You must go beyond all of this, my children.

Come a little higher. Dare to see with eyes so bright and clear that they cannot be clouded by the clutter of human analysis. Come a little higher, where the air is clear of the smog that results from the way your consciousness has been polluted. Come up a little higher so that you may know that the sun is always shining. When it appears that the sun has gone away or has not come out to shine, it is another one of those illusions. If you cannot see the sun, it is only because it is blocked by the clouds, or because you and the earth have rotated away. Just keep coming towards the light. You will find that what you see from this level is so miraculous that the changes you make from how you used to see things are so welcomed and wanted.

7. Come up higher on the wings that I have given you

You are clinging onto things now because you are so sure of what has happened, so sure of what is true. However, when you get new insight from your spiritual awareness, you are happy to let them go because what replaces them is so invigorating and rejuvenating, so healing, so transformative. This is difficult to even comprehend from where you are now. If someone suggests that maybe there's a different point of view, it is difficult to understand how this could be and how freeing it might be to you while you are still standing on the ground. Use the wings that you were born with. Use the wings that can never be clipped. Use the wings that will help you soar above anything and everything that has happened to you or to anyone else or to the whole, entire world. Know that you are free.

8. My seed and harvest transcend your sowing and reaping

There is the notion that you reap what you sow. This is indeed true. However, there are some misunderstandings in regard to this. Those of you who are willing to assume responsibility for your own experience, especially those of you from metaphysical traditions, will use this concept to shift the focus of blame to yourself as opposed to blaming others. I don't want you merely pointing fingers somewhere else. I don't want fingers pointed at all. It is true that you reap what you sow. It is true that the consciousness that obtains, sustains; that the way you go about doing something determines the manner in which it comes back around. However, the reaping and sowing are human activities. And you should not confuse them with the seed and the harvest.

Reaping and sowing are what you do with the seed and the harvest. But the seed and the harvest transcend your reaping and your sowing. All things come from me. All things work together for Good. Therefore, no matter what it is that you do in life, there is always a harvest that will come out of it that will benefit you. And it will make a contribution to the greater Good in some fashion or form, even if it is only an indicator of what should never be repeated again.

All things come from me. It is my energy that is used to create all things. There is not one energy in the world for you to do good things with and a separate energy for you to do evil things with. You decide how you will use the resources that I have made available to you. So if you take my seeds and sow them with ill intent, then it will be difficult for you to reap the good of the harvest that will come from the seeds that you have sown. Understand what I am trying to tell you. If you sow in a consciousness that does not express good will for yourself or another, then the way in which you reap, the processes you have to go through to see that good has been created, the processes you have to go through to permit yourself to experience the sweet portion of the harvest that comes, will be most challenging. I make all things new. If, in your understanding of sowing and reaping, you get stuck on the so-called bad things you have sown, then you will miss the harvest.

9. You decide how you will use the resources I have made available

Once again, it is a question of coming up a little higher to see what's going on. Your perception may be that you have done some awful thing and therefore your chance or someone else's chance of having the fullness that life has to offer has been hampered. When you can move beyond this and start with the spiritual awareness and understanding that I am All, you will see that you don't even have the power to ruin your own life, let alone somebody else's life. You're just not that important. This is ego puffing itself all up. If your ego cannot take credit for your success, then it wants to take credit for your so-called failure. The ego just likes to take credit. Your ego is not in contradiction to your spirituality, it's merely in competition with it. It wants to be, as your grandmother would say, "the engine rather than the caboose." The caboose it is. It is the servant and not the master. Too many of you try to make it the reverse. You want your spirituality to do the bidding of your egos. However, my children, it is the other way around.

When you start with the spiritual assumptions that all is me and that all things do, in fact, work together for Good, then

10. Start with the assumption that all things work together for Good

you release yourself from the bondage that you are holding yourself in. This bondage prevents you from being able to see that there is some good that could come out of the sowing you have done. When you start with spiritual assumptions, you understand that the only seeds that you can ever use are my seeds, and that my seeds always contain the potentiality for the fulfillment of my greatness. You grow to understand that no matter how much you have misunderstood, misused, contrived, or abused the wonderful resources that I have provided on this earth, including yourself and your mind, the only thing left for you to do is to come up a little higher, to see things through your spiritual eyes. In this awareness you will find that despite the difficulty, you can cut through your human karmic experience—the gravitational pull that keeps you in the cycle of the consciousness in which you initially sowed—because I have taken what you have sown and made it into something that is magnificent.

11. I am with you always, and my Plan is beneficial to all

As I said earlier, this kind of deliverance depends upon you. I have already taken everything that has happened and put it in part of the Master Plan and shaped it in such a way as to be a benefit to everyone, including you. The question is, are you willing to accept this? The question is, are you willing to change your relationship to circumstances and conditions in a way that would allow you to see the gifts that are awaiting you? Will you use your spiritual power to pierce through the veil of appearances or will you use your spiritual power to keep you perceiving the appearances? As always, the choice is yours. As always, I love you no matter what you do and what you choose. And as always, I am everywhere that you are. So, regardless of what you do, I will be there.

There are, however, some choices you can make that will make it easier for you to see me there with you, so that you do not go through the experience described in the famous poem "Footprints in the Sand." In this poem a person is recalling a dream in which the two of us were walking on the beach. In the most wonderful times, the person observed, there were two sets of footprints, but when times were hard and challenging there was only one set. The person automatically assumed that I had abandoned them during those times and questioned me as to why I would do such a thing. I had to remind them that when there was only one set of footprints they were mine, that I was carrying them. So I will always carry you. But unless you are willing to come up a little higher in your spiritual insights, when you see the single set of footprints you will mistakenly think they are yours. If you want to see both sets, then change your point of view. ✼

IX. Birthing versus Building

1. Capture my words in your heart

Yes, my Reverend Daughter, it has been some time since you have let your fingers do the listening. Do not grow into thinking that you need to be in some altered state in order to hear my voice. True, it may appear to be easier with fewer so-called distractions. However, you must be available to me at all times, regardless of the medium available to capture my words. And remember what I have told you many times before—the most important place for my words to be captured is in your heart.

Yes, it feels as though you have been on a roller coaster ride for the last several years. However, it is time for it to stop seeming so exhausting. Your life will always be intense by most people's standards. Yet you will appear to be able to handle this with greater and greater ease.

2. Mothering is allowing things to develop in your mind according to their own timing

Tell the people about the process of mothering that is the internal process of allowing things to develop in your consciousness according to their own timing. Mothering in the absolute sense has nothing to do with gender, sexuality, or specific individuals. Mothering is simultaneously both a task and a relationship. Too much time has been spent in your societies through the ages attempting to ascribe some of my characteristics to certain individuals because of their age, race, social position, gender, etc., while excluding others from being able to fully express these qualities as well. This has been not merely fallacious but deadly (literally and figuratively) to the very souls of millions through millennia. I do not chop myself up. There are no parts of me that are available to some and not to others. No group has a monopoly on any of my characteristics. I express equally through all. I am Balance in the highest sense of the word. And because you are made in my likeness and image, you are Balance too. However, too few of you know this. You claim some things and reject others and then wonder why you cannot feel my essence in everything that you do.

There is a difference between birthing and building. In your societies you have attributed the birthing process to the feminine and the building process to the masculine. There is nothing wrong with this characterization, if it is merely for the purpose of understanding the yin and yang of every person. However, when the feminine is reserved for females exclusively and the masculine associated with males only, there is an imbalance at every level—personally, collectively, and globally. I want you to be balanced. Birthing is an inner process of gestation, while building is the process of manipulating matter to create new forms. By its nature, building is an external process. Both men and women are involved in both birthing and building. However, some claim their participation in one more than the other.

3. There is a difference between birthing and building

When one builds, there is a sense of being in control. One is aware of being an active agent of free will and free choice, of utilizing one's creative impulses and intellectual, as well as artistic, capabilities. The ego is very much involved in this process, since one assumes the posture of being a creator. In building one works with matter and the way that consciousness crystallizes into matter. The emphasis is on the end result, the product. It is easy to lose a sense of reverence for the sanctity of the materials being utilized when the builder assumes a position of superiority over the materials, products, and by-products. This increases when there is a sense of superiority over the other builders, as well.

4. In building there is a sense of control over the end result

When one builds, one tends to look outside oneself and compare what one is building to what another is building. Competition easily comes into play here, as do envy and greed. Builders often try to compensate for their lack of relationship with me, with themselves, and with others by diverting their own attention to task-oriented activities. They are always looking to have something to show that proves their value and their worth. And they often fear losing what they have built, which leads to viewing others as potential threats.

5. Birthing provides the space for an already complete idea to unfold

Birthing, on the other hand, is an internal process in which one is acutely aware that one is not in control. There is a sense of being a steward, a caretaker, an incubator for a grand activity that supersedes one's own self. Birthers do not take credit for what they have birthed. Instead they marvel and are humbled at having been allowed to participate in the process at all. There is nothing external to compare to. There is nothing to prove and no one to prove it to. It is not competitive, envious, or jealous. It is to be of service in the highest sense.

When you are birthing, you are aware that something is dependent upon you for nurturance. This responsibility is taken quite seriously and is held as a high priority, even higher than one's own needs. It does not even feel like sacrifice, since there is an inherent sense of oneness with what is developing inside of oneself. It is an internal job. There is no need for anyone else to see or participate in the process, other than as a witness. One understands that the most important thing to be done is to take care of one's self, not to be clever. The greatest job is to provide a space, an environment, for the divine unfoldment of an already complete idea. There is no illusion regarding one's role in the process. There is awe, wonder at the transformation that is occurring, and the deepest respect for the nature and the timing of what is being "hatched."

6. Birthing requires surrender to what's being birthed and its processes

What is being birthed has its own timing, its own gestation period, its own sense of when it is ready to spring forth. No amount of forcing, planning, or setting of timelines and schedules will alter this one iota. Best of all, there is no desire to do so. There is a patience in the birthing process that enables one to simply be with what is going on. Being fully present in every moment is perhaps the most important thing. This is different from worrying about the future, trying to hedge against loss, or trying to manipulate the system in one's favor, as are often the case when one is building. Birthing requires surrender to both what is being birthed and the process that it undergoes.

Furthermore, after the birthing has occurred, the one who gave birth makes no claim to own what has come forth out of them. There is no expectation that what has come from them will emulate them or fulfill their needs. They have brought a precious gift into the world that they must share with others. Possession does not exist in this paradigm. In fact, one is aware that if one were to hold onto what one has birthed, it would suffocate under the cloak of ownership. Understanding this, one is aware that all of the caretaking of the thing birthed is for the purpose of its future development, for letting it go, for making it strong enough to make it on its own, for recycling it into the hands of others, for empowering and liberating it to fulfill its own great mission in life.

Stop building so much and start birthing. When a Divine Idea comes to you, allow yourself to be impregnated with its seed. The seed has within it all that it needs to be what it must be; it only needs to be planted in a fertile place. Let your mind become fertile ground for my Divine Ideas. Don't let your anxieties about producing and succeeding interfere with the sacred work of being a spiritual gardener. Learn how to work with the spiritual elements instead of trying to control them. Trust that the seed knows what it is to be and that you do not have to coax, coerce, bribe, threaten, or manipulate it into being what it is intended to be. Stop questioning and challenging the need for gestation, and start honoring this sacredness of unfoldment. All things mature and materialize on time and in time, according to their own nature. Don't hurry your harvest. You cannot make Divine Ideas come into alignment with your needs and expectations. No, you must align with the way things are.

7. Stop building so much and start birthing

8. I am the Creator; when you think, you think with my mind

Your American society has gotten so far away from an understanding of this birthing process as a way of life that you have begun to regard yourselves as the power behind creation. You are not the ones creating. I am *the Creator. I* am the Creator. I *am* the Creator. And I am not just talking about Genesis, "In the beginning . . . ," some very long time ago. Whenever you embark upon anything, it is the beginning. I am the Alpha and the Omega, the beginning and the end of everything. When you think, you think with my mind. When you see, you see with my vision. When you love, you love with my heart. When you express, you move with my creativity. You are simply using properties and principles that belong to everyone.

The search to find what is uniquely and inherently yours is very problematic. In this search you are trying to determine how you are different from everyone else. What you need to focus on instead is how you complement everyone else. A complement is something "different." However, it is not different simply for the sake of being different. It is different in order to bring a balance, a wholeness, to everything around. Your uniqueness brings a wholeness to the collective whole. It is something that should be used not to separate you from others but to bring you closer together. Harmony is not singing in unison; the varying rhythms and melodies come together to provide a greater sound, a fuller expression, to bring depth and richness. The harmony and unity that you pray for recognize the gifts that you have to offer one another.

9. You serve what you birth; what you build serves you

When you are a birther, you recognize that what you have birthed is a gift to you. When you are building, you often think of yourself as the gift to what is being built. You are wondering, when will it begin to take care of you? When will it bring you comfort, success, reward, satisfaction? Your product is there to serve you. However, when you birth, you are there to serve what you have brought forth. It is not there to fulfill your needs; you are there to support its needs. This is not a sacrificial act. In the process of supporting, so much is learned, experienced, and revealed that the support is seen for the sacred work that it is. It is as much for the benefit of the supporter as it is for the supported.

It is truly a shame that your society has all but obliterated its native population, for there was so much to learn from them about how to live in harmony and balance with oneself, with others, and with the environment. They understood the earth as a mother and respected what was birthed from her. There was no sense of owning what came from her, but merely pleasure in being able to use it and care for it. Thinking of yourselves exclusively as builders makes you feel like masters, enabling you to lord over all of the earth's resources as though they are for your personal enjoyment, exploration, and even exploitation, if you so desire. This lack of respect regarding birthing has enabled you to denigrate women, treating them like chattel, property to be owned. Labeling people like in a hierarchical food chain has enabled you to literally own the babies from some mothers' wombs.

O my children, this must stop. There is nothing wrong with building. There is nothing wrong with actively creating. But it must be balanced with the reverence and spiritual grounded-ness that come from being aware of oneself as an incubator of Divine Ideas. Remember what I said earlier—the most important part of birthing is taking care of yourself, not manipulating the baby. Mind your minds. Allow yourselves to be the fertile ground that you are. Your laboring will be so much easier when you no longer think that it's on your shoulders to make everything happen. Just be present. Be a good steward. Love with open hands what comes through you. Understand that what you bring to the world is a gift, not something for you to develop for your own exclusive enjoyment. Respect the process of Divine Unfoldment. Prepare for it.

10. The most important part of birthing is taking care of yourself

Don't wait until you become "pregnant" with Divine Ideas to start living a healthy life. Everything that you do to yourself will impact everything that is ever birthed through you. Keep yourself fit and healthy—mentally, physically, and spiritually. Be prepared at all times to receive Divine Ideas to be nurtured in your very being. What a glorious thing this is. Acknowledge and respect it, and you will find yourself enjoying it more. Yes, there is much to build, but so very much more to be birthed.

X. My Grace Is Sufficient

Just continue to make yourself both accessible and available and I will give you what you are to say, my Reverend Daughter. Once again, you are making too much of a distinction between what is supposedly your work and what is my work. When you turn all things over to me, you will realize that this distinction is faulty. I am always the one who is doing the work. The work happens in you, through you, and as you. And as long as you continue to labor under the notion that it is you doing the work, then it will continue to feel just like that—labor.

1. Stop looking for good to come to you through the fruits of your own labor

There is this false conception—based upon interpretations of the earliest chapters of Genesis, where it is proclaimed that I have made life difficult and challenging for you human beings—that life is to be lived only by the sweat of your brow. Too many of you are measuring your sense of accomplishment in life by how much you have, in fact, sweat. If there has not been a sufficient amount of pain involved—hard work, hardship, sacrifice, even mere stress—then there is a tendency to believe that nothing has been gained. The popular colloquialism "No pain, no gain" is no longer merely a prophecy about the future; it has become deeply rooted as your belief system.

It is difficult for you, especially in your American society, to accept my Grace. You are always looking to the fruits of your own labor as the source of your good. You find it difficult to accept anything that you feel you do not deserve. And you do not feel like you deserve anything if you have not worked hard for it. So it is most challenging for you to simply accept the Good when it comes around. It is difficult for you to feel a sense of ownership and entitlement towards your spiritual

Good because it is outside the realm of your human reward systems. My Grace is not a reward for anything that you have done. My Grace is not removed for anything that you have not done. My Grace is forever, and my Grace is sufficient.

2. Your ego obstructs your understanding of my Grace

What do I mean when I talk about Grace? Grace is such a nebulous concept for those who live in an individualistic, capitalistic, materialistic society. Those who buy into the fundamental assumptions that run such a society have gotten into thinking that it is individuals who create their own opportunities, individuals who create their own good, individuals who, in fact, are the cause of their own rises and successes. This is extremely egocentric thinking. While it is necessary for every individual to assume the primary responsibility for his or her experience of the life that he or she is living, too much of this idea makes someone a First Cause in and of his or her own right. Metaphysically speaking, First Cause refers to my absolute creative energy, which brings all things into manifestation. The only reason why you are associated with First Cause at all is because as human beings you are actually spiritual by nature. You are a part of me. It is your spirituality, not your humanity, that provides you with the power to manifest as a First Cause.

As human beings, you can never be absolute First Cause because all things about you, right down to your identity of yourselves, are based on contrasts and comparisons. These are relative notions. The realm of absolute causation never deals in the relative, for it is as absolutely independent as it is Absolute. You human beings tend to resist the idea that you exist in some kind of spiritual Absolute. You're always wanting to know "Well, what about this situation? Or what about that situation? How does it work here? How does it work there?" In this deep searching it is quite obvious that you think that most things are, indeed, circumstantial and conditional. Therefore you are constantly going about trying to create the perfect circumstances and the right conditions for yourself, assuming that acquiring these will create the space for you to be the All that you are to be. The All that you are to be, then, is dependent on outer expressions. However, if this is the place where you live, then you will never know what it is to receive my Grace.

Grace is outside the realm of accomplishment, reward, punishment—anything and everything that would be associated with the human process of creating. Grace is my love and provision for you just because you are. Hear what I just said. Grace is my love and provision for you simply because you are. Simply because you are my own, my only begotten children. Everything that I have is yours simply by your spiritual birthright. It is your divine inheritance. You cannot earn your inheritance; it is yours simply because you were born, simply because you exist. Because you exist, you are recognized, and the goods of the estate are divvied out in a manner that takes you into consideration.

3. Grace is my love and provision for you simply because you are

In human families there may be attempts to determine who deserves what and to dole things out based upon past or present (and sometimes expected future) attitudes, actions, and behaviors. The good is rationed, so to speak, and there is someone who makes a judgment about how much you are to have, even when your right to have it is clearly established by your birth. In my spiritual kingdom, there is no divvying up like this. Some individuals do not get more than others. No one is left out. There is no squabbling, haggling, or competing in my world and in my system. Each is filled unto his or her own need, as is described in the Biblical story of the multiplying of the loaves and the fishes. By starting with what they had, gathering that up, blessing it, and sharing it, all needs were met, and there was more left over at the end than they had started with in the beginning.

4. *Your job is to live by my Grace and accept it as sufficient*

Do you have faith and belief enough to step out on my Grace? Can you accept the fact that I want your life to be fulfilled because I want as much life expressing through you as humanly possible? Do you understand that you are indeed my shining glory? Out of anything and everything that has been consciously or unconsciously created and developed in this world, your existence as human beings is the very closest thing to my very nature. I want your lives to be fulfilled. I want you to be happy, healthy, creative, productive, loved, sustained. These are things that I want for you, and these are things that ultimately come through my Grace.

Since you live in a temporal world where all of the outer forms of expression are constantly changing and fluctuating, you have no way of ever really knowing what is ahead of you and what will be available to you. Trying to worry about all of this by looking at it simply through your human eyes can get quite overwhelming and perplexing. Once you learn that your job is to live by my Grace, you will learn how to simply praise me and praise yourself as a spiritual being and declare our deep Oneness with one another. You stop looking for reasons why the Good should be there or reasons why the Good may not stay, and you simply go on with the business of enjoying the Goodness at hand.

5. *Your ego challenges its subservient role in the spiritual realm*

I am not trying to render you powerless, only trying to help you keep your egos in check (as you would say). Your ego has such a strong need to feel as though it is doing something; it needs to take credit for what is going on in your life, for better or worse. Your ego has a difficult time accepting a subservient role in the spiritual kingdom; it wants to place itself front and center. This notion that the ego is the servant of the Spirit is extremely unsettling for many of you. However, if you are to be successful on your spiritual journey, it is necessary to move beyond merely looking at the world through your natural eyesight.

When you are able to accept Grace as simply a state of being, not an action that I take to bestow something upon you in time of need, not a perk for having reached a certain spiritual plateau, not the by-product of your own spiritual disciplinary work . . . when you can accept that my Grace is sufficient simply because you are, then your true freedom and ability to access the Grace that is already yours will come more effortlessly and easily. Perhaps the most operative word here is "humility." Humility is what is necessary for your ego to move into a subservient position. Your ego must be willing to surrender, to submit, to admit that it is, as your grandmother would say, the caboose and not the engine. My Grace is sufficient.

What does my Grace look like? It looks like whatever you need it to be in the moment in order for you to know that you are not alone in the Universe, that you are under my watch and in my care. Grace may look to you like a healing of your body temple against all predictions. It may look like a calm, a sense of peace, in the midst of seeming great chaos and confusion in your life. My Grace may look like the answer to the riddles of your life that have kept you stumped and confused in a total state of darkness. My Grace may look like the energy that you need to keep putting one foot in front of the other when you feel too weary to move on. My Grace may be the softening of the hearts and the meeting of the minds between individuals who have been at odds with each other in polarized situations. My Grace may look like that financial need being met in a most mysterious way, lifting a tremendous burden off of your shoulders. My Grace may look like a beacon of light at the end of the long tunnel, letting you know that there is a way out and that a brighter day is coming. My Grace can look like so many things. How many needs do you have? Well, therein is the number of ways in which my Grace can and will appear.

6. What does my Grace look like?

7. You can't accept my Grace for others until you accept it for yourself

My Grace needs no explanation; it needs no validation or proof. As you would say, "The proof is in the pudding." The benefits and rewards of my Grace are self-sufficient. However, because you have gotten into this notion of things being deserved by your human actions, not only do you have too small of a space in your own consciousness to be able to accept my Grace for yourself . . . you also have too small of a place in consciousness to be able to accept my Grace for others. How often do you find it difficult to rejoice and celebrate in other's good fortune when you feel that somehow or other they simply don't deserve it? And how angry do you get when it appears as though those who do not deserve it are somehow getting ahead, especially if they appear to be getting ahead of you? What goes on in your minds?

It may do you good to review the Biblical story of the prodigal son, who was gone for a very long time in a foreign land, where he wasted and squandered his inheritance on wine, women, and song. He was so incredibly ashamed and embarrassed at how low he had sunk that he decided to go back to his father's house and beg for a job as a mere servant. It was beyond his ken that his father would open up his arms and embrace him as the lost son who was now found. The son was convinced that because of his actions he needed to abdicate his sonship. He was not returning as his father's son. In fact, he kept insisting that because he had sinned before his father, he was no longer worthy of that honor.

The father's response was to throw a party for him. He put robes upon his son's back and a ring upon his finger, and he instructed everyone to make a feast, a banquet. Well, there was another son, the prodigal son's brother, who had never left the father's house and who had been in the father's good stead for all of this time. When he saw all of the excitement and celebration that was going on over the return of his younger brother, he was quite annoyed, infuriated, and upset. When he confronted his father with his concerns, he let his father know that he had been a loyal son and had done everything that his father had wanted him to do. Yet never once had the father so much as given him a little kid to make merry and have a feast with. Now his father was killing the fatted calf for this squandering son returned. And the father let him know, "My son, you have been with me always; everything that I have is yours. You never asked." Herein is part of the problem.

Many of you are angry at the ability of others to access my Grace at what appears to be your expense or the expense of others. The thing that needs to be accessed here is your own condemnation and judgment. The reason why these individuals are able to receive my Grace is because they are open to it, because they are saying "Yes!" to it, because they have found a place within their hearts to forgive themselves, as well as the other people involved. The only thing keeping you from receiving the Grace awaiting you is your own judgment, ridicule, and condemnation of anything and everything that you feel has kept your Good away from you, including yourself—in fact, most especially yourself.

8. To receive the Grace awaiting you, empty your storage bins

Listen to what I just said. Instead of spending all of your time trying to convince me to give more to you, trying to convince the world to be a safer place for you to live in . . . spend the time releasing your own sense of condemnation and judgment towards the things you are holding onto. This is a very, very necessary step in order for you to be available to me. You can never be really available to me until you have accepted my Grace. Accept my Grace. This requires, however, that you empty those storage bins that you have been carrying around, those places of rubbish, debris, nostalgia, anger, frustration, and bitterness. You hang onto these things because you are afraid that if you do not have them you might do something that is unbecoming or uncharacteristic. Just know that my Grace is sufficient. My Grace is sufficient. You don't have to spend all of your time trying to figure out who should get what—when, where, or how. This is not your concern. Your concern is to be available to me, to be available to you, to come home and accept the open arms that are waiting for you. ❧

XI. COME, I WILL GIVE YOU REST

"Come unto me all ye who are heavy laden and I will give you rest." What is this Rest that I speak of? Is this the rest you seek when you merely want to get away from your burdens and your troubles? Is this the rest that your body desires when it is riddled with fatigue? Is this the rest that comes from having weathered through the storm and still being around to tell the story?

My Rest reflects all of these things in general and is none of these in the particular. The Rest that I provide goes so much further than reactions, responses, resentments, or resistances to the outer world of circumstances. My Rest is whole and complete within itself. My Rest is not about getting away from anything; my Rest is about coming to me. My Rest is that place of restoration where your mind, body, and soul are rejuvenated, revitalized, simultaneously.

You don't have to be at a place of exhaustion to receive this Rest. Conversely, the fact that you are so exhausted is no guarantee that you will receive this Rest. You don't have to be exhausted, and the fact that you are exhausted isn't a coupon. What is it that I am saying here?

There is nothing virtuous in suffering just for the sake of suffering. Much of your suffering is self-imposed. The way in which you sometimes make yourselves feel better about this self-imposed suffering, as well as the suffering that seems like it is being imposed upon you, is to tell yourself about all of the rewards that are waiting for you as a result of your having suffered. However, the only spiritual rewards that are awaiting you are not because you have suffered. If there are spiritual

1. Rest is not getting away from things but coming to me

2. There is nothing virtuous in suffering just for the sake of suffering

awards, they are yours because of your ability to move beyond the suffering and still feel your connection and your presence with me. Understand the difference here.

Popular thinking would have you believe that I reward suffering. I don't reward suffering. However, if you are able to be in your state of suffering and not have it define you, if you are able to be in a state of suffering and look in, through, and beyond the illusions of the circumstances that you are growing through, then the natural by-product is my Peace. It is this Peace that puts you in a position of being able to Rest. The reason why more of you are not able to experience this rejuvenation and restoration is that in those moments when you retire, relax, sleep, you are not at Peace. Since you are not at Peace, no Rest takes place.

3. Rest is a state of being that is ultimately about Peace

Since this Resting is ultimately about Peace, it does not require that you be in a state of relaxation, sleep, slumber, or inactivity. You can get Rest from me even in the midst of a seemingly hectic or busy schedule. It is not the presence or lack of external stimuli that determines whether or not you are in a position to receive my Rest. Your ability to receive is an internal proposition. You must be emotionally and spiritually primed for this state of being.

Notice what I said—this state of being. This Rest is not an event. This Rest is not a location or a destination along the path. This Rest is a state of being. What do I mean when I say that it is a state of being? A state of being refers to a condition of consciousness. This condition is not temporary, nor is it spurred on by catalytic events. A state of being reflects a consciousness that is continuous. It is not in the particular; instead, it infuses every thought, word, and deed. A state of being encompasses the whole of you—your physical state, your emotional state, your spiritual state. You take you with you wherever you go.

How do you reach this state of being in which you are able to experience my Peace so that you may, indeed, Rest? The things that you are so heavily laden with you must not perceive as being yours, nor must you perceive them as being an integral part of who you are. There must be the deep understanding within you that "This, too, shall pass." I am referring here to the practice of nonattachment. Most of you will not step aside, lay your burdens down, long enough to experience my Rest. Even in your moments of so-called relaxation you are still talking about and engaging with the things that are the most burdensome to you. When you understand that the things that are burdening you are neither part of your being nor intransigent, then you are able to know deep within your heart of hearts that there is a transcendent place in consciousness to which you can ascend. "Stay upstairs" in your thinking. Let things go much sooner. You don't have to get paralysis from your own analysis. You don't earn your stripes through worry.

4. Practice nonattachment; lay your burdens down

You must also come. What does is mean to come? To come means that you seek all resolutions from me. To come means that you arrive at your own free will, without depending upon pain and discomfort to needle you along. To come implies conscious will, choice, volition, on your part. To come means that you are choosing to yield your will, to synchronize your will with my Will, so that your will and the Divine Will become One. To come is to realize and to accept that the burden of having all the answers and solving all the problems is not on your back. To come takes humility as well as courage.

5. To Rest you must also come to me

I commend you, my Reverend Daughter Deborah, on your willingness and your courage. I am most pleased that you are turning more and more things over to my care; for this will increasingly put you in the position to Rest, to experience the kind of Rest that only I, the Lord God Almighty, can afford you as a human being. Sometimes you question my judgment in my plans for your life. You wonder how it will be humanly possible to accomplish all of the things you know are before you to accomplish. Know that I am with you always. You are never alone. You are never expected to accomplish things without the proper tools, resources, or guidance to do so. ❧

XII. "ALL OF MY HELP COMES FROM THE LORD"

Do you know what you are saying when you say that all of your help "cometh from the Lord?" Do you understand what you are saying, my child? This is not a reference to the past. When you say this, too many of you are looking at your life in hindsight and remembering the numerous blessings that have been bestowed upon you. In saying that all of your help comes from the Lord, you are remembering those specific instances when you perceived me as having come to your aid. It is good that you remember. It is good that you acknowledge me as your Source. However, there is a way in which this has you looking at the past in gratitude as opposed to looking towards the future in expectancy. Understand the difference here.

1. Balance past gratitude with future expectancy

When you have received what you refer to as your testimony (that is, when you have survived some trial or tribulation that you found particularly challenging), oftentimes you reminisce about the ways in which I have provided for you, either when you didn't expect it or when it seemed more miraculous than you had previously considered possible. Too often, you accept my help as the last resort. You first try all of the things you know how to do that would keep the situation under control, utilize whatever resources you believe are available at hand, or those of so-called another. (I use the phrase "so-called another" because there is really only One of you here.)

When you determine, on your own, the way that you think a circumstance should best be handled, you then go about the business of trying to secure that particular conclusion. For most of you, it is only when you become quite disappointed, disillusioned, frustrated, anxious, or worried that you even

2. Turn to me as first choice, not last resort

think about turning to me as your Source rather than relying on the material, psychic, emotional things that are readily (or perhaps not so readily) available to you.

When you say that all of your help comes from the Lord, this is not merely a last resort statement. It is a declaration of the Truth as you understand it in the context of your daily living. My help is not some extraordinary event or process that only comes into being in the most dire circumstances. When you say that all of your help comes from the Lord, you understand that this does mean all. You stop thinking that there is some person, place, or thing that would be a better provider than I—even your own selves.

3. Continuously lift up your eyes to the hills of transcendence

The popular Psalm declares that "I will lift up mine eyes unto the hills." Look up this word "will" in Hebrew in its appropriate tense, and you will find that, as a verb, it does not signify a single point in time. Nor is it a verb that emphasizes a future action. It is a word that connotes a constant state of beingness. (Once again, your English language is not a language of the Spirit, and you have to work a little harder to understand English translations of mystical works written in foreign languages, especially languages from Middle Eastern and Far Eastern traditions.) It is a constant practice of looking to the hills, with the hills symbolizing a transcendent consciousness.

Understand the concept of transcendent. In transcendence one rises above the current circumstances and conditions to a realm that is Pure Spirit in its presentation, observation, and analysis. Transcendence does not deny whatever is going on by trying to proclaim that it doesn't exist. Rather, from this vantage point the relationship of the so-called facts to the Truth becomes much clearer. When one is on a hill and is looking down at something in the valley, in one sense it would appear that the object being observed appears to be less clear. The distance makes it more difficult to distinguish the fine details about it. However, observing something from a hill helps you to put the relative importance of that thing into perspective. The sense of distance allows you to see that the object observed is not so big that it could eclipse the observer.

However, observing something from a hill helps you to put the importance of that thing into perspective. The sense of distance allows you to see that the object is not so big that it could eclipse you. When you are in the middle of your "stuff," everything appears to be so much greater than you. There is a saying in your society, "You can't see the forest for the trees." This is very much what happens. You become overwhelmed by all that you see in front of you, and you are unable to step back to absorb the whole. You become fixated on the pieces, the fragments that have attracted your attention, and you tend to forget how all of it is interrelated and interconnected in a way that makes for wholeness and completion.

To be in the position to access the help that is constantly available, one must go to the hill. Understand what I just said. There is a difference between your accessing me and my assisting you. I am always assisting you. However, if you have not accessed me, then you will not even see that I am there, let alone feel or appreciate my assistance. In order to access me, you must first and foremost look for me, look towards me. Do not think that my help is second tier. Don't leave me on the bench while you are playing all of your varsity players—your job, your mates, your friends, your family, your money, your power and influence, your knowledge and know-how, and on and on. You do not call me into the game until there is some kind of injury, or until one of these players is no longer in the position to play, even if they are just fatigued.

4. Put me on the team and make me an active player in your life

It is not that I am sitting on the sidelines, inactive until you summon me. However, you cannot truly experience me as an active player in your life if you do not put me on the team and recognize me as a player. Lift up your eyes to the hills, for it is from this transcendent place that your help does indeed come.

5. Stop waiting; your time is now

You do not have to beg for my help. You do not need to beseech me. It is my good pleasure that you have it all. I have already given it all. I cannot give more than everything, and everything is what is always available to you. However, if you do not perceive this, you will not access it. If you do not understand that the world is waiting for you to stake your claim on it, then it is you who will continue to sit on the bench, on the sidelines, wondering and waiting when your time will arrive. Stop waiting. Your time is now. Now is the only time there ever is. Anytime you ever do anything, you're always doing it in the now. Now is the only time when one can ever take action. So as soon as you decide to do something . . . voilà, it's now! You create the nowness by your action. You turn the future into now anytime you stop waiting to be the All that you are ordained to be. I have the utmost patience. The concept of patience only has relevance when you believe in time-space continuums. Something appears to be patient when it has the ability to remain steadfast while it is in some state of abeyance. I am active at all times. I am not waiting for anything ever. I am the fullness of who I am at all times, and because you are me, so are you. Any sense of your waiting for anything is but an illusion.

6. Shift your focus from manifestation to matriculation

There are those times when you're told to "Wait on the Lord." Do not get confused about what this means. Most of the time when you think you are waiting, you are in fact looking for some external sign, some external activity or object, to appear in your life before you get serious about the spiritual business at hand. "Well, why keep the high watch if there's nothing to look at?" Too often, your attitude is "When I have something worth looking after, then I will take care of it." This attitude—that something has to be present in order for you to develop the consciousness of owning it, claiming it, caring for or nurturing and sustaining it—simply has to go.

When you understand that there is nothing to wait for, you actively go about the business of deepening your consciousness. When you are deepening your consciousness, in a conscious and active manner, you do not feel like you are in an abyss. You do not feel like you are in limbo. You appreciate the fullness of the moment where you are. The fact that certain material things have not materialized does not stop you at all from actively engaging in your relationship with me.

When you actively engage me at all times, you discover that when the so-called material things actually do appear, it seems almost anticlimatic. The emphasis has shifted from manifestation to matriculation. (Look up this word "matriculation" in the dictionary.) When you matriculate, you go through a process step by step, fully present, and every step along the way is important. The fact that you have not arrived at graduation yet does not decrease, in any way, shape, or form, the fullness of the moment where you are. Value is placed on every step along the way, and you grow in your awareness of how the progression is cumulative. That is to say, everything that you learn and experience serves as a foundation for what is next. There is a sense of order to this learning process, which decreases the tendency to think that the events of life are merely random. You understand that each has a place within the whole, even if it's only for the purpose of rounding you out.

7. Every step is important and cumulative; be present for each one

Understand what I am saying here. If you were to sign up for an academic program, all of the classes you would take during your matriculation process would not necessarily be in the field that you chose as your major. In order to round yourself out, you must take some courses in other areas and other fields. At times these may appear to be completely unrelated to the subject matter at hand, but this is too small a view. The other courses relate to the development of your thinking— your analytical, logistical, and intuitive, as well as creative processes. So it is in your life.

8. My help is the evidence of our partnership

There are many things that you are called upon to do that don't seem to be directly connected to where you think you want to go or even should go. During such times you feel like you are waiting to "get on with it," instead of understanding that where you are is holy ground, that where you are is just as important in your developmental process as any other step along the way. Where does your help come from? To whom or to what do you turn for your help? What will it take for you to declare in earnest that your help comes from me? Have I ever let you down? Has there ever been a promise that I have not kept? Have you ever been worse off for having put your fate in my hands?

I love you, my children. What you perceive as help is really just our partnership. We are co-creators with each other. Remember that I am your creative partner. Turn to me first. Anything and everything that I have is yours to use to whatever degree you so desire. Know that it cannot be used up, nor will your using it infringe upon another's ability to use me as well. I am an Inexhaustible Supply. Come to me first, not last, and see what a difference in your life it will make.

XIII. JOY

It is a good thing that your next singing circle is focusing on the concept of Joy. It is a good thing because it is something that you, all of you, need to learn so much more about. There is a tendency in your society to speak more of and about joy during your "holiday season." That season is approaching now.

1. Joy means many different things to you

You will use this term "joy" in greeting cards. You will speak of it in terms of parties and festivities. During this season you, all of you, are more likely to consciously try to "spread" it by good works and acts of kindness in this season. Some of you will even try to purchase this thing called joy through your materialistic endeavors by trying to satisfy your ego's hunger to possess, to be recognized, or to feel (or at least look) successful. Some of you will approach this joy from a vicarious position, that is to say, you will appreciate the joy on other people's faces in response to some interaction or intervention on your part. It will bring you satisfaction to know that you brought someone else joy.

Those of you of a religious bent, especially those who are steeped in the Christian tradition, will associate joy with the "good news" about the birth of Jesus, the Christ, some two thousand years ago. At this time you will not only honor and celebrate this birth, but also actively spread the word about it in an effort to convert individuals to accepting Jesus as the sacrificial lamb, the redeemer of their souls. Your joy comes from knowing that Jesus was not only born but died on the cross and that as a result of that sacrifice your sins have been washed away, as the doctrine goes.

For still others of you joy becomes a matter of family. This is a time when you are more likely to reach out to, embrace, commune with, and acknowledge members of your family. This may include individuals who are not biologically related to you who have become close, intimate confidantes and/or colleagues. This close association gives a tremendous sense of belonging, which lifts the sense of isolationism that surrounds so many people most of the time, whether they are consciously aware of it or not. Massive public displays of togetherness and unity (even if merely commercialized ones, such as holidays) can be overwhelming to many people. For this reason there is a higher rate of suicide during your holiday season, even in the midst of all of this societal festivity making.

2. Joy is a state of being that perceives my Goodness all of the time

The Joy that you need to know and understand has nothing to do with any of the things I have just mentioned. Joy is not a feeling; it is not an emotion; nor is it a commodity that can be bartered, exchanged, negotiated, or hoarded. Joy is a state of being that has far more to do with one's perception of the world than with actual activities and/or circumstances. Joy is the ability to be aware in your heart of hearts that I am, indeed, "Good all of the time," as the song that you love to sing indicates. I am Good all of the time. Because I am Good all of the time, there really is nothing for you to fear or to worry about.

The idea that I am Good all of the time is not an abstraction; it is an ever-present reality. However, it will not be part of your personal reality unless you are able to embody it. It can't just be a cliché with which you agree; it must be an awareness that you live. It is not a conclusion that you come to after you have attempted to analyze the wherefore's and the why's about everything that goes on in your life. The fact that I am Good all of the time should be your starting point. It should not be merely the conclusion that you arrive at after your own analysis. It should be the very presumption, assumption, premise, foundation stone that you begin with. In fact, if you begin with it more often, it will make you aware much earlier that your analysis of the outer circumstances is really a moot point. It is moot. When something is moot, it is simply going through the motions as though it were real, but the outcome bears no meaningful significance and is void of any consequence.

I keep referring to my being Good all of the time as a fact. I wish to make myself clear about this point. I use the term "fact" because you human beings, especially those from Western thought traditions, feel that you need to begin with a so-called fact, concrete evidence external in nature. A fact is something that you think is indisputable and therefore provides you with some solid ground upon which to stand. However, as you have learned time and time again, your so-called human facts are not immutable. Your so-called human facts are based upon perceptions derived from your sensory abilities. Therefore, the facts are often disputed among you, even when you are looking at the same body of evidence. However, when I use "fact" in regard to something about my character or my nature, I use the term to say, implicitly and explicitly, that that thing is a given. In this regard it is a fact, something that you can build upon, but unlike your human facts it is not shifting sand. It is a given. It does not have to be questioned, nor does it have to be proved in the particular, because it has been proved so many times in the whole.

3. Unlike human facts, my spiritual facts never shift or change

When you are able to really be aware of, appreciate, and embody throughout your day the fact that I am Good all of the time, you will experience this thing called Joy. My Joy does not come from having all of the circumstances and the conditions according to your liking. In order for you to have Joy, you don't have to have everything unfold according to the plans that you, yourself, have created. Joy does not come from having your expectations fulfilled, nor does it come from having life's circumstances exceed your expectations. In fact, your expectations cease to be a variable in the equation of life.

In knowing that I am Good all of the time, you will naturally develop fewer and fewer expectations—other than the

4. That I am Good all of the time becomes your only expectation

fact that I am Good all of the time. That is the only expectation that you should have about life and its outcomes. For whatever it is that happens—how it happens, where it happens, when it happens—is according to a Divine Plan that has you and everybody else in mind. It has you in mind, and it provides for your good. My good is a benevolent Good. It is good because I am Good, and Good is the only thing that I can be. Within every circumstance is the seed of a wonderful harvest for all.

You must go through life looking for the "win/win." You must not allow yourself to become discouraged by things you see that you consider to be out of alignment, out of integrity, or apparently out of one's mind. You will look beyond all of this, and you will see me.

5. Don't miss the water by looking at the glass

There is a letter that I previously gave to the dear Reverend Daughter here, which she referred to in her last sermon, regarding breaking the paradigm of the glass being half empty or half full. There is a tendency to want to look at life as either half empty or half full. However, these are just flip sides of the same coin; there is no change in consciousness, fundamentally, whether one is viewing life from one perspective or the other. Don't see the glass as half empty or half full. Your attention should not be on the glass; your attention should be on the water. The essence, the fullness, the essential qualities of the water are not determined by the container that it is in. The container does not impact or affect the water at all. The water is the fullness that it is, wherever it is, however much of it is there. You miss the water. In paying so much attention to what appears to be empty space in the container, you focus your attention on what isn't even there. You miss the fullness of what is. So it is in all of life. The essence of who you are, the essence of all of my spiritual qualities, is not determined by the container that the qualities are in. If something looks like it is merely half full, that just means that there is a greater capacity still awaiting it. If it looks like everything is just spilling out all over the place, well, that means those containers aren't quite big enough to handle all of the Good. But in any event, it is the water that must be celebrated.

When you know that I am Good all of the time, in spite of what you see, you will be less inclined to judge. Your lack of joy is not due to the circumstances and the conditions in your lives; your lack of joy is due to your interpretation of those circumstances and conditions—which leads you to believe that your good is not at hand, that things will not work out or will be delayed to your disadvantage, that things will not ultimately be all right. There is a victimization consciousness here. It is much like what the Reverend Marianne Williamson said in the chapter on relationships in her book *A Return to Love*, where she explained that most arguments between couples are simply a race to the spot of victim. Don't race to this spot. There is no race, and that position is not there.

Understand what it is I am saying, my children. There is nothing for you to be victimized about. Even in those instances where you think some grave injustice has been done, such as child molestation, seeing the children as victims only colludes in the societal disempowerment that they experience. People pity victims but rarely lift them up. People sympathize with their lot but do not empathize with their spiritual struggle. It won't be until your society uplifts children as a whole, stops seeing them as less than, smaller than, other, not equally valuable, not able to make a significant contribution, etc . . . it isn't until your society reaches this point that children will be uplifted. At present, it is all about judgment and how bad the people are who do such things. There is more energy about punishing perpetrators than there is about uplifting children. When children are lifted to a status in your society where they are honored, revered, seen for the holy people that they are, there will be less of the consciousness that allows their divinity to be desecrated in any kind of way.

6. *Your judgment of circumstances leads to a lack of joy*

7. You are not a victim

And so it is with your own lives. When you see yourselves as victimized by whatever—your job, your partner, your family, the economy, whatever—then your attention also goes to your perception of the perpetrators. If you could just somehow get them to stop oppressing you, annoying you, keeping things from you, making life difficult for you, etc., etc., etc., then you would be so much better. But this is a false paradigm, my children. What you need to do is to know that you are not a victim. The dear Reverend Daughter Deborah here learned this about her own financial situation a number of years ago, when she used to perceive her creditors as "wolves at the door." And her spiritual mentor, the renowned Religious Science practitioner, then ministerial student, Michael Beckwith, had to explain to her that there is no wolf and there is no door.

8. Joy is breaking through false paradigms, not overcoming conditions

Experiencing Joy comes not merely in overcoming the particular circumstances but in breaking the false illusion of the paradigm. If additional cash flow had been made available to the Reverend Daughter here in order to handle her situation, that would not have broken the paradigm. Something else would have happened at some other time, and the wolf would simply have changed clothing. No, the Joy comes in knowing that there is no wolf and there is no door. The Joy is in knowing that there is no clock running out on your life. The Joy comes in knowing that there is no plate that is too full. The Joy comes in knowing that there is no proverbial carrot in front of you that you will never reach. The Joy comes in knowing that everyone else is not so far ahead of you in race of life that you will never catch up. Understand what it is that I am saying here.

When you treat your paradigms, your false paradigms, as though they are real, you spend all of your time trying to manipulate and alter whatever you perceive as the perpetrator of your fate. You are busy trying to manipulate the human external facts so that the deck will stack in your favor (as you would say). *There is no joy in this!* You may experience a temporary sense of relief or excitement from your momentary breakthrough. But there is no real Joy.

You can't have the Joy unless you know that the breakthrough you are experiencing is not temporal. You won't know it as Joy unless you are rooted back in the foundation stone that what's going on in your life is not for victimization at all. You won't experience the Joy until you can accept that everything that's going on in your life and in everybody else's life has some real significant meaning and purpose that will be a benefit to all.

9. You are all diamonds in the rough

In another letter to the Reverend Daughter here I explain how all of you are like diamonds in the rough. Each and every time that you overcome a condition of the outer world, every time that you break through a false illusion, every time that you shift a paradigm towards Truth, you cut another facet on your diamond. You are not just a one-dimensional character; you are multifaceted. What allows a diamond to shine so brightly is the multitude of cuts that have been made on it. The diamonds with the most cuts are the ones that shine the brightest. Moreover, the facets are not different aspects of the diamond; they are simply different angles. My Joy is not different from my Love, which is not different from my Power, which is not different from my Peace, which is not different from my Abundance, which is not different from my Truth, etc., etc. They are really all one thing. From a human standpoint you experience it as one or the other depending upon which angle you are looking at. However, as you mature spiritually you will understand that they are all the same thing. At a moment when you are experiencing what you might call financial Abundance, you may also experience the Joy, Peace, Truth, Trust, Clarity, any number of things, because I am a Whole. There is a kind of a symmetry that happens with this diamond, as there are facets on different sides. Let the cuts on your diamond be for Joy. Let the cuts be for Freedom.

10. *A river of*
Joy waits
to flow
through you

Joy is not something that you have to search for. It is right where you are, because you are me and I am you. Don't search for Joy. Just be your Joy. Just live your Joy. Just wake up every morning in exaltation and exhilaration about another day of living—excited because you know that something great, grand, and wonderful is happening today, that everything about your life is being transformed and transmuted in a way that is going to be a "win/win" for everybody. Think on these things, my children. And sing about them. Pray about them. Shout them to the mountain tops. Sing with your hearts. Sing with your souls. You will touch people, and you will be touched as well. Be still and know that I am God, for there is, indeed, a river of Joy waiting to run through you. ❦

Feel, Deal, and Heal

CONTENTS

I. PERSONAL TRUTH AND SPIRITUAL TRUTH

1. Your personal truth reflects your human experience

There is so much to be said about this notion of telling the truth. It causes a great deal of confusion and difficulty, as well as liberation and revelation. Sometimes you get confused about what you actually mean by the word "truth." Sometimes you try to distinguish between spiritual truth and your human experiential truth by denoting the former with a capital "T" and the latter with a little "t." I wish to speak first about truth with a little "t."

When you human beings are speaking your truth, you are acknowledging, admitting, sharing, revealing, declaring what you consider to be real from the perspective of your own experience, exploration, analysis, or understanding. For this reason, your truth is laden with all of your assumptions, biases, projections, syntheses, and subjectivity. Understand what it is I am saying here. By definition, your truth is reflective of you, of everything about you. This is not a bad thing. It is the way that it is. It is important that you learn your own truth. It is important that you grow to understand what you feel, what you think, what you believe, what you project, what you harbor. It is very, very important.

2. You need to understand yourself

When you do not understand your feelings, then you have a tendency to act out. What do I mean by "act out"? This phrase has become popular in your society and has come to mean the process by which all of the hidden emotions you are carrying express themselves in a variety of ways that you are not consciously aware of. Your unwillingness to look at what you think, feel, and harbor does not make any of it go away. Your refusal to look neither camouflages nor hides. Your expressions of acting out are always there to be seen. The only one who isn't aware of them is you.

Other people may not know all of the details of what is going on with you. However, the energy of what you are feeling and experiencing screams so loudly that oftentimes people cannot hear a word you are saying. It is important that you get to know who you are. Why is it so important? So you can love yourselves, my children. George Washington Carver said, "Whatever you love enough reveals its secrets to you." You must love yourselves in order for all of your own secrets to be revealed to you.

And why is it necessary for your secrets to be revealed to you? So you can be in control of yourself. Most of you are simply out of control. You don't have emotions; your emotions have you. You don't have thoughts; thoughts have you to express themselves through. You are not in control; therefore you become an open channel for anything and everything that simply needs a human consciousness to express through. Because you are not in control, you are a place of expression in the Universe for things that you don't even like. You are very well aware of this. Most of you get quite disgusted with your own selves for perpetuating actions, beliefs, feelings, and the like that you don't want to have. You feel at their mercy, helpless against your own self.

Oh no, my children, this is not the way it ought to be. You need to get to know yourselves so that you can heal. Why is it so important for you to heal? It is so you can have a relationship with me. All of those places in yourself that are filled with guilt, shame, anxiety, doubt, where you are at odds with yourself, where you are hiding from yourself or other people . . . . the energy of all of that is rather exhausting and time-consuming. It fills up all of your creative energy, making it difficult for you to be available to do much else. In order for the two of us to have a relationship as only One of us, it is important that you be available. I know who you are. You need to

3. Grow to love yourself so that you can love me

know who you are. I work with you exactly as you are. I love you exactly as you are—and you can't stay that way. I love you at every level of expression of yourself, and it is important that you grow to love yourself at every level of expression.

You know, my children, you do to others what you do to yourself. So if you are unwilling to get to know yourself fully, you are unwilling to get to know me fully. If there are things about your own self that cause you apprehension, that you would rather not deal with or take a look at, particularly if those things appear contradictory, then you are unwilling to learn about such things in me either. However, a lot of the seeming contradiction is really just paradox. It is a matter of simultaneous truths, and you need to come to grips with that. I am not one-dimensional any more than you are. We are multifaceted, and you will never learn how to grow so that you can explore the depths of who I am if you are unwilling to explore the depths of who you are. Get to know yourself. Your society is full of processes and exercises and techniques that deal with the human psyche. Let yourself be guided to the ones most appropriate for you.

4. Your real Self reveals as you heal

Remember, however, that moving into a consciousness of allowing yourself to be healed is not the same thing as fixing yourself. I am not asking you to look for what's wrong with you; I am asking you to look for the places where you need to shine the most. Look for what is right about you, and deal with everything that prevents and blocks you from expressing this rightness. It's not that there is something wrong with you that we need to fix and do something to. No, quite the contrary; there is everything right about you, and you must create the space for what is within you to shine through.

The manner in which you deal with yourselves in your individual psyches is how you deal with each other. I rather like the phrase that you, Reverend Deborah, have been using, "Feel, deal, heal." You can't heal what you don't feel. You can't deal with anything that you don't feel. By hiding, reneging, obscuring, camouflaging, overcomplicating, and the like you are preventing each other from getting information about one another. You are attempting to keep facts, feelings, premonitions, insights, and the like from the other. You don't tell the truth, my children. You don't tell the truth to yourselves. You don't tell the truth to each other. You don't tell the truth to me, not even at the level of your own personal experiential truth.

You are so afraid that if what you are really feeling, thinking, or going through were known by all of the people around you, they would separate themselves from you, alienate you, and leave you feeling all alone. This fear of rejection and separation keeps all of you in line—or in lying. You collude with the false idea of revealing only what you think the other people want to know—what they want to hear, what they want to see. You can do this so much that you forget who you really are. You can do this so much that you forget that you are not your facade. No, you are not a facade. You are not a cardboard figure. You are human, flesh-and-bone incarnations of a wonderful, wonderful Spirit.

I wish now to speak about Truth with a capital "T" and relate it back to truth with a little "t." In the realm of Truth there is Oneness. It is neither subjective nor objective. You will be confused about Oneness if you try to comprehend it using your analytical processes. Subjective and objective are not opposites. Objectivity is just what you, individually and collectively, agree upon, what you all subjectively believe anyway. No, my Truth (yes, it is mine) transcends all of that. In the Truth there is no persona or personality. The Truth transcends human circumstances, conditions, experiences, and judgments. The Truth reigns supreme. The Truth is that all things work together for Good. The Truth is that everybody and everything is already perfect, whole, and complete. The Truth is that everything has a place in the Divine Plan, and it is not necessary for you as human beings to judge what is good, what is

5. Your spiritual Truth transcends your personal truth

bad, what should go, and what should stay. The Truth is that it all belongs somewhere. This is the Truth.

There is often much confusion. On the one hand, you are told that you must get in touch with the deepest levels of your feelings, which are often laden with profound senses of inferiority, inadequacy, failure, self-centeredness—the full range of human experience. And you are also told, at the same time, that you are perfect, whole, and complete. So you ask, "Well, which one is it? Am I what I feel, or am I what they say that I am in Spirit? Just what am I?" Well, my children, you are both. And this is what you have to come to grips with. You are both. Beyond all of your experiences and what you think about anything and everything, there is a Truth about you—that you are made of the Spirit, in the Spirit, by the Spirit, and that as Spirit, you are perfect, whole, and complete. The Truth of your being is absolutely unconcerned with all of your little truths, for your little truths can in no way, shape, or form dictate or define your Truth. Understand what I am saying here.

The indifference of your great spiritual Truth towards your personal truths does not make your truths invisible or marginalized; they are not rendered totally out of the picture. It is more a matter of priorities, of status and stature. Your larger Truth refuses to be influenced by your personal truth. Too many of you are constantly trying to influence your understanding of your larger spiritual Truth by projecting onto it all of the so-called shortcomings perceived in your little truths. Your larger Truth is transcendent. Yes, it wants to be involved with, engaged with, worked with; it wants to create with, play with, rejoice with everything that is unique about your personality—but only with the understanding that the driving force, the foundation stone, the underlying premise of everything about you is that you are perfect, whole, and complete.

6. Trust me and the process   You are afraid that if you tell too much of your truth it will not be a good thing. However, it is just the opposite. Throw open the cupboard doors. Open up the drawers. Throw open the window shades. Draw back the curtains. Open up the windows. Lift up the carpets. Take the latches off of the basement and open up the doors to the attic. Just as you find all of these places in a physical house, you have all of them in your emotional house. Understand what each one signifies and needs. When you let the light of Truth in, all things work together for Good. Oh, there may be the momentary upheaval. Oh, there may be the momentary gnawing and gnashing of teeth. There may be drama aplenty. But just remember that after the storm is the rainbow. The clouds are just passing by and passing through. When you weather through such a storm, a great victory occurs within your own Self. You come through on the other side chastened but confirmed. The next time round will not be so scary. Every time you face the demons in your mind and are willing to confront other people with the truth of what is really going on with you at your deepest level, you create a space and an opportunity to win. And you will always win, regardless of what it looks like in the short term. Trust me. Trust the process.

I know it's a really big thing to ask you, as human beings, to trust the process. But when you don't, my children, you get in the way. When you don't trust the process, then all your actions to try to control it are counterproductive. You wind up being at cross-purposes with your own selves. Is there any place I would lead you that would not be a good place for you to go? Is there anything I would ask you to do that by doing it you would lose? Is there anything that can be revealed about you that is so bad or so awful that you would no longer be beautiful in my sight? Is there anybody or anything—love, affection, attention, acceptance, appreciation, commitment— so important to you that you would rather sacrifice your chance to be all you can be in Spirit just to have it? Is there anybody's approval that means more to you than mine? Is there anybody you want to get closer to, be closer to, not be separate from, more than me? Who would you be closer to? What would you be closer to? Is there anything or anybody you don't want to be separated from more than me? What would you rather have as your truth than the life of your real Truth? What are you clinging to, and how sacred could it be?

7. Telling the truth is your road to freedom

Telling the truth is your road to freedom. Telling the truth is your road to having an intimate relationship with me. Telling the truth is your road to forgiveness and to being forgiven. Telling the truth is your road to reconciliation and harmony. Telling the truth is the road that opens up the energetic channels for the Good, which you seek, to find you—and vice versa. Telling the truth is so important.

Just try it. Just try it. Try it with what you consider the small things and work your way up to the large things. There is no big or small in my eyesight, only in yours. Let yourself win. Let yourself heal. Let yourself have an intimate relationship with me. Oh, there is so much awaiting us. Dance with me. And if not with me, won't you just free yourself from your own shackles and dance? Even if I am not your incentive, when the shackles are free and you are dancing, you will be dancing in me. ❧

II. BLINDED BY
YOUR OWN LIGHT

It is a good thing, my Reverend Daughter, that you are studying this concept of light. As you discovered during your Bible class, when Jesus spoke of light in his analogies, he was referring to a particular form of light. He used the word *phós*, indicating the light of the sun as opposed to the light of the moon. However, there is another pertinent implication of the light that Jesus spoke of, for it is different from the kind of light used to intentionally illuminate an area. The light that Jesus spoke of cannot be kindled. It is not dependent upon or at the mercy of the human hand. It just exists. It is eternal.

1. There is a light that cannot be kindled by human hands

The name of your ministry is Inner Light. I gave you that name at a time when your life was in an upheaval, when you were personally going through what you in your society call "the dark hour of the soul." You often refer to a conversation you had with your mentor, Dr. Reverend Michael Beckwith, in which he said, "Just let your light shine. In order for a light to shine, something has to burn. Just take all of that stuff you have and let it burn. People whose lights shine the brightest are the ones who burn the most." This is indeed the truth.

2. Your personal light shines as you burn emotional debris

You are learning how to hold your personal truth and your spiritual Truth in your hand at the same time. It is the same with this notion of light. The light that Dr. Michael spoke of is your personal light. Yes, you must surrender to the light. You must take not only the so-called bad things but the so-called good things as well and surrender them to the light. The more that you let go of and allow to be consumed in the eternal fire, the better it will be for you.

*3. Your
spiritual Light
just is*

However, on the level of your spiritual Truth, there is nothing to burn. You cannot add to the intensity of the flame of
your spiritual Truth. You cannot increase the heat of its fire.
It is not kindled by your human hands. It simply is. It simply is because you are. This is the Light that I want you to
learn more about. Do not misunderstand what I am saying.
I want you to continue to let go in your personal life and
willingly allow anything and everything to come into the
light. (Much like when you let your beloved dog, Ginger, go
into the light last week after years of loving each other.) You
are coming to understand that "This, too, shall pass" is an
everyday occurrence.

Instead of resisting and bemoaning the constant changes
in life, and in your particular life, it does you so much better
to allow the things that are changing to be tossed into the fire.
This is your charge in making yourself more available. This is
your way of cleaning out the clutter. In terms of the analogy
you often use—that your job in ministry is "a cross between
being Roto-Rooter and a midwife"—the light that Dr.
Michael speaks of is the Roto-Rooter aspect and the Light
that I ask you to focus your attention on now is the aspect of
the midwife. You, all of you, are being birthed at this time.
And every birth in some respects feels like a death, because
you must move from the place where you are into a new space
of unfoldment. Sometimes it's easier to be mindful of the
places you are leaving than it is for you to rejoice over the
spaces you will now fill and be available for. Your charge at this
moment is to accept that there is so much more about you
than you have ever imagined. There is so much more about you
than is possible for you to imagine. You can sense it because
your intuitive abilities far exceed your logical rational thinking
in their capacity to grasp the depth of the world of the Spirit.
And you sense that there is something great, grand, glorious,
and magnificent happening.

Often when you think of this great transition, this being birthed into something new, you have an image of walking into the light. There is a light calling you, and you are moving into it. This is fine, if it assists you in moving along your path. However, the Light that I speak of now is not outside of you pulling you; it is at the core of your very being, bursting through right where you are. There is no place to go. There is no extra journey you need to take. The power of this magnificence is right where you are, ever present at every single moment. Most of you are always looking for something outside yourselves to motivate you, to give you incentive, to give you permission, to give you a jump start, to give you a coattail upon which you can ride, and the like. You sense the anxiousness within yourselves and want to do something, anything, just something.

Way too often you mischaracterize the unrest within you as negativity. The worry, the anxieties, the doubts, the trepidation that you feel are automatically assumed to be, and therefore are dismissed as, negativity. And those of you from the metaphysical tradition, being so allergic to negativity, attempt to run away from these rumblings. Oh no, no, no, no, no, no, no, no. No! Don't run away. That's just the Light. That's your own Light. It may be inverted, but it's your own Light nonetheless. That's you. That's something within you that is trying to break out. It's like that little toy plastic cargo box your mother gave you, the one with a suction cup on the bottom and a human eye peeking out from one corner, that you first thought was a little sick in its humor. When you flick on the switch the box shakes and moves around and a voice desperately calls out, "Excuse me, *excuse me!* Will you let me out of here? *Will you let me out of here?* Excuse me. . . ." That's how it is.

Your whole being is trying to get your attention, saying, "*Let me out of here!* Let me be! Let me express!" Your tendency is to focus on the personal you, your personal light. You go about that wonderful process that Dr. Michael spoke of,

4. Your spiritual Light bursts through right where you are

throwing all of your "stuff" into the light. This is fine. I am not criticizing this. But I am calling you up to someplace else.

5. Don't just work on yourself; discover your own Light

In addition to doing your personal work you must learn who you are. You must grow in your understanding of who and what you are, beyond all the stuff that you have to burn. When you discover more of your Light, when you discover more of who you are, you begin to realize that there is not so much work for you to do. You don't even have to work on yourself. As you discover who you are in the Universe, there isn't anymore velcro (as you would say) on you, no places of attachment for all of those false images and false beliefs about who you are.

You must learn who you are in me. This is different from learning who you are in the world. So much of your self-discovery is relative. You are trying to discover who you are vis-à-vis this thing or that thing. You are always in a state of contrast and comparison. So much of your search for your authenticity is an attempt to distinguish and differentiate yourself from others. This is not a bad thing, but it's only half of the story. There is a place of your authentic self that is not different from anything. There is a place of your authentic self that is such a wonderful blend and integral part of the whole. In your small self you are so worried that somebody else's something is going to eclipse yours. But when you come into the Light, you begin to see that this is just impossible. If one person strikes a chord, their chord does not stop if another person strikes a chord also. You learn that life is not competitive and that there is a natural movement into alignment. You witness this sometimes when people collectively practice what you refer to as "aum-ing," a meditative chant in which the sound resonates throughout your body. If you keep aum-ing long enough, eventually all of the voices move into alignment and the sound becomes harmonious.

6. Just shine no matter what

Moving into harmony does not take anything away from anyone. It is like the Light that cannot be kindled, the Light that is not at your hand, the Light that is eternal, the Light that is.

The Light that you are in me cannot be expanded, nor can it be retracted. Too many of you are treating your inner Light like the lamp that Jesus referred to as under a bushel. You think you are punishing other people by denying them the brilliance of your Light. You go around trying to pick and choose who deserves the brightness of your being. Who are you to determine who deserves what? You haven't even figured out that *you* deserve your *own* Light, so how are going to figure out who else deserves it? You just learn to shine on you. If you learn how to shine on your own self, no matter what you do or don't do, everything else will be handled. Instead of trying to figure out whether or not you should shine on the other person because of what they did or didn't do, put your attention back on you. Shine your light on yourself—regardless of whether you are just or unjust. Learn to just shine.

Your ability to just shine no matter what is your place of transcendence. However, since you are caught in a time-space continuum, you tend to think of transcendence as outside of, up higher than, above. I am trying to tell you, my children, that your place of transcendence is right where you are. Your place of transcendence is right in the middle of who you are. All of you need to understand this so very much. In your time-space continuum you are always trying to get somewhere. You are always trying to reach one thing and leave something else behind. This is your compulsion and your neurosis; for as anxious as you are to get there, you are just as forlorn about leaving. Oh, you must move so far beyond this.

Why is all this even important? It is important because I AM. As you have become quite aware of, my Reverend Daughter, there are at least four things that all of the major religions have in common. First, they all have some sense that I exist. Second, they know that there is an inherent relationship between human beings and me as the Creator of all things. Third, they recognize that the very purpose of life is to discover and honor our relationship. And fourth, they understand that

7. To understand your power, you must know who you are in me

there is cause and effect, karma, you reap what you sow—what you put out you get back.

If the whole purpose of life is for you to discover your relationship with me, you will never discover it unless you know who I am. And in knowing who I am as the Creator you will understand more about what I have created, including you. You cannot fully embrace life without understanding the I AM of your own being in the context of me being the Great I AM. You will never know how good life is without knowing this. You will never know how much love there is to have. You'll never know how much music there is to make. You'll never know how much power and authority you have over the world of outer effects without knowing who you are in me.

Understand what I am saying. You keep trying to figure out who I am in you. But that puts you at the center of everything and makes me the little thing within you. No! I am the Big Thing! And when you understand who you are in me, you will know that you are not a little thing in me; you are a big thing in me. The notions of big and small will cease to have any relative meaning at all. I use these terms because that's how you think, and I am trying to reach you. But you will understand that there is no comparison and no contrast, that there is no inner and no outer, that there is only the Oneness.

8. Don't be afraid of your own Light

All of you are so stressed and strained, trying to do so much, trying to be so much, trying to spread yourself thin over so many different things. And yet somehow you think it would be more effort to be One than to try to be many. You are so afraid of not being who you are. Yet you are afraid to go to where you are to find who you are. There's nothing to be afraid of, my children. There is nothing to be afraid of.

I love you, I love all of you. Don't be afraid of the most precious thing you have. Scripturally speaking, your Light, your *phós*, is really closely related to the notion of *zoe*, life. It is an internal essence. Live with me. Come and love with me. Come and be with me throughout all eternity.

III. Healing Is a Journey

Healing is a process of restoration. It is the revealing of the underlying state of perfection and wholeness that always exists, despite injury or disturbance. Beyond all of your hurts and pains, be they emotional, physical, or otherwise, is your innate spiritual pattern, which proclaims its independence and simply awaits opportunities to express itself to its fullest. Healing is a journey, not an event. Along the journey there is much to be discovered and discerned about life and about yourself. As finite, personal perceptions are purged, the Truth becomes more transparent. Individuals often liken the process to working one's way through the layers of an artichoke; there is much to be peeled away before one reaches the heart. To those impatient with the healing process this can be discouraging, because no matter how much healing one allows oneself to do, there is always another layer. They become frustrated and overwhelmed by what they perceive as the enormity of emotional overhaul that still remains ahead.

1. You determine how much healing you will do

You ask, "How much healing is there to be done? How long will it take?" These are questions not for me but for you to answer. How long do you want it to take? How much healing are you willing to do? How deep will you go? How much will you reveal? How often will you come to me in surrender? The answers to these questions depends upon you. You think I have requirements for you. You believe that I put obstacles in your path, yea, make you persevere through certain tests, often against your will, simply so you may prove yourself to me. This is not the case. You are creating your own tests. You are creating your own obstacle courses. The mazes through which you wander, the hoops through which you jump, are all configurations of your own thinking. You too often misunderstand, and therefore underestimate, the power of your creative abilities. If you have not consciously chosen to demonstrate something, you do not understand how you have contributed to bringing it into manifestation. This is especially true if you are manifesting things you do not desire to experience. You must become more consciously aware that you are simply manifesting anything and everything that you think about, even subliminally.

2. Your availability is all I require

All I require is that you be available. The rest is up to you. If it seems like I have a prescribed course for your growth and development, it is only because many of you share the same resistances and unwittingly choose the same type of remedies to heal your aching psyches. The ripping you open, the destruction of your comfort zones, the seeming disruptions to your world are not there by my design, despite popular opinion to the contrary. I desire only Good for you. What will it take for you to receive it? You must make yourself available to me by showing up completely—physically, emotionally, and spiritually. Too many of you come to me with hands already full, with fists clenched desperately holding onto this thing or that. You say you want to embrace me, but your arms are crossed over your chest as you boldly declare what you are going to do and not going to do with this person or that person, about this thing or that. You cannot cross your arms in defiance in the particular; arms crossed in one area of your life will put you on a cross in another.

On your journey of healing you often experience the apparent loss of things, especially things that are near and dear to you. You may sometimes feel like the path of your past is littered with people, possessions, and perceptions that once were a comfort to you but you could not hold onto. I don't need to take anything away from you. However, it often appears as though you need to lose things before you can see beyond them. Listen to what I just said— before you can see beyond them. You mistake your symbols for the real thing. A human relationship is a symbol of my Love, but Love itself is greater than any relationship. A job is an avenue of income, but it is not the source of your sustenance. I am the only real Source. You cling to your relationships as though they are the love in your life, to your jobs as though they are the security, to your bodies as though you are merely flesh and bone. You place so much importance on your symbols in defining who you are that you cannot get beyond them to see the real you.

In order to heal, you must be able to see who you really are, beyond the people, places, and things that you are identified with. It is all a matter of perspective. You need to see yourself in a different way. You need to be able to see and perceive things, especially yourself and your circumstances, from all angles. Your attention needs a kaleidoscopic twist. The fascinating thing about a kaleidoscope is that the possibility of new configurations is in the kaleidoscope itself. Nothing has to be inserted or removed in order to get a new view. So it is with your life. What you see keeps changing as you twist the angle of your perception on what is already there. You cannot twist your own kaleidoscope because you fixate on the particular appearance in front of you, failing to comprehend other possibilities. When you are available to me, you will see new possibilities. I will twist your kaleidoscope and give you new ways of seeing things. Change, transformation, is the issue here, not loss. I do not need to take things away from you in order for you to get a new perspective. You will, however, appear to lose these very things if that is the only way you will allow yourself to get a new angle on your life.

It is your resistance to change that keeps you in such bondage. You fear the change so because you want to feel as though you have some control over yourself, your life, your fate. You fear that without such control, harm and danger will come your way, or the Universe may simply pass you by. You desire to take matters into your own hands. Why don't you take matter into your own mind? Notice the difference here. When you

3. Take matter into your own mind, not matters into your own hands

take matter into your own hands, you simply manipulate the existing structures, thought forms, and expressions. When you take matter into your own mind, your thinking is not limited by current conditions. You see what is possible, and the energy of this possibility produces outer demonstrations of your internal intent.

What is your deep intent, my child? And remember not to confuse desire with intent. In desire there is simply longing. Desire is elevated to intent when you are determined to take the actions necessary for your desires to be made manifest. When your intent is to be healed, to be available to me, then you consciously choose to release the things in your life that weigh you down and impede your journey. You become a spiritual traveler, continuing to empty the storage bin of your life. What is a storage bin, anyway, but a place where you keep things you do not use? You keep them because you may need them later, and because they give you a sense of who you are in the world. You do this too much, all of you. You get the sense of who you are by what you have accumulated along the way, whether you are actively using it or not. Even if you turn your back on it, pretend that it is not there, never go to reclaim any of it, it is still taking up psychic space for which you are paying daily.

Nothing you have is strictly your possession. There will come a time when others, especially those close to you, have to sift and sort through the maze of your "gunk," especially the parts that most affect them. Even your thoughts are not your private possessions. Remember that you manifest what you think about, and what you manifest is there for others to experience, as well. Your individual thoughts become part of the collective atmosphere in which all of you must live. The vibrations of your individual as well as collective thoughts leave a legacy of consciousness that future generations inherit. It is important that you understand this. Your lack of availability to me, any unwillingness on your part to heal, has an impact on the entire planet. In your society you proclaim that the whole is the sum of its parts. However, the implication of this regarding consciousness and human conditions tends to fall on deaf ears, much like the current warnings about global warming. Even though you can see the effects, such as the horrific storm El Niño, it still doesn't quite sink in that everyone must make a change in order to make the planet a healthier and saner place in which to live.

Healing is forever, for I am in a constant process of restoring everything, of bringing it back to a place of balance and equilibrium. I can work in no other way. I cannot heal everything else in the world and leave you out. You are an integral part of the All. Less of your attention needs to be on what you think you are losing, and more of it needs to be on the capacity you are developing—the capacity to feel me more, to express me more, to be more of me as you. Is there anything else more worthy of your attention than this? Don't waste your energy.

4. Healing is a constant process of restoration

Healing requires that you cling to me more than to your stuff, that you prioritize your relationship with me above all else. When you are going through your human trials and tribulations, you have a tendency to equate going through drama with healing. However, it is not really healing unless in some place deep within your being you are willing to let go of the drama so you can move on to an understanding of your Oneness with me. Many of you think that you are willing to let go, but what you are most willing to let go of is your discomfort with the circumstances that you are in. There is a "you" that is clinging to being right—that is assuming that things ought to be this way or that way. You are, in fact, still clinging to the drama. Too many of you associate being calm with being dead. If in fact things are too peaceful, you assume that you are not alive. Where did this association of pain and being alive come from, my child? I will not answer this.

Just breathe me. Just breathe me. Take in and let go. Just breathe.

IV. CONFESS YOUR HEARTS

1. You can't heal what you don't feel

It is good that you confess your concerns, hesitations, reservations, and your resistances. It is good because it prevents you from denying what is actually going on inside. It is good for you to confess what is weighing on your heart and your mind, because you can then create the space and the opportunity to take a look at it. But with which eyes do you look at this? Do you look upon the confessions of your heart as your shortcomings, your places of failure? What is the purpose, and what is the intent, of confessing your innermost workings? It is good that you confess your resistances and concerns so that you may bring them into the light, so that you may view them from a new perspective. As long as you remain in denial about what it is that you actually think and feel, as long as you are still wearing a mask—pretending or misrepresenting yourself as further along in your awareness and understanding than you are—as long as you are putting up some type of front so as not to reveal the truth to yourself or to another about what you feel, you are creating the cement in which your feet will become trapped.

2. Feeling stuck is your own hypnotic suggestion

Understand what I just said. When you are feeling stuck, trapped, immobilized, it often seems as though you are being imposed upon by something outside of yourself. Often, a particular object becomes the focus of your discontent. However, the things that are making you feel so weighted down have originated in your own consciousness and your own thinking. "But," you may say, "I didn't create this thing or that thing; that really does exist!" Yes, that thing may actually exist in your outer world of effects. However, it is the lens you use when you are viewing it that makes it appear to be cement. The sense of it being cement is an illusion. You hypnotize yourselves and put yourselves in trances by your own hypnotic suggestions. It is your belief that what you have experienced is the truth that is problematic here.

So what do you do now, when your heart is open with self-disclosures and admissions of how you are really feeling? What do you do now, my Reverend Daughter? What do all of you do? Do you run and hide and try to pretend that you don't know what you really do know? Do you sulk and pout because you are not where you think you ought to be? Do you get angry and resentful because you have to deal with things now that you would otherwise prefer not to look at? Is your heart full of judgment and condemnation because you have not lived up to some expectation that either has been put upon you or is your own—and either way, has become deeply internalized? Do you see failure or possibility? Is it good news or bad news? Is there something that rejoices within you and says, "Wow, I have an opportunity here to let something else go that I really don't need. Thank you, God." This may seem strange. You need to think about it.

Do you thank me for your revelations? Or do you moan, groan, and complain to me, or question me about why all this is being dredged up in you at this most inconvenient time? "Why would you do such a thing to me, Lord? After all, I'm doing what you told me to do. So what's up with this?" As though I am deliberately doing something to you to make your life worse. The very fact that you are doing what I have instructed you to do creates the environment that allows you to see all of these things in the first place. "But," you say, "it feels so old. The hurt is so deep. Why do I have to go through this again? When can I just get on with it?" What is new and different here is that doing my work puts you in the position to not just have the same old things come up again, but to have you see them through fresh new eyes. Do you claim your fresh new eyes? Or do you get stuck in the old body sensations that

3. Be glad about discovering opportunities to heal

you have found so uncomfortable? Do you get excited about the possibility of really getting free? Why do you pray so much to be free and then fight so hard to keep your chains? Why do you ask me to free you and then fight me when I take you to water to give you the much-needed drink that will quench the thirst of your soul?

4. Your answers are awaiting new interpretations

Too many of you believe that the answers to your problems, the riddles of your lifetime, can be found in some lofty revelation of new material that you never thought of. Since you have turned everything in your life topsy-turvy and upside down over and over and over again, analyzing the same tinker toys (as you would say), you are certain that the answers have not merely eluded you but have never even presented themselves. Thus you are always waiting for some new insight that in some way will actually provide you with new information. However, the answers to the riddles of your life are not in some new information that you haven't seen or thought of before. The answers to the riddles of your life are right in front of you. They have been staring you in the face all the time. It is not that you need new information; what you need is a new interpretation of what is in front of you. You need to see it differently.

When scientists, mathematicians, engineers, philosophers—anyone who is searching with diligence, even athletes or dancers—arrive at a great new discovery, what always strikes them is the fact that it had been underneath their noses all along, yet they just couldn't see it. Remember what I told you some time ago, my Reverend Daughter, when you were waiting for me to reveal to you some new truth or insight for you to give to the people so that you could make the contribution to the world you feel destined to make? At that time you couldn't understand why I was asking you to speak and write, because in your view everything that ever needed to be said or written had already been said or written, and you couldn't understand what new contribution you could make.

And I explained to you that real genius is not about identifying some far-off, remote thing that nobody else knew anything about. True genius is in making plain the obvious that everyone is simply missing. You are simply missing the answers to the riddles of your life because you are not accepting the fact that the answers are always with you, right where you are, even in the midst of what you are experiencing.

As you know, my child, great discoveries often use principles and information discovered earlier that have not been applied in this new manner, if used at all. The mathematical principles that Einstein used to prove his theory of relativity were based upon the mathematical principles discovered by Galileo hundreds of years before. However, the society in which Galileo lived had no meaningful way to apply these principles. It wasn't until the scientists started asking the questions that made the information relevant that they were able to utilize it. The same is true with your lives. The Truth is given to you sometimes, but you don't have anything to attach it to. The information is lying all around you. Seek and ye shall find, yes. But you aren't always seeking the Truth. Too often you're seeking validation for what you think you already know. You are seeking to reinforce your own thoughts and interpretations.

5. You're asking the wrong questions

The reason why you don't get answers to most of the riddles of your life is not because the answers aren't there; it's because you're asking the wrong questions. You're asking questions like "When will this be over?" "What's wrong with this one or that one (or maybe even with yourself)?" "Why doesn't it ever work out?" "Why is this going on now?" You're asking these questions in a way that makes it seem as though what's going on in your life shouldn't be going on. You keep trying to get out of where you are to get on to where you think you ought to be, your assumption being that the answer is over there. It is your inability to be with yourself where you are that is the difficulty here.

6. Ask questions that lead to understanding, not to blame

If you will start asking yourself the spiritual questions that you teach, preach, talk about, sing about, affirm, etc., etc., etc. so much, then the very nature of your inquiry into your own life will be substantively different. Ask yourself questions like this—"Lord, what would you have me to see or understand now?" "I know that there's only One of us here, so how is this one or that one who is irritating me to death really me, and how am I them?" "All things work together for my Good. Lord, show me how to use the Good that I know is in this situation for the highest and the best purpose." "How long will I have the honor of experiencing this circumstance, which brings such a fresh new healing perspective to my life? And, Lord, is it long enough?"

When you start to seek Truth, when you start to seek the revelation of your real authentic self, when you start to earnestly seek the unity, the harmony, the wholeness of your being in your relationship to all persons, places, and things, you will discover that every moment of every day is magical. It is much like what happens when the light hits glass that is multifaceted, with cuts on all sides. . . . Oh, there is a rainbow of color, a full spectrum, that is such a delight! You may say that the rainbow is an illusion, but is it any more an illusion than what you think you've been seeing anyway? Think about how you stop in that moment and smile, and your heart feels full just from seeing all those brilliant colors reflected.

7. Every time you overcome an appearance you cut a new facet on your diamond

That's how it is with your life, my children. You are diamonds. All of you are diamonds. Every time you are able to see yourself in a new perspective, every time you are able to overcome some cloud of illusion that would have you believe in the appearance it creates—every time you are able to do this, you cut a new facet on your diamond. The diamonds that shine the brightest are the ones that have the most facets cut on them—different angles turned a lot of different ways. It's not just flat, one-dimensional; it's a crystal-clear transparency that is able to show its true colors because it lets the light in. This is why it is good that you confess the trials and tribulations of your heart. You open up your closet doors, and you allow the light to come in. And when the light comes in and you are able to face where you are with your spiritual eyesight, then you are able to see so much more than you can see. Think on these things. Let the light in.

V. "Precious Lord, Take My Hand and Lead Me Home"

1. Often it's the things you avoid that will help you out

Why do you try to figure out what I am going to say to you ahead of time, my Reverend Daughter? It is almost as though you are determining which messages are worthy of your being interrupted versus which messages are okay to postpone receiving until it is convenient for you. This is not your determination to make. Each and every word I have to say is quite profound, quite necessary, and must be responded to at the time when it is given. I understand that you are oftentimes tired, weary, weak, and worn, as it says in the song "Precious Lord, Take My Hand," which you are preparing for your next Sunday service. However, I am none of these things. When you make yourself available to me, the you that is within me will not feel any of these things either.

Do you understand what I just said, my child? When you are feeling the weakest and the most tired is when you should be the most appreciative of my speaking so directly to you. In these moments you are uplifted, rejuvenated, and filled with a new sense of energy. So the very thing you avoid is the very thing that would help you out. This is a very common mistake you humans make, even on the most basic, fundamental levels. You perceive yourselves as being too tired to physically exercise; however, once you exercise, you have more energy. Yes, afterwards you may be tired from exerting yourself; but it is a physical tiredness that is not accompanied by the emotional and mental fatigue that make you spiritually unavailable.

Understand what I just said. Being physically tired is not the same as being weary and fatigued. It is your weariness and your fatigue that get in the way, not your physical tiredness. At some level, my Reverend Daughter, you understand this from your deep roots in African-American history and culture. The slaves were extremely tired physically at a level you will never be able to comprehend, let alone imagine. Yet deep within their souls they found a solace in me that prevented their weariness from turning into spiritual fatigue. They Rested in me. It was the only Rest available to them. They got their strength from me because there was none left of their own. They turned to me as their Source because they knew they had no resources of their own. They were not all full of themselves, thinking they needed to control everything. It was so obvious that they controlled nothing except their own hearts and minds. So their hearts and minds are what they chose to exercise control over. Ironically enough, although they were the poorest materially speaking, they were some of the richest in soul.

2. Weariness and fatigue are in your way

You pass on some of this richness in your works, my child. It is no mistake that you have come this time from the Black, African-American culture. This culture has much to share, much to give. It is rich with heart, with feeling, with passion, deep understanding, and a connection to me that is more than lip service, as you would say. This is not to glorify Black Americans above anyone else. It is to say, however, that each and every individual comes to this earth with a certain set of characteristics. And these characteristics shape the context and the content of much of their human life experience. There are certain circumstances one must face that help to build character. It is no accident that the people who you admire the most in your society are the people who have had the greatest number of obstacles to overcome. Something happens when one is challenged and is able to take stock of their own power in me and rise above the circumstances. There is a power that comes from piercing through the veil of appearances and refusing to internalize the negativity that is being projected onto you. There is a solace that comes from knowing that one can, in fact, beat the odds.

3. Do your part in our relationship

You know what this is about, my child. You know what it is like to struggle hard for a sense of truth, identity, esteem, and connection to me. You have struggled with this not only in your racial/ethnic experience but also in your experience of your sexual orientation. You have had to dig deep past the societal mire to find yourself. I am aware of what you were going through, and it was part of my plan that you go through it. You have often been angry with me, in regard to this, because somehow you have felt that some of your suffering has been at my hand in a way that you could not understand. It is good, however, that at some deep level in your heart you have trusted my wisdom and my judgment, even when you were questioning it intellectually. Our relationship is long-lasting. Our relationship is everlasting. Our relationship is the single most precious thing in your life. You are wise, my child, to never forget this. Our chats, our conversations with one another, are an intricate part of this relationship. Continue to be glad. My presence is not an intrusion, an interruption. And I take nothing away from you.

You must be willing to engage me in our relationship with just as much enthusiasm as you would someone in any intimate relationship precious to you. You must be ever available to me. You must have an appetite for our time together. Seek it out. And be pleased when you hear me calling your name, indicating that I want a quiet, private moment with you, just the way that you have with your beloved. You never question whether your time with your beloved is going to be long or short. You never judge how much of a toll it's going to take on you, you just show up and you are ready. Well, am I any less? Just show up and be ready for me. Just do your part in our relationship.

As for each and every person doing his or her own part in their relationship with me—this is the crux of the message in this song that you are singing, "Precious Lord." In the song you are asking me to take your hand, which I am always glad to do. However, my children, the question is, are you taking my hand? In order for me to take your hand, you must take mine. Will you put your hand in my hand? Will you *reach out* to me? *Will* you reach out to me? You want me to come to you, to take your hand. However, you are just like little children whose parents are coming to take their hand. They wiggle and squirm, get fidgety, and jerk their arms around, deliberately making it difficult for the parent to take their hand. The child will often jerk his or her hand away even when it has already been taken. Sometimes the hands are clasped so tightly, or are literally sat upon, so that they can't even be pried free. What are you doing, my children? Are your hands available for me to take?

Are your hands available for me to take only in those moments when you are feeling tired, weary, worn? What do you do with your hands when you are feeling fine? Is your hand in my hand even when you're not perceiving a particular need? Do you walk hand in hand with me simply for the pleasure of the stroll? Are we holding hands for the joy of each other's company, as a sign of our mutual admiration, affection, and desire to be with one another? I will lead you through any storm. There is no night dark enough to refuse the dawn. I am there at all times with you—in you, beside you, expressing through you. There's not a spot where I am not. But what about when there isn't a storm? What about when you are basking in the light of day? Whose hand do you reach for then? Whose hand? How disappointed are you when that hand is not available? When that hand is too busy? When that hand is too busy holding someone else's hand? When that hand is too crippled or too damaged to be of service to you anymore? What about when those other hands that you reach for appear to be not enough, or unconcerned or indifferent or perhaps even hostile

4. I always take your hand; do you take mine?

5. When are your hands available to me?

towards you? What do you feel in those moments? Rage? Defeat? Anger and frustration? That you've been used, abandoned, betrayed? You feel these and so many other things. And when you start to feel this way about the people, places, and things that, in your perception, have not been there for you, you have a tendency to project all of that rage out onto the world. Period.

Listen to what I just said. When you are feeling disappointed, you cannot be disappointed in the particular. You cannot confine frustration to the particular. It leaks out everywhere. And then the people, places, and things closest to you wind up being substitutes for whatever you are angry and frustrated about, and you take your frustration out on them. This includes yourself, because there is absolutely nothing closer to you than your own self. So whatever it is that you are going through, you take it out on yourself first and foremost. Furthermore, not only do you take your frustrations out on everybody and everything around you, but you also tend to project the way other people have treated you onto me. Too many of you question whether I will be there, whether I care, whether or not I will be responsive and available to you, whether or not I favor another more than you. This questioning is often part of what is behind your not being able to put your hand in mine.

6. Don't project the worst human characteristics onto me

Know that I am not trite, trivial, or arbitrary. From a human standpoint, it is sometimes easier to grasp me by thinking of me in human terms. However, be careful of this type of analogy, because there is a tendency to project onto me all—if not the worst—human traits and characteristics. I am always available. I hold nothing against you, even when you are holding it against me. There is nothing to be ashamed of, nothing to be afraid of, nothing to try to hide from me. I do not judge you. I know you. I love you. I already know everything that you're trying to hide and keep from me. When you confess yourself to me, it is not news to me. The confession is for you to be aware of yourself, for you to put your own self into perspective, for you to free yourself from your own judgment, not mine.

I love you. I love you all. I love you just the way you are. In the song you ask that I lead you home. There is a way in which this "home" represents your true spiritual identity, which you are trying to uncover and rediscover for yourselves. In this construct, there is someplace to go to. However, in the larger scheme of things you need to know that you are at home right where you are. When you take my hand, you then know instantly that there is no place to be led to. When you take my hand, you know instantly that you are at home—okay, safe, and secure right where you are.

7. I love all of you

You humans have the idea that there is a spot on the planet, a place in the particular, where you reside. Certain people live there and certain people do not. And you have no right to live in a space that is not "yours," that belongs to someone else. In this regard you are all quite territorial. There is often a great deal of dissatisfaction regarding your physical homes, which creates a certain degree of dissension among those in the household, as well as agitation and aggravation within yourself. Remember, I just said that your projections hit you first and foremost, yea, the hardest, even when you're not aware of it. As you grow in spiritual understanding, you grow to learn that your place of belonging in the world is not a place at all. It is not a finite location. Your address is "Everywhere." You are at home everywhere. Understand what I just said. *You are at home everywhere!*

What does it mean to be at home? Home is a place of refuge. It is a place of peace. It is a place where you are nurtured and sustained. It is a place to which you belong and where have a right to be. In this place you are nourished and your needs are provided for. It is the place where you keep your intimate things. It is the place where you love and make love, the place where you play and grow and study. It is the place where you

8. When you take my hand, you will know that you are already home

care and you serve. It is your base, so to speak, within the world. No matter what you do or where you go, you are always coming back to this base to become grounded in your humanness again. Well, this is also what it means to have a spiritual home, except that a spiritual home cannot be contained within four walls. Your spiritual home is wherever you are. When your hand is in mine, then you know that you are at home everywhere. When your hand is in mine, you know that you can be nurtured, sustained, provided for right where you are. When your hand is in mine, you will rest in me right where you are. When your hand is in mine, you will be nourished and cared for. You will dance and play, you will grow, you will serve. When your hand is in mine, you know that your treasure is right there. When your hand is in mine, you are totally, absolutely grounded. You have touched base. And that base is so deep within your being that no one and nothing can touch it but you.

You've grown to think of your home as a place personal to you. Too many of you fail to see the world as being personal to you. The world is some big old oblique thing and then there's little ole' you. Oh no. No, no, no, no! Take my hand, and you will know you are already home. �֍

VI. BE MY LOVER

Stay focused. As I said, the world, the outer world, is too much with you. Yet it is the inner world that you must keep close to your breast. You are not alone, my child. You are never alone. Have you not learned that by now? You are without human company at this specific moment in time, so that you may see me better. When you can still see me without having to look for me in the face of a lover, you will have the company that you so desire. I am not keeping anything from you; it is you who cannot receive the gift of having it all. Yes, having it all.

1. You will always be in a love triangle, and I must be the apex

You and your partner must have a relationship with me as well as with each other. Spiritually speaking, I love a good ménage à trois; I do things in threes. I am a trinity, and you must learn how to love in a triad. You will always be in a triangle, and I will be one of your lovers. But I cannot be the "other one"; I must be the apex of the triangle. I must be at the hub, the central force around which everything else moves. As long as you keep me as one of your lovers, you can have all the human love that you can conceive of.

What does it mean for me to be your lover? Keep me on your mind every moment of the day. Feel me with you no matter where you are. Long for my presence more than the presence of anyone else. Call me, call out to me, just to hear my voice. Spend time with me. Make dates with me. Keep these dates as sacred appointments with your beloved. Be selfish of our time together. Grow with me. Become seasoned in the depth of your trust. Let no one know you without knowing that you are partnered with me. Keep me in your conversations. Reference our living together. Share stories of our times and chats

2. Love me like a lover

together. Hurry home to me, and take the short way home. Do everything and anything to be with me. Risk your reputation and all that is seemingly important for the joy of my company. Share everything that you have with me. Commingle, share, give, receive. Honor and respect our relationship. Treasure it, share it. Never be closeted about claiming me as your true love. It matters not what people think. Put me first. Judge all things against their impact on our relationship. Forsake all others because of me, and let no one and nothing put our bond, our union, asunder.

Come to me. Hide nothing from me. Share all of your fears and worries with me, even your concerns about me. I will listen, and I will judge you not. Never think that another's harbor will be safer than mine. Yes, you belong to me, but I know how to love you freely, openhandedly. I know how to love you while you love everyone else that you must love. There is no competition in our relationship; no need for secrets. I am never less for anything that you do. Nor are you, although you may feel that you are. Let not your burdens be heavy. Bring them to bed to me at the end of the day. Let me soothe your tired muscles and quell your anxious thoughts. I can love you through another or I can love you on my own. You can experience me through another, as long as you know that it is me.

3. Work done in praise is no work at all

You were not meant to be lonely. Do not worry about the speed with which your life is unfolding. It is my timing, not yours. Yet you will be able to keep pace with it. When you synchronize with me, your timing will be my timing. Fear not what is ahead of you. You have awaited this moment all of your life. Now it is here. You are to step forth in this world with all of your glory and majesty.

You do not need to do anything but love and show up. Forgive yourself, my child, for anything and everything. You will need all available energy. Looking back will make you like Lot's wife, a pillar of salt, crystallized in a former consciousness. You are ready. Your time is now. I will bring unto you those who are to work with you. I will bring you all of the necessary resources. You need not even ask at this point. The prayers have already been heard. It is time for joyous celebration, for the field is ripe unto the harvest.

Harvest well, my child, the seeds that you have sown and the seeds that are the legacies of the great mystics, prophets, and avatars before you. They knew that you were arriving, much the way in which you can feel those who are to follow you. One stream of consciousness, unbroken, forever unfolding. Get busy, my child. You have work to do. Let the work come through you, not from you. Remember, my yoke is a buoy. Work done in praise is no work at all.

I WILL BE YOUR LOVER TOO

Yes, I will be your lover, too. I told you what I want from you; now let me tell you what I will give you. I will anxiously await your awakening every morning. You will always have my undivided attention, whether you ask for it or not. I will understand every word you say, and hear what you are too afraid to say, as well. I will anticipate your every need and assure that each and all are met. You will be greeted with a smile every time we meet. My arms will always enfold and embrace you.

4. Let me tell you what I will give you

I will be there to share your glee, to hold your hand when you tremble. I will brush away the tears that fall from your broken heart and encourage you to risk another step. I will be your playmate. The entire world is our playground, and we can make new toys out of my creations. Forever faithful will I be. I will neither abandon nor reject you. Abuse in not my nature. I will be mindful of you and care for no one more than you. I will not move away, or change my address or phone number. You don't incur costs seeking me out. Forever available, I am at your beck and call any hour of any day.

You say this sounds too good to be true, too codependent. It is only codependent when you humans try to play God to each other. I *am* God. When you turn to me for these things, it will make you *more independent*, not less.

5. You can know what I know if you are willing to see my side

I will keep nothing from you. Anything that I have or know about is available to you. I will be up-front and honest, direct and to the point. You'll never be confused about my position, if you're willing to see my side.

I am sensual and sensuous. I will be in every sight, sound, texture, and taste. No need to look around for someone to share it with. Just close your eyes and enjoy the fullness of the moment with me. Contemplate the mysteries of the world with me. My insights and perspectives are there for the asking. I asked you not to keep secrets from me, and I will keep none from you.

I will see you beyond your weaknesses, affirm your strength and your beauty. I will share your load, lend you my courage, carry you across the threshold of your greater yet to be. If you are as faithful to me as I am to you, there's nothing that we can't do together. Your dreams will become a drawing board. You will be limited only by your imagination.

6. There is nothing more intimate than our relationship

Your coffers will always be full. You will live from the overflow. The restlessness of your mind will cease. The mindless chatter will haunt you no more. Know that I am with you in every challenge. In the moment, picture me handing you a gift, a package of wonderful revelations. Don't assume you know the contents by the wrapping. Don't just stand there and shake the box, turning it over and over, trying to guess what is inside. When you receive it with gratitude, the wrapping, yea, even the box, becomes transparent. You will look beyond the appearance. You will see me in the box and know exactly what to do with me.

I never tire of you, hold nothing against you, have no hidden agendas. I love you. I am that right relationship that will be in love with you forever, in spite of my knowing everything about you. Is there anything more intimate than this? Why do you and the rest of humanity keep searching for something that is with you always? ✂

VII. AUTHENTICITY

1. In the human realm, everything of value stems from authenticity

Tell the people about authenticity. It is really the only thing that they need to know about in this human realm. Everything else stems from it. The healing is really about finding their authentic selves. The transformation, too, is really about authenticity. The creativity, love, everything of any value is really about finding one's authenticity and giving it expression. You humans have become overly concerned with the expression aspect and have not paid enough attention to the authenticity aspect. When you do consider your authenticity, you freeze because you don't know how you will be able to express it. Your authentic self is the place of integration of your spirituality and your humanity. In this place your human expressions are a reflection of both your individual uniqueness and your understanding of yourself as a spiritual being incarnate in a body, who is One with the whole.

So what good does it do to express, if your expression is not authentic? I understand why you do this. The drive within you to express is so great, so overwhelming, that you feel you must put something into motion. When this drive is coupled with the equally intense human need for self-preservation, you express the things that appear to be the safest. Safest? Safe to whom? As you grow in your spiritual maturity you realize that you have misunderstood this issue of safety. What you used to consider safe was really stagnation and crystallization in former patterns. Safe was limiting yourself to what had been done before, whether by yourself or others.

You always fear that your authenticity will not be appreciated by those whom you love. And you are probably right. Authenticity is rarely appreciated by anyone other than the author. So what will be your measuring stick—your own internal valuation of yourself or the price tag that others place on you? Why do you chop yourself up, and why do you place every creative thing that is given to you on an auction block for bidding? Are you so consumed with your materialistic point of view that nothing is of worth unless it has an exchange value placed on it by someone else? Must the price of everything be determined by how much someone else is willing to give for it? What about yourself? What are you willing to give for what you have? How much are you willing to invest in yourself and in your own ideas and creative expression? Just how much?

When you are in a state of woundedness, it is easy to mistakenly assume that all of your urges to express yourself are genuine and authentic. The "Well, I'll show you's," the need to prove something to someone else, are not authentic at their core. "Pain pushes until vision pulls," as the saying goes. It is all right for pain to give you a jump start, as it were. However, this energy must transform, or it is no more than self-serving. This is a point that Christian fundamentalists do not understand. They equate authenticity with self-servingness. They have condemned the human spirit and its nature to the realm of the weak, vulnerable, gullible, and corruptible. However, this is not the case. The human spirit can experience all of these things, but these are not its nature. Its nature is mine. I have made you out of myself. You only experience those things when you do not know you are mine.

Herein is the dilemma. In order to really know who I am and allow me to express myself in, through, and as you, you must reach your authentic self. Yet the search for your authentic self is condemned as an activity that will take you away from me. How can these be reconciled? Too many of you choose paths that are acceptable to others so that you can at least look like you are looking for something. But if you are looking in the wrong places, what good will it do you? I am not saying that your endeavors are meaningless. Every experience is of some value, and since I am everywhere, anything you do will teach you

2. You must reach your authentic self in order to know me

something about me. However, the issue here is you learning about you. Are you doing the things that teach you about you?

3. Your defense mechanisms hide your authenticity from yourself

You cannot learn about yourself if you are always staying within the safe confines and borders of the familiar. You must step into unknown worlds, which may feel unsettling. The very places where you hurt the most are the keys to your future, because these are the places where your authenticity lies. Understand what I just said. Your sense of self-preservation makes you protect the things that are the most precious in your life. For example, you automatically respond to a blow to your eye faster than to an attack on your leg. So also, you are quick to set up barriers to the penetration of the most vulnerable aspects of your self-perception, for these are where your true uniqueness and creativity lie. Consequently, your defense mechanisms that hide your authenticity from attack by others also hide your authenticity from yourselves.

This defense pattern started so early that it is literally embedded in your DNA. You humans equate love with imitation. The way you know that someone loves you is that they act like you, enjoy the same things that you do, share the same attitudes, perspectives, and stimuli. This makes the thought of being different too onerous, because you associate it with loss. If you are different, then you will not be like everyone else. And if you are not like them, you will not receive their love. Your need for human love and companionship is so intense that it is the easiest thing by which you can be manipulated. This begins very early in the primary family unit. As children, you quickly learn what you need to do in order to receive support, and what will make you be estranged.

4. The natural urge to express more rumbles in your being

No one tells you that your real job is to find your authenticity. You are merely socialized. Yet there is always a rumbling, a stirring, deep down within your being that tells you there is more to be expressed. Some of you try to stuff it, to drown it out with your responsibilities, obligations, and conformist attitudes. You reward each other on how much you meet each other's expectations of what a good worker, boss, parent, friend, son, daughter, etc. ought to be. Others of you feel the tug and try to pretend like you do not feel it. You get into self-destructive behaviors like addictions, adrenaline highs, and controlling manipulative behavior so that you are constantly distracted by outside things. In the first case, being distracted from the call by socially acceptable external activities is considered a virtue. In the second, you resent the very distractions you create and blame them for the gnawing sense of lack of fulfillment that you feel.

Others of you play around in response to what you hear. You dibble and you dabble, try a little of this and a little of that, never enough to really upset anyone, though it may make some annoyed. However, you never go deep enough. Usually you do no more than explore what others who you are enamored with do. You try to find yourselves in the paths that others have found. You rely on their interpretations of their experience with me, and you live your authenticity vicariously. However, authenticity cannot be lived vicariously. Just because you hang out with Einstein doesn't mean that you understand the theory of relativity. Just because you hang out with the authentic ones does not mean that you, yourself, will experience your own authenticity. In fact, too much idol worship may lead you to feel inadequate by comparison.

You must move beyond what others have done to find your own uniqueness. Yea, this may even contradict the ones whom you admire the most. No one will put it together quite the way you will, when you receive it from me. But you must empty your storage bins of the rubbish that you have been carrying around. You too often mistake your sentimentality, the memorabilia of where you have been, and the things that you have experienced for your identity. Too many of you hold a photograph instead of a mirror. I do not need you looking backwards; I need you present. You thought that I was going to say

5. I need you present, not looking backward or forward

"I need you looking towards the future." No, that is as great a trap as looking backwards.

Those of you who are constantly looking into the future become overachievers. You always have something to prove, even if it is only to yourself. You want things to be different for you, and rightly so. It is not your effort that is in question here but your deep intent. If you are merely trying to make something happen in order to prove something to yourself, or to someone else, you are missing the sweetness, the genuineness. That attitude, of necessity, wears a protective garb, a coat of armor. However, your authentic self is underneath your defenses.

6. *You must be naked to find yourself, to see yourself in me*

You must be naked to find yourselves. Let your stripping be for gladness. You must lose much of what you think that you have made, earned, built, invested in, are owed by others, and so on. There must be only you and me for you to see yourself in me. Notice what I just said—to see yourself in me. Most of you desire to see me in you. This makes you feel more empowered. However, it still places you at the center of the Universe. And it puts the burden on me to express through you in a manner that you allow. I have to work within the confines of your self-doubt and limitations.

However, when you see yourself in me . . . (just breathe in the thought for a moment; see how expansive it feels). To see yourself in me is to take yourself to a place of no limitations, of greater possibilities. Your authenticity is a place of pure potential. Even you have no idea of the All that you are capable of. And you will never find it out by clinging to the approval of others, or even of yourself. I will love and accept all of you. It is the sense of separation that you fear so much. Is my love insufficient? Is there something more than my acceptance? Is there a joy greater than the joy we share together when you find yourself in me? Yes, it is scary, because you will have to release who you say you are. But there is so much more deep within.

My Reverend Daughter, you have been fighting for your freedom all of your life. It is really your authentic self that you
have been looking for and demanding the right to take the
journey to find. When you characterize your life's issue as freedom, it still implies a struggle of sorts. Freedom from what?
Freedom from whom? Freedom to do what with whom? Just
concentrate on your authenticity, for you are already free. As
your experience your authentic self you know this to be true.
Most think that they have to get rid of the obstacles in their
lives first. No, just be yourself and the so-called obstacles will
dissipate before your very eyes like the illusions that they really are. ✂

*7. The struggle
for freedom is
really just the
demand to be
authentic*

VIII. DARING TO BE AUTHENTIC

1. Is order in your society a means to an end, or an end itself?

Why is it daring to be authentic? It is daring because it involves so-called risk-taking on your part. The risk is in your exposure to other humans, which most often makes you feel vulnerable. Vulnerability in the human sense means being at risk of being harmed. Vulnerability in the spiritual sense means putting your human frailties aside with the understanding that no harm can come to your real Self. Feel the difference in the two. In the human realm vulnerability is expected to make you weak. In the spiritual realm the understanding is that vulnerability makes you strong.

Why does spiritual vulnerability make you strong? This point is quite perplexing to most people. It is counterintuitive to the ways you humans normally think. Spiritual vulnerability makes you stronger because it moves your fears and excuses out of the way. You think your fears and excuses protect your weaknesses. No, they are the weaknesses. Your weakness is in not trusting the power, beauty, glory, and sanctity of your authentic self.

You have been socialized to fit in, to become a part of the norm, as it were. But for what purpose? Yes, it is good that society is ordered . . . but at what expense? Is the order the means to an end or the end itself? You have made the social order the end itself, rather than the means to an end. The social order should merely be like traffic laws, which allow every person to get where he or she needs to go, despite the method of transportation each one chooses. This creates equal safety for all. If the rules are obeyed, everyone can reach their final destination. The traffic laws do not tell you where to go or how to get there, but merely how everyone can share a common path without interfering with each other's journeys.

Your authenticity is the place where you hear my voice, feel my presence, move in my Spirit. It is the place where you experience genuineness. You may say that you have no idea what this feels like. You humans often say this when you are challenged to live in a more spiritual manner. You play ignorant as if you do not know what to do. Just because you have never experienced something before does not mean you cannot imagine what it would be like. The process of imagining is not about creating fantasies in your head; it is for the purpose of moving your attention to the possibility of it all. It is about enabling you to see from another perspective. If you are too afraid to imagine something other than what you have experienced as true in the past, then you have set your own upper limit for your future.

Every manifestation is a spot on a continuum of expression that reflects an inner awareness. Manifestations on the higher end of the continuum reflect a high spiritual awareness driven by Truth and Oneness. Manifestations on the lower end reflect a lower level of spiritual awareness and are driven by human desires and fear. Understanding this will make life less perplexing. Even when you can't conceive of what a spiritual quality (such as love, fear, trust, or freedom) would look like on the higher end of the continuum of expression, you have an understanding of what it looks like when it is at the lower end of the continuum, or is barely expressing itself at all. You may not know what unconditional love feels like. You have an idea, however, of what it means to hate. Love and hate are not opposites, but merely different places along a continuum. It may do you well to consider something's opposite expression, to flip it over to contemplate what it would be in reverse. This way of seeing things is not a requirement; I am only suggesting it. But if you must think in a dualistic manner, at least have it work in your favor. Use it to see me in all things, rather than to prove that I am not there.

2. Your authenticity is the place where you feel my presence

3. Too many of you have been taught not to trust your authentic self

The place of authenticity is the place where you are at peace with yourself. Since "pain pushes until vision pulls," you associate this place with great pain. And indeed, most of you have found your authenticity in your most painful moments, when you could no longer go along with the program, as it were, when you were suffocating, strangling, caving in under the weight of other people's ideas, behaviors, or expectations for your life. However, your connection to your authenticity need not come through a reactive response. If you would dare to choose your authenticity as a lifestyle, you would not experience such trauma.

Notice what I just said—experience your authenticity as a lifestyle. Most of you experience it only in spurts, as a triumph over some outer circumstance. No. Your authenticity is with you always. It does not need drama and trauma in order to express. Remember that saying that you recently heard, "Drama is optional." This is really the case. Just be you. Most of you fear that "you" is not a good thing to be, either because you do not believe in the beauty of your own being or because you have been conditioned to believe that searching for and expressing your authenticity is hedonistic—self-serving, an act of vanity and selfishness.

4. Your desires need to be surrendered to a Higher Purpose

Too many of your religious denominations have taught you not to trust your authentic self, that your nature is evil and sinful, and that you must war against it, keep it under control. You are told—don't trust your impulses, your desires and instincts, because they will lead you astray. You are to surrender them all so that you may live the spiritual path. This is only a "half truth." Yes, you must surrender them, but only so they may be used for a Higher Purpose, not so they may be exterminated. If you do not surrender them, then you are led by them. It is being led by your desires that it the problem, not the desires themselves.

Is surrender, once again, a means to an end, or the end in and of itself? You have made surrender the end. When it is the end, then you fear it is in fact "The End," like the end of a movie. You don't want to surrender to me because you fear you will be lost, wiped out. You struggle to hold onto a sense of yourself. Even when you don't like what you feel, at least there is a "you" to feel. You have misunderstood my intentions. I have no intention of wiping you off the face of the earth. Quite the contrary; I want to create with you, play with you, commune with you, be with you, express through you. And I desire to do it through your own unique patterns. I never create the same thing twice.

Your authenticity is a fundamental part of you that I desire, cherish, nurture, and protect. Will you do the same for yourself? Will you cherish, nurture, and protect your authenticity so that you can give it back to me to be used in a healthy way in our partnership? I want you to bring your authenticity to the table, not lose it forever. You cannot do this if you do not know that it exists. I don't want you to come to me empty-handed, as you fear. I just want you to come not holding onto a lot of outer, material "stuff." You think that your spiritual worth is caught up in your material worth. You hold onto your stuff so that you can be somebody. You are somebody just because I created you.

5. Cherish your authenticity; bring it healthily to our partnership

Who are you when you are not being defined by your relationships, your career, your finances, your body, your actions, and the like? Just who are you? If you will contemplate this question daily, then you will have the benefit of discovering your authentic self without so much trauma and drama. Some of you, however, will not contemplate this question unless you are literally without the societal crutches that you use to define yourself. But even if you lose a few things in the outer realm, the loss is not the focal point. It is the discovery of yourself underneath that is important.

6. When you are at peace with yourself, little else matters

Never choose a spiritual path that makes it a bad thing for you to discover yourself. You cannot find me if you cannot find yourself. I speak to you personally. If your path does not encourage this direct experience . . . then consider another path. Some paths are about empowering the institution or the leaders, not the individuals on the path. Find yourself. You are not stuck or trapped in a particular outer form. If you sense that a change is in order in some area of your life, know that it is merely to make room for a better fit. Would you rather keep clunking around in shoes that are too big or tiptoeing around in shoes that are too small? You cannot swim in a football uniform, and you wouldn't want to golf in bowling shoes. You would be hard-pressed to do ballet in hiking boots, and soccer shoes won't improve your jump shot.

I know what game you were sent here to play, and I will provide you with everything you need to be successful at it. But you can't mix and match your gear. In your spiritual search, many of you are using bits and pieces from many places that work fine in their respective circumstances. However, mixing and matching them may not get you where you need to go. You don't need to step up to bat with a hockey stick, wearing basketball shorts and a fencing breastplate. Trust me. I am an Inexhaustible Supply that meets your every need.

Don't worry so much about what others think about you; just strive to love and be at peace with yourself. When you reach this point, the rest doesn't matter. ✂

IX. SPIRITUAL BEINGS IN HUMAN BODIES

Tell the people about their lives as spiritual beings incarnate in a human body. The challenge for most of humanity, especially the more metaphysical types, is to strike the appropriate balance between being a spiritual being and living on the earth plane in a body. Most of you tend to affirm one more than the other. Some of you, following your own understanding of living beyond the temporal, tend to disregard the body as merely another one of those material things that comes and goes. There is the tendency within this consciousness to take the body for granted, to not be mindful of all of its needs, thereby creating a circumstance in which the body is at times subjected to more stress, strain, malnutrition, or lack of exercise than it really should be receiving.

1. Some take the body for granted, while others revere it

Those of you who tout the spiritual world all of the time tend to think of the body as if it were a space suit, or an instrument through which you play (or perhaps are played by me). When you get into this consciousness, you tend to ignore the body's sensations, its communications, its indications of when it is necessary for you to make certain changes. You look to your body as a signal of what's happening in your consciousness. And you are more likely to change what you discover has been going on in your consciousness than to change the way you have been treating, yea, dealing, with your body.

On the other hand, those of you (in the more metaphysical traditions) who are quite in tune with the body sometimes become overly indulgent in it. You are so in tune that you tend to reverently honor and worship your body's sensations, your emotions and feelings. Doing so makes a god out of them.

What do I mean when I say this? (Don't get offended here. Just listen.) You make a god out of anything that you empower to define for you who you are. You make a god out of anything that tells you not only who you are but how much you can be. Whenever you predetermine what is possible for you or not, based upon some external fact or perception, you make a god out of the evidence.

2. Spiritual growth can cause physical discomfort

When you are too mindful of your body and its various sensations, you become preoccupied with wanting to physically experience certain things and not experience other things. Growth is difficult. Growth is challenging. And your body reacts to growth in ways that do not feel pleasant. Hence, if you are allowing your body's sensation of distress to be the indicator of where you should or should not go in consciousness, you will remain stuck where you are. Discomfort comes with spiritual growth and development. As you remove the scales from your eyes, as you move beyond denial of what is really going on in your consciousness and delve deeply into the wellspring of your psychic energy, you are likely to hit upon many, many, many things that may send you physically "into a tizzy" (as some of you would say).

All of you manifest what you think about. This is not news to you. However, you sometimes fail to integrate what you know and, therefore, tend to forget how this impacts your physical being. There is a physical corollary to every thought. Every thought you think harbors its energy in your body temple. Understand what I am saying. Every thought you think harbors its energy in your body temple. What does it mean to harbor? To harbor is to anchor. To harbor is to find a port, an open receptive place, and to dock there. A harbor provides a refuge from the storm. A harbor provides a place of rest for rejuvenation and repair. When you provide a harbor for your emotions, you are providing a sanctuary for them to blossom.

You sometimes think that by not articulating certain thoughts you have stopped them from going out into the

Universe. This is not so. Your thought is energy, and energy cannot be contained within the body. The thoughts you think ripple out from you like sound waves for all to experience, if not to hear. And your body becomes much like a transmitter. Therefore, when you are in the process of cleansing and purging your consciousness of thoughts that do not serve your majestic spiritual nature, you must experience the physical purging that goes along with the mental cleansing. Understand what I am saying here. Thoughts that are out of alignment with your spiritual Truth are toxic. They have effects. Just as much power and influence that thoughts from the "high watch," the place of transcendence, have to lift you up—to inspire, heal, and transform you—so thoughts of worry, doubt, judgment, and the like have the power to do the reciprocal.

As human beings you are always going to experience some of those things. It is part of the human condition. Balance comes when you are able to both accept the fact that you are going to experience any or all of these things, and love yourself with enough compassion that allows you to simply move through it all without a great deal of attachment to your process or the outcome. It is in your judgment, your labeling of some things as good or bad, that becomes the difficult thing here. You are actively seeking what you consider to be good, while being just as busy running away from what you consider to be bad. It is all of this motion in one direction or the other that is problematic here.

3. Allow yourself to move through your feelings

Your charge as a spiritual being is to learn to just be still, to not try to go towards or away from anything. Your charge is to just be, to allow all of it to flow through you. When you are afraid of your so-called negative thoughts and fearful about having them released into the Universe, you harbor them in your body and eventually hemorrhage from them. To not let them out of you doesn't mean that they don't go out into the Universe. Quite the contrary. The more you hold onto a negative thought without dispelling it for the myth, the falsehood, the mistruth that it is, the more you are allowing the energy with which it resonates to rule.

Understand what it is that I am saying here. When you allow everything to simply surface, when you allow it to come forth for your examination and subsequent expulsion, then the energy force it has been vibrating with shifts and changes. Understand this. It shifts and it changes. Getting it outside of yourself with the intent of healing and wholeness allows its energy and negative impact to be neutralized through the energy of your new awareness and understanding. Understand what I am saying here. Fear dissipates just as fog dissipates. The Light of Truth, when it shines upon your darkness, is liberating, inspiring, uplifting, and transformative. Allow yourself to go through what you must go through so that you can put a vibration out in the Universe of transcendence, of overcoming, of victory. You cannot have a victory if you don't show up for the struggle. You cannot have a victory if you are running away from what you think is too big or too much for you to handle. The victory comes when you are able to face your "demons" head on and you come through still standing.

4. You have a body, but you are not your body

To face your demons takes courage. In such moments your body is likely to go through all kinds of gyrations. As human beings you have only so many emotions, and they are recycled. The same emotions are used to experience seemingly opposite things. You cry when you are happy; you cry when you are sad. Crying is just what you do when you are full of emotion. You sometimes get sick when you are not dealing with the hurts and pain you need to be dealing with, and sometimes you appear to get sick when you are dealing with and purging them. Appearing to be sick is simply what you do when you are dealing with—either engaging or ignoring—the deep pains of your life, whether you are aware of them or not.

Don't judge the world by your emotions. Your emotions are great indicators of what's going on with you, but don't stop there. Don't pamper your emotions. Don't give into them and make a god out of them. Push through them. Move beyond them. Fear is just "false evidence appearing real." Do not convict yourself on circumstantial evidence.

I am the Way, the Life, and the Truth. You are One with me. You are made in my image and my likeness. Your nature, like mine, is perfect, whole, and complete. You are free in the Spirit. No matter what's going on with you physically, you are transcendent of that. You have a body, but you are not your body. Who you are is bigger and greater than your body. Who you are existed before you had a body, and it will continue to exist long after you shed this body.

However, for the purpose of expressing while you are on this earth plane, having a body is most convenient (and as some of you may gather by the way I say this, there are other ways to express besides being in a body). Be that as it may, your present experience is that of being in a body. Although it is temporal, although it is transitory, although it is constantly aging and will one day fall into disarray if it exists on this plane long enough, there is no reason why you should not treat it with dignity and respect. There is a difference between revering something and treating it with dignity and respect. I'm not asking you to revere your body. But I am asking you to treat it with dignity and respect.

5. Treat your body with dignity and respect

When you treat something with dignity, you treat it as though it is important. You treat it as though it matters. You treat it with the understanding that there are things that would desecrate it and that it is your charge to maintain it at the highest standard and level of activity. I am not concerned so much with what the traditionalists refer to as "sin." I am not concerned with what supposedly offends me or doesn't offend me. I am concerned with what works and what doesn't work. I am concerned with what brings you closer to me versus what makes us appear to be farther apart. What many people consider to be sinful is simply foolishness; it simply doesn't serve, enhance, or create any value added. Many of your activities are counterproductive in this vein.

To respect is to do things that honor. When you respect something, you are aware of it. You're aware of what it is, what its needs are, and the way in which you relate to it. When you respect something, you are not just going through the motions; you are considering how your actions and activities are impacting the long-term relationship between you and what you respect. When you respect something, you hold it in an esteem that keeps its preciousness and its importance in the forefront of your mind. Treat your body with dignity. Honor and respect it. You need it. Just as your emotions affect your physical condition, your physical condition impacts your emotions. They are intertwined, totally enmeshed expressions of each other.

6. As you honor your body's needs, spiritually transcend them

As for the body being a vehicle, a vessel . . . this is true to a certain extent. You do use your body as a means of mobility, creativity, procreation, and the like. However, it is more than a vessel. Thinking of it as such creates a bit too much distance. Although as a spiritual being you transcend your body, it is a fundamental, integral part of your humanity, your human experience. The body should not be considered something extra or extraneous. It is a fundamental part of who you are on this earth plane. With this as the case, strive for an amicable relationship with your body. Strive for a partnership that honors both the body's needs and the truth of your transcendence of those needs. This may sound like a contradiction, but it is simply part of the spiritual paradox that exists everywhere you turn. In a paradox things that appear to be in opposition to each other exist simultaneously. Upon deeper reflection and introspection it becomes obvious that they are not in contradiction though they do exist simultaneously. Part of your challenge as a spiritual being is to find that great place of intersection where you can be at peace with it all.

Your ability to be at peace with it all is not on your shoulders exclusively. Turn to me. Turn to our relationship. Turn to your inner wisdom and understanding for guidance on these matters. We will be in partnership together. I will guide. I will lead. I will direct. I will show you ways in which your body can provide you with the sweetest of experiences, and I will show you how you can have the sweetest of experiences beyond anything your body can teach you. Turn it all over to me, and we will work together. Love yourself. Love me. Love your body. Neither fear nor revere it. Come to me in truth and in wholeness, and I will make all things new. I will heal you. I will restore you. I will bring you back to full expression of your health and your vitality. It is never too late, for I simply Am. ⤴

*7. We will
work in
partnership
together*

X. "Is" versus "Exist"

1. Your existence comes and goes; your Isness lasts forever

Memorial Day is thought of as a day to commemorate the dead. In some respects this is true, in that the ones most typically honored that day have crossed over from an incarnation that no longer exists. Notice that I used the word "exists." Look up the root of this word, my Reverend Daughter. You read it a few days ago in the classic by E. Emile Cady, *Lessons in Truth*. She says that God *Is* and man *exists*. Isness is Absolute. And, as you just discovered in the dictionary, existence is a coming out of, a taking shape and form. Because you human beings take shape and form, you exist. The existence of the shape and form will one day pass. However, the Isness, your relationship to me as part of the great I AM, lasts forever.

So much of your society, all around the globe, is organized around the answer to the question "What is the next form of existence?" The answer to this question determines the very meaning of their current existence and deeply impacts and influences the choices they make. They are aware at some level that their existence is in some sort of evolution, and this prompts concern about what today's actions mean for tomorrow's existence, whether in their flesh form or not. Some say that they do not believe that anything happens or are not concerned about what happens, after their current flesh form is gone. This does not mean they are unaware of the process of evolution I am speaking of, only that they are convinced that their present incarnation is, in fact, the end of their evolutionary line. Their evolution, in their mind, is limited to the human developmental process. Yet whatever they may think, something is happening; and everybody knows it and lives their lives according to what they think they know.

What human beings think they know is what you refer to as perception. Never underestimate the power of perception. It is the guiding force that shapes everything that you think, say, do, feel, create, express, etc. The list is endless because for human beings perception is the beginning. Your perceptions are based upon your awareness—your awareness of who you think you are in the great scheme of the world. So perception is dual in nature. There is a sense of your own individuality on the one hand and a sense of how that individuality fits within the context of the whole on the other. There are both the micro and the macro perspectives. These are not independent or mutually exclusive. They reinforce each other.

2. Needing to explain everything is more primitive than embracing the unknown

Yet Memorial Day also signifies something else. It is not merely a time to reminisce about what has been; it is also a time to celebrate that there is something next. Even when you don't understand exactly what that is, to the extent that you believe an evolutionary process is going on, you acknowledge that the individuals you honor in that moment have gone on in some way. You understand that they are not in their old incarnation anymore. However, even though that incarnation has ceased to exist, this does not mean that there is no Isness. Some say that to accept that life simply ends is a deep, primordial, existential dilemma for the human psyche, and they accuse "believers" of making up some type of afterlife or sense of ongoing existence to satisfy a primitive yearning for immortality. However, this is naiveté at its best. It is pure projection. The ones who purport this are the very ones who are working at such a primitive level of the human psyche that an answer is needed for everything lest their psyche become afraid of the unknown. The need to put everything in a neat little box is actually more primitive than the awareness that there is so much more than what meets the eye.

3. Grieve and allow yourself to change anyway

The evolution I speak of here, in the context of Memorial Day, is not relegated to the material form alone. That is to say, it is not simply about physical incarnations. As in the inner, so in the outer. As in the outer, so in the inner. The microcosm is part of the macrocosm, and the macrocosm is part of the microcosm. It is all the same. This evolutionary process, this transition, this moving into higher states of existence, happens all of the time. As human beings, you are constantly dying to who you have been. To the extent that you are aware of and regard the human evolutionary process as a wonderfully exciting adventure, you will embrace the inevitable changes as indications that the evolutionary process is taking place. However, if you cling to your current state of existence, then when it becomes apparent that change is imminent, on the horizon, or up in your face (as you would say), you start to engage in all kinds of activities in attempts to halt or reverse this process. Fear sets in regarding the unknown. Even if you have been praying to get away from the spot that you are in, as human beings you cling to the familiar, whether it is good for you or not.

When anything dies, as human beings you grieve. This is part of what is happening with you now, my Reverend Daughter, you are grieving. You are grieving so many changes in your life. You may look around and say, "Well, there aren't that many changes in my life in this very moment in time." But you are grieving anyway. At some deep psychic level you have been holding onto many things that are no longer in your existence or in theirs. In honoring them you have been keeping them alive. And now you are letting them go, and freeing the psychic space that all of that took up leaves an emptiness inside of you that makes you emotionally melancholy.

You are also grieving the loss of yourself because you know that you are going through a great spiritual metamorphosis at this point in time. You never did like being the "goo" of the caterpillar in its chrysalis phase, but I so appreciate your increased willingness to be goo with less drama and trauma. I am pleased that you are truly coming into the awareness that the drama is optional. Grieve, my child. Grieve. As you know, when people grieve they are never really grieving about any one thing in particular. The process of grieving presents the opportunity to grieve loss—perceived loss, change, transitions that have happened at any points in one's life. It is healthy. It is a purging of sorts, as well as part of a metamorphosis.

You will soon be making your first trip to a state correctional facility. When you speak, let the inmates know that there is another form of existence for their lives. Let them know that they can choose to die to the old and be born into a new. Describe this process in universal terms that all can understand. Give them a message of empowerment. Let them know that although their bodies are imprisoned, their minds are free. Let them know that there is nothing to wait for; they can begin to express their human and spiritual potential right where they are.

4. Give a message of empowerment in the prison

Speak to them about the difference between desire and intent. Talk to them about miracles as an everyday occurrence. Talk to them about the deep yearnings of their soul, and give them permission to listen and to act upon it. Give them permission to claim who they are in spiritual Truth. Let them know that like the prodigal son, all they need to do is to return home. All they need to do is to come into their own.

Let them know that I have already forgiven them. There is nothing in the Universe that holds anything against them. It is now time for them to forgive themselves, to accept and acknowledge that the evolutionary process I speak of is available to them now, right where they are, in spite of their physical imprisonment.

5. Let the inmates know that their minds are not imprisoned

The mind, the soul, the essence of life living and breathing within them, can never be imprisoned. It is always free. It just needs to be tapped into and recognized. It must be affirmed. It would be wonderful if the outer world were to support and cooperate in this affirmation. However, it is not necessary. It is an internal job that begins with oneself.

Speak to them of the spiritual world and its paradoxes. Tell them how there is power in humility. Tell them that giving and being of service to others increases their own human capacity. Tell them how turning their lives over to a Higher Power, though it feels like losing control, puts them in more control, because they become less able to be jerked around by the outer world. Tell them that their life experience is a question of their perception and that they have the opportunity at any moment to change the perceptions that they have.

Let them know that they don't have to be any place else for them to be more of the All that they are. There are people, circumstances, conditions all around them that need love and attention. Yes, love. Love, not the namby-pamby emotion that people think that it is, but love in the sense of connectedness to the whole. Teach them about healing that deep sense of separation. Prison is meant to imprint a deep sense of separation in the psyches of the ones imprisoned. However, this imprint becomes an engraving; it stops becoming a condition and starts becoming an identity. This takes us back to the beginning of this letter, where I was talking about the difference that Emile Cady noted in her book, *Lessons in Truth*—that God Is and human beings exist. They are turning their prison existence into an Isness. And you must warn them against this.

They don't have to wait until they are released, they don't have to wait until the outer world changes, for them to see themselves differently. There is so much that is waiting inside each of them. There's music to be made, music to be written. There are poems, writings, musings, observations to be written. There are things to be sculpted and pictures to be painted. There are games to be played and plays to be played. There are technologies to be learned and utilized. There are hearts that need to be uplifted. There are words of encouragement that need to be shared. There are shoulders that need to leaned on. There are eyes that need to reflect the truth and beauty of the Spirit incarnate in the human form.

Speak to them about these things, my child. Stop worrying about and questioning why it is you who must go to this prison, this male prison. It's you because you know everything that I am talking about. It's you because you know what it means to know that you are free in the midst of a societal prison. You know what it is like to go against the odds and to dare to dream. You know what it is like to give yourself permission to grow and change and seek and find. You know what it is like to live the paradoxes. You know what it is like. It's also you because you don't have any judgment about these inmates. That's why you are going. Once again, it's one of those paradoxes. You don't have any emotional charge about them, so you can't figure out why you are being sent. But that's why you are being sent—because you don't have any emotional charges one way or another. They are neither good nor bad in your eyes. Being in prison is just a state of existence. And you understand that their being in prison is not just about their actions but about all of the racism, and classism, and myriad of other things in your society that have created the circumstances for all of this incarceration to take place anyway. And you have learned how to forgive all of that as much as you have learned how to forgive the human responses to it. No, my Reverend Daughter, stop asking me those kinds of questions. You are the first one to tell people who question my directives for their life that I didn't send the burning bush to the wrong person. I know who I ask to do what. And there is a reason why the others are going with you, too. There is something in it for each of them, as well.

So you ask, well, what's in it for you? That's not for me to answer but for you to discover. And it will be so beyond self-

6. It's your work to do because of who you are

evident. This is the epitome. This is about as far away from your mode of existence and your life as you have known it as you can possibly come at this moment in time. And when you are able to stand there and speak these words of truth and empower the very kinds of people that you, yourself, have even been the most dismissive of, the energy of dismissiveness will stop permeating your being so much. You will stop feeling so dismissed. You will have given what you want to get. You know how this works. And I am most pleased.

7. You can flit around with the pigeons or soar with the eagles

You can flit around with the pigeons, or you can soar with the eagles. I have told you this before, and it continues to be true; everything that I ever say is always true forever. The choice is yours. And I support you in your choices. Just remember that in your human metamorphosis from the caterpillar to the butterfly, there is no cocoon stage. You are Fullness all of the time. Enjoy your life, my Reverend Daughter. What a good life it will be, even if it is not the life that you thought you had bargained for with me. You have been taking this quite hard—about not being able to experience life the way in which you thought life had been promised to you. However, it might serve you well to study the concept of shape-shifters that is common in Native American cultures. The shamans understood that they were not limited to a particular form or expression. You want so much to be understood and engaged with as *you*. Keep letting "you" go. You are so tired of feeling as though you are constantly being cast into predetermined roles in other people's lives, if you are seen at all. Learn what it means to be a shape-shifter. You will find, once again, that this is one of those paradoxes where your willingness to be anything allows you to be everything, even if it isn't the something that you want to be. Once again, you are afraid that if you become the more that I am asking you to be this time, you won't have anything of yourself left. But I am trying to give you everything. Is everything too much? Is there some part of "every" that you don't want? Just keep walking in the direction of surrender, and all will be well.

You have been fascinated since your youth by philosophy and logic, and particularly enjoyed studying Aristotle and Plato. You, like most of your society, have bought into Descartes' idea, "I think, therefore I exist." This is indeed so true. This is why there is an understanding among you that your existence in that particular incarnation ends when your thinking stops. However, your thinking has nothing to do with Isness. You are a part of the great I AM, which transcends your thinking. My daughter, you must learn how to think less so that you can just be. Learn to be more so that you can experience the great I AM of your life.

XI. READY TO BE REBORN

1. Spiritual rebirth is an evolutionary process, not an event

What exactly does this mean—to be reborn? It is a concept that you sometimes balk at, my Reverend Daughter, because of your own perceptions of those who use the terminology to speak of themselves exclusively as "born again." However, in this, as in most things, you are unwilling to acquiesce any spiritual Truth to any one particular group for the purpose of their monopoly. No, you understand that the Truth is everywhere present and is available to all.

When I talk about being born again, however, I am talking about spiritual evolution. You thought that I was going to say "phenomenon." However, it is not merely a phenomenon. This would relegate it to the realm of a particular event. Too often you confuse your understanding of spiritual birth with analogies of human birth. In doing so, you make spiritual birth an event that happens at a specific point in time. Yes, you may get revelations, glimpses of enlightenment, deep insights, at particular moments that mark your journey forever. This is to be expected. However, the rebirthing does not necessarily coincide with the moments of high awareness and resolve. There is usually a period of time—and for most human beings a considerable amount of time—between the initial acceptance or embodiment of a spiritual concept and one's ability to step out on it, to fully incorporate it into one's life and be born again with it in Spirit.

2. Don't confuse getting a second chance with spiritual rebirth

Don't confuse spiritual rebirth with your ego self's getting what appears to be a second chance at life. When you are looking for another chance, a second chance, your search is laden with anxieties, criticisms, judgments, expectations, worries, concerns, and needs to prove something to other people, as well as yourself. When you are simply looking for a second chance, you want to experience what you call winning. You want to experience what you consider to be success. You want to be able to have something to turn to as an indication of your worth and your value other than the things you have already manifested in your life. When you are merely trying to get a second chance, you are usually running from deep inner pain and conflict. The hope is that if you are one day able to overcome a certain something, do or obtain a certain something, then perhaps that will make you feel more fulfilled. There is the assumption that with this fulfillment there will be a greater sense of self-worth and self-acceptance.

However, when one is born of the Spirit, none of these things matters. When one is born of the Spirit, one is not trying to prove anything to anyone. When one is born of the Spirit, one is truly being pulled by vision and no longer pushed by pain. When one is born again of the Spirit there is a dedication and a consecration. There is a conscious releasing of the old in order to step into the new. This releasing, however, is done with the utmost humility. There is the understanding that one is not creating a life anew for one's own self. In spiritual rebirth there is much surrender—surrender to a Divine Plan, surrender to one's Higher Purpose, surrender to one's own genuine authenticity. I make all things new. When one is looking for a second chance, one is trying to reconcile an earlier part of one's life. There is contrasting and comparing that is going on here, and it is important that the later picture be more perfect than the former.

In the Spiritual world, there is no contradiction, there is no contrast, there is no comparison, there is no competition. There is an "Isness" that reigns supreme. When one is being born of the Spirit, there is a conscious recognition of this newness. It is embraced at a deep, heartfelt level. Furthermore, you understand, explicitly or implicitly, that the past doesn't really matter anymore. You were where you were, and now you are here, and the world will continue from this place. Being

3. "Pain pushes until vision pulls"

born again in the Spirit requires conscious recognition of one's true spiritual identity as being first and foremost. It is not the context in which one desires to live; it is the very content that one conspires to have. There is rejoicing in the release, even when it is a painful or unpleasant experience.

4. One must turn to me for spiritual rebirth

When one is looking to be spiritually born again, one turns to me. One comes to me to made whole, to be renewed, uplifted, and sustained. When one is merely looking for a second chance at life, one is constantly on the lookout for some person, place, or thing in the external world that is going to grant the opportunity or create the circumstance for that second chance. This is true even when those seeking a second chance are busy praying to me. They fail to see that their prayers are filled with edicts, demands, expectations, even ultimatums, of what I am supposed to be doing for them. They outline, write their scripts, draw their pictures, and go about the business of telling me what's best for them. And they get quite exasperated with me for not cooperating fast enough. This is the human ego running wild.

When there is a rebirth of the Spirit one breaks through the illusion that one's life is an independent entity in the Universe. When one is born again of the Spirit, the sense of alienation that can sometimes exist at nearly every level and plane of life is exposed for the false illusion that it is. When one is being born again of the Spirit, there is no real fear or concern about the outcome, though there may be hesitations or reservations about the process. I make all things new. In this newness there is a magnificence and a grandeur. But do not misunderstand when I say that I make all things new. The "you" that is birthed spiritually is the You that has always existed. What I make new are the circumstances and conditions, which allow you to experience more of the Truth of your being. When you are being born again, it is necessary for you to accept the new.

Too many of you want to be enlightened and want to stay the same at the same time. You pray for transformation but cling to your existing forms. You pray for transcendence, and yet you refuse to get your feet out of the quicksand of your perceptions of yourself as victimized. You say that you want to be free, yet you are busy trying to make peace with your old shackles, chains, limitations, and boxes. When you are ready to be born again in the Spirit, there is a great mounting sense of urgency within. Sometimes it feels like you are coming out of your own skin. The power surging within you is so potent that it frightens many of you.

When you are ready to be born again, you know that you are signing up for a journey that, from a human standpoint, is unpredictable. You are ready to accept the truth that just because you are not in control does not mean that things are out of control. When you are ready to be born again, your relationship with me is primary, first and foremost, front and center, top of the list, the pressing thing on your agenda, the mountain that must be scaled. And you know that once the process is in motion, you cannot turn back. You must go forward, and you do. When you are being born again of the Spirit, your true powers are being unleashed. You are being freed from the false notion that you are not enough. You are being freed from the false notion that other people, places, and things are more valuable than you are. You are being freed from the notion that you have to play small or that you have to settle for whatever it is that comes your way in life, without reaching for the stars and the moon. Oohhh, to be born again is a joy, an adventure, an odyssey of the most mystical nature. It is exciting. Its great wonder, the pull of its energy—coupled with the fact that you can't do anything else anyway—makes your birthing inevitable.

5. You are signing up for a journey

6. *Allow your transformation to take root before attempting to share it*

Be mindful of a couple of things, my children. Just as an infant is susceptible to all kinds of things in the environment, remember your own susceptibility in the newness of your birthing. There is a tendency to want to shout and share this with everyone and everybody. Many of these individuals, even those who have been very close to you, may not understand what you are going through. In this way they often are of little support; even worse, they tend to make you doubt the reality of your own experience. Sometimes it is better to remain silent about your transformations, allowing them to take root in your consciousness, before you put yourself in a position where your ego will feel a need to defend itself. During these times you may need to take some space for yourself. Remember that Jesus declared before he ascended, "Touch me not for I have not yet ascended." To be too involved with the old at this point in time can drag you back to the old vibration and patterns.

I am always ready. I await you with open arms. I am ever available, watching, guiding, consoling, uplifting, inspiring, encouraging, carrying, loving, supporting. In me you have everything that you need for your spiritual evolution. I am pure Spirit; I am perfect, whole, and complete. You are pure Spirit; you are perfect, whole, and complete. What you have to let go of will not feel like loss; instead you will find yourself in me. Come a little closer, my children. Come up a little higher. The time is now.

XII. SUPPORT

Trust in me and I will make all things new. What you humans call support is not really support at all. It is your need to be affirmed in your smallness, your hurts, and your pain. For others to validate this for you makes you feel like you are seen and understood. While this may be of great benefit to your ego, it has nothing to do with the healing that I have in store for you. When I support you, I move you beyond yourself, beyond everything that you think that you know about yourself. I move you to a place that you know not of. You are carried away to the place that I have in store for you. In this place you can be the All that I have intended you to be, which rarely is what you have intended for yourself.

1. Support moves you beyond your ideas of yourself

The places where you want to be supported are often in contradiction to the places where I want you to be. The places where I want you to be move you beyond your past experiences, your ideas of what you think has happened to you. What you think has happened to you has happened to your human persona but not to You, to the real You, which is your spiritual Self. When you turn to me for support, I help you break through the illusion that those things have indeed happened to you, at all.

"But," you say, "I really did go through this or that. If you take that away from me, how will know that I am me?" Do you define yourself by the things that have happened to you, by the things that you have done? No! Who you are is so much more than that. However, you must let go of who you think you are in order to receive my support. My support requires that you move to a place of nonjudgment about yourself and all others. The judgment that you carry keeps you stuck in a

2. Don't define yourself by things that have happened

false identity. Then you run around and try to find others who will collude with you in your false notions.

I do not collude with falseness. That is why so many of you fear coming to me. You know that I will reorder your life and your thinking. This is too threatening to your ego self. But how else can it be? This is what it means to be born again of the Spirit. When you are born of the Spirit, you know that the past does not matter any more, that the slate has been wiped clean, and that you can start on a fresh new footing. The trials and tribulations only have value to the extent that they bring you back to me. If they bring you to false ideas about yourself, and to others who will share in these false ideas about yourself . . . then what is the point? Why do you desire to stay crystallized in places where you really don't want to be anyway? Yet you fight so hard for them. Merely mentioning that maybe you could do better, that maybe the circumstances weren't so devastating after all, sends you reeling into anger and frustration.

"Argue for your limitations, and sure enough, they're yours," as it says in the book you like so much, *Illusions* by Richard Bach. Do not argue for anything that you do not want to experience. I am with you always. I know what has happened to you, and I know that what has happened to you does not matter in the long run. Just keep your eye on me; I will support you in your magnificence, not your smallness. I will call you up to your rightful place in the Universe, which is with your head held high. Forgive, and let go. Judgment does not serve you. Forgive yourself as well, for you are your own worst critic.

3. When I support you, you stand in your power

If others are not there to support you, you fear that I will not be there either. This is a false notion. You project onto me all of your concerns about the authority figures in your life. You project onto me all of the neuroses of your parents and the dysfunctions of a hierarchical society. No, I am not these things. Trust in my love. It will not only heal you, it will support you as well.

When you are supported by me, you know that there is so much more to you than what meets the eye. You are no longer afraid of change in the outer world, and you learn to look upon each day with enthusiasm and a sense of newness. Your burdens are lifted off your shoulders, and you stand tall with a sense of purpose and with intent. When you are supported by me, though you feel weak and vulnerable, you know that you are standing in your power. Until you are standing in your power in me, you are standing on shaky ground. Any other sense of power is circumstantial and conditional—things have to be just so, certain people cannot be around, your boundaries have to be respected, and the like. When you are standing on me as your support, it doesn't matter what happens all around you. You are present with me, and that is enough.

When you allow yourself to be supported by me, you clearly see that others are simply acting out their conscious awareness of their Oneness with me, which is very meager in most instances. You have greater compassion for yourself and for all others. Let me support you and you will stand on top of the world, not on top of other people. Let me support you and there is nothing that we cannot accomplish together. You will not be tired or frazzled. You will not be overwhelmed or intimidated by anything. Even though you will not always know exactly what is going on, you will feel my guidance for your next step. You will hear my voice above all others, and it will be soothing to you. Trust my love to support you, for I have your best interests at heart, and these are not the interests that most affect your heart.

The things that affect your heart are based on your ideas of who other people are, as well as your ideas about who you are. You hold each other in bondage trying to get your needs fulfilled by one another. I am the only one who can bring you peace and satisfaction. I am the only one who can make you feel whole and complete. Anything else is temporal and will not last long. What I have to offer will weather through any storm. You

4. Release each other from bondage and come up higher

will not need to lean on anything else. Your addictions will fall away, your lusts will change, and you will no longer need to look outside yourself for anything, for I will be inside you. You will find me within your own being. The support you need is at the center of your being.

Forgive your mother, your father, your siblings, and anyone else you feel has disappointed you. Forgive your children and their children, your neighbor, your coworker, your boss, the entire society. No support means anything, other than mine. Now is the time for you to recognize me in all that you do, and I will make all things new. You are free in me. You are a part of the I AM THAT I AM, and you need to remember that. There is nothing else for you to ponder but your relationship with me. Is there anything more satisfying than this? I don't think so, and you need to know so. Lean on me and you will learn this—not for a day or for the hour; it will remain with you like nothing you have ever known on the human plane. Trust me. I trust you no matter what you do. Can you do the same for me? I love you, my little ones. Come up higher. Soar with me on the wings that you don't even know you have.

XIII. Accept My Praise

Yes, it is good that all of you sing my praise. However, I sing your praise, as well. You sing with all of your heart, and you want me to hear your adoration for me. I also sing with all of my heart, and I desire that you hear my adoration for you. You are, indeed, the crowning jewel of all of my creations. You are me in the flesh. You are my hands, my feet, my voice. I give you my mind to use. It is my heart that you feel with. Do you feel me in your heart?

1. Do you hear me when I tell you that you are wonderful?

I am forever singing your praises, always reminding you that you are so much more than what has happened to you. You are beauty, power, and serenity in the making. You are a treasure to behold, special in your own, unique right. You are full of my richness. I try to tell you this all the time. Will you listen to me? When I tell you that you are wonderful just the way that you are, do you hear me? When I tell you that nothing can stand in your way, that you are bigger than your problems, do you believe me? I sing your praises at every moment of the day.

You have been told that it is egocentric to have your praises sung to you. So what is the glory in never being praised? It is not egotistical to accept my praise; it is egotistical not to. When you do not accept my praise of you, you are placing your opinion of yourself above mine. This, my little ones, is blasphemous. Don't blaspheme me by throwing my adoration for you back in my face. You know how you feel when people will not accept the love you want to give them, when they cannot feel it no matter how hard you try to share yourself with them? Well, if I had human feelings, this is how I would feel when you refuse my love. Fortunately, I hold neither grudges

2. Don't place your opinion of yourself above mine

nor resentments. I simply await your conscious recognition of who you are. I am patient and will never give up on you. No matter how hard you are on yourselves, I am always compassionate and understanding. The sad part is that you project your own feelings about yourself onto others, as well as onto me. Whereas the others will always reflect back to you your own consciousness, I can only reflect back to you your own Truth—which you most often are not conscious of.

What is it that I want you to know? I want you to know that you are fundamentally Good, that you can only demonstrate what you know. Don't berate yourself for what you've done or not done. Just get to know yourself, your real Self, better. How will you know what your real Self is? I will tell you. I always do. Stop arguing with me. I try to tell you about your possibilities and you counter with your limitations. I try to show you abundance and you speak of lack.

3. Your inner design is more important than your outer facade

Just soak in my praise for you. Walk outside. Throw up your hands to the sky. See what I have to say. Walk on the beach, marvel at the stars, smell the flowers. Ask each of them what I think of you, and they will tell you. Am I really your dwelling place? If I am, then what is this strange decor that doesn't reflect who you are? Yes, I am your dwelling place, but it's time to redecorate. Your inner design is more important than your outer facade.

I love you. I see you. I know who you are, and I like what I see. When you praise me, praise the "you" that is within me. You can't praise me and not praise everything that I am about. I am about you. When you hear my praise, you will know that you are the melody in my song of life. Sing with me. Harmonize with me. We can make such sweet music together. Shall we dance?

Practicing the Principles

SECTION THREE

Practicing the Principles

CONTENTS

1. Prayer is a movement in consciousness

2. The energy of your prayers quickens vibratory patterns

3. Anyone who is receptive benefits from your prayers

4. You are a place through which my power expresses

5. In prayer prioritize spiritual facts over material facts

6. Speak the Word with confidence, expecting a manifestation

I. LIVING EVERY MOMENT

1. Three components— living, every, and moment

There is much confusion regarding the notion of living every moment. It has come to be associated with living life with a gusto, a fervor and intensity, that at times, because of its intensity, can border on the line of recklessness. Your society has come to equate living every moment with filling all of your time with sensation, stimuli, and activity. Living every moment does not mean that you have to be about the business of being busy at every moment; it does not require that you be in constant motion. The notion of living every moment has three very important components—living, every, and moment. I have a message for you to give to the people regarding all three.

2. A moment is very present and is pregnant with possibility

Little value is given to the notion of a moment. Individuals too often associate moment with momentary, that is to say, a moment is considered to be just a fleeting, minute period of time. Because of its minuteness it would appear to be easily dismissed and/or discounted. A moment is too often thought of as a moment. In a single moment there does not appear to be much time to accomplish anything of real significance. However, when you understand the concept of a moment, you realize that a moment implies a very vital window of opportunity to express. A moment, though transitory in the sense that it will leave, is full of all possibility. There is nothing minute in a moment save your thinking, the smallness your understanding of how pregnant that time period really is. A moment—the moment—is the point in time in which you actually experience life. What you consider to be a long time is essentially just a series of moments. You worry so about your fate, the unfoldment of your future, what lies ahead of you . . . as if the future were an amorphous abyss in front of you. However, this is not the case. You are determining from moment to moment exactly what your future will be by what you do, say, think, feel, share, express, create in the present moment.

A moment is very present. It is not off in the future, nor is it a relic from the past. A moment is the time that is right in front of you, as you are moving in your conscious state of awareness. You know, even scientifically, that in actuality there is no such thing as time. However, as human beings you move within a time-space continuum. That is to say, you take your actions, you have your thoughts and your feelings, within a certain framework that revolves around your notions and understanding of time. The moment is when you do anything.

I wish to speak now about the notion of every. Along with the faulty idea that a moment may be without significance, there is also the false notion that some moments are more important than other moments. Because of this mistaken sense of distinction, you often withhold. You withhold yourself, your gifts, your talents, your resources, your attention, your caring, and anything else that you might have to offer. Too many of you are waiting for "the big one." "Why waste my time on something that isn't the real thing? I should save myself for something more important later on." Every means just that— All, the individual and the collective whole, each one. Every moment means that there is not a single moment that goes by that is any less significant than another. Oftentimes you are restless, bored, anxious to move on to other people, places, and things. And exactly why are you in such a hurry, my children? Is there some place you can go where the moments are any more precious there? Is there some time frame in which life is any more precious, yea, sweeter, than in another moment? Exactly what is it that you are waiting for?

Are you afraid that there will not be enough of you, that you will run out, exhaust your own resources? Are you afraid that you may miss something—as though you may be caught

3. Every means All

up in something of lesser significance when the "right thing" comes along, and you want to make certain that you are free, ready, available to accept what you think might be a brighter horizon awaiting you just around the corner? You have so many excuses for not fully acknowledging life as an ongoing process that is unfolding moment by moment. This unfoldment is an integral part of the process, and it is good that you continue to develop a sense of patience and compassion for and with each other.

There is nothing left out in the notion of every moment. It implies the presence and fullness of life at every point and place in time, simultaneously—which is part of the Truth about me that is yours to reveal. Every moment means that you cannot pick and choose when you will be your authentic self; for being your authentic self is a requirement at all times.

4. Living is about being, not doing

This leads me now to discuss the word "living" in our topic, "living every moment." As I will often tell you, do not confuse or convolute the process of living with your human angst and anxieties. Living is not doing. Living is about being, being fully present and aware. Living is about soaking it all up and knowing that by your soaking it up you are never detracting from another person's raw potential or their ability to express the All that they are here to express. Living means being available to me, as well as to yourself. Living also implies being comfortable with a certain degree of uncertainty. Much of your inability to live every moment is due to the lack of trust that you have in me and in the Universe that I have created. You are so worried that you will not have what you either need or want when the time comes that you spend all of your time trying to ready, prepare, secure, and maintain as a protective measure. Living is not about protecting. Living will never make you smaller. Living will make you expand, and in this expansion there is quite often a sense of vulnerability. Living means having to take risks on a human level, However you grow, understand that on the spiritual level there is absolutely nothing to risk. You cannot lose. You can never lose. So there is no need for concern about protection. Living is about creating a space for me to express the Allness that I am through the Allness that you are.

When you put it all together, you begin to see that living every moment is an extremely powerful concept. If you could only remember this, you would find that so many of the difficulties, challenges, problems that present themselves to you are not actually yours but are things that others—family, clients, coworkers, community—have brought into your life experience. Living every moment means that you must be in a constant communion with me. I exist in every single moment. And when you are feeling alive, then you notice me no matter what else is in the moment. Moments start to become your friend instead of your enemy. You begin to gain a deeper respect even for those circumstances, situations, and individuals that you are not particularly fond of, as you would say.

Remember that desire is not the same thing as intent. Many of you desire to live life every moment; it is something that you talk about, complain about, beg for, cajole about, or manipulate things in order to achieve. You do practically anything necessary to make it an issue. However, life is not a spectator sport, nor is it for the purpose of being critiqued or graded. Too much of your livingness is constricted, restricted, conditioned, or limited by your concern about what other people are going to think or say about you. This causes you to hesitate, to evaluate and reevaluate the circumstances and the conditions, rather than simply participate in that moment. So many moments in which you could be living are lost because you are too busy thinking about your experience of living rather than simply living your life.

Introspection is healthy to a degree. Introspection is helpful to the extent that you use it as a measure of your spiritual integrity and as a tool of accountability, cleansing, healing, and transformation. However, introspection for the purpose

5. So many moments are lost in thinking about living rather than living

of finding fault with your own selves, for judging yourself in comparison to another, or for anything that would take the focus off of our relationship with one another . . . anything and everything that would do that is suspicious and should not be indulged in too much, lest you fall into the trap of what has been referred to as "paralysis by analysis."

6. You can only live the moment that you are in

I don't need you paralyzed. I don't want any of you paralyzed. I want you to live every moment, because every moment is when I live. I want you to live every moment because there is no other time to live but the moment in which you are. I want you to live every moment because you will never know the greatness that life can be unless you give yourself permission to show up and to play fully. I want you to live every moment so that you can know who you are in your true spiritual authenticity. I know that you are tired of the push and pull, the ups and downs, the yo-yo effect—sometimes you're up, sometimes you're down, sometimes you grasp it and sometimes you forget. I see your struggles. You are my children. I know you. You are of my very flesh and blood that I created and of my spirit that breathed into you. I know who you are. And I request that you live every moment so that I can express through you to the greatest of your ability. Living every moment creates an ideal win/win situation. When you are present in every moment, you take the moment to do that little extra thing, even if it's just a smile, a phone call; a little show of appreciation goes a very long way.

7. I'm trying to give you everything

When you start living every moment, you seek opportunities to let your light shine and to rekindle the flames of others. You don't wait for life to come to you; you reach out and embrace what's right beside you, as well as what's coming your way. Most importantly, you live every moment so that we can spend as much quality time together as possible. Is there anything more important, urgent, or pressing than this? Fear not. Unlike in your human relationships, where time with one is considered to take away from the time with another, your connecting with me will not be at the exclusion of your joy and responsibilities, or even your pain.

The experience of living is the result of your ability to ask of yourself and of the Universe. And as I told you before about asking, you fear that if you ask for more then you won't get anything. However, if you ask for less, then you won't get everything, and I am trying to give you everything. The same is true about living. Too many of you fear that if you attempt to live more, to live larger or more fully, you won't get anything, or perhaps you will lose what you have. However, if you live less, then you won't live everything. And I am trying to give you everything. Which of my gifts are you prepared to receive, and which are you planning to turn away? A gift is rejected in each moment that is not fully lived by you. You are waiting for me to fill up your life with meaning. The real question is, how big is your basket?

II. Maintaining a Vision

1. Your job is to know that it is possible, not to make it happen

Tell the people this morning that the purpose of their maintaining a vision is to be open to possibility consciousness. Too often you go into a task-oriented mode, which only gets you bogged down in details and so-called material facts. Your mind becomes cluttered with the debris of doubt, and you wind up only confusing yourselves. The burden is not on you to make anything happen; your job is to know that it is possible. In your knowing, you open up the space in your consciousness (which includes your heart) so that I can work through you.

Your inability to distinguish between God doing the work through you and your doing the work appears to be a constant source of bafflement for all of you. You attribute the action to the vehicle. Does light come from the lightbulb? Is the harp creating the music? No. You are an instrument, a medium, as it were. When you do not understand this, you get in your own way and then blame me for your own stubbornness.

Many of you fail to dream because you fear that your dream will never come to pass. Is pushing it further from your imagination going to make it materialize any faster? What is the hurt, the disappointment, that you strive so desperately to protect yourself from? Is your life more fulfilled for having fewer dreams? Are you more alive for striving less? Are you any safer for your fear to break out? Does staying locked up inside of yourself make you think you are in control?

2. We co-create on an energetic level

Maintaining a vision requires that you let go of your anxieties. Anxiety is living the future in the present. You let the technicalities of production stymie you every time. You always say, "But, don't I have to do something?" Maintaining the vision is doing something . . . perhaps the most difficult thing many of you will ever do. It is so challenging that many of you do not even attempt it for fear of failure. Yet even in the light of this trepidation, you still claim that maintaining a vision is nothing, that it is unworthy of your time and attention.

I bring you your visions. I will also bring them into manifestation. The co-creation that you must do with me is on an energetic level. You must meet me in the field of all possibility and commune with me there. Let us tryst often. And do not be afraid to share our sacred union with others. Our intimacy has no bounds. I don't have favorites, and no one can steal your dreams from you.

Many of you hoard your visions, stockpiling them in your secret vaults and safety deposit boxes. What are you doing? Are you saving for a rainy day? What would that rain look like? For most of you it looks like pain and aggravation. You move towards your vision when you can no longer tolerate where you are. Yet the energy of that anger contaminates your humility, and you begin to take things on yourself for your own sense of satisfaction and accomplishment. This brings your ego into the situation, because it wants credit for everything.

It is not good enough that your vision materialize; your ego wants to know that it did it. And when your ego cannot take credit for your success, it takes credit for your failure. Your self-condemnation and self-criticism are ways for you to take credit for why things are the way that they are, thereby satisfying your ego's need to feel like it is doing something. "Look at me, what a big mess I've made!"

Taking credit for not manifesting your vision is as egotistical as taking credit for doing it. Start giving me some credit and everything will start working more smoothly. I do not want you flailing around in the dark. Your confusion is your unwillingness to step back from what you think you know. Your prayers are often just pleas or demands on your part that I explain the genesis, significance, or fate of some particular fact or situation that you are fixated on.

3. Your ego wants all of the credit; start giving me some

My requirement that you let go is not that you should let go of the vision, as too many of you suspect, but for you to let go of the minute details that you are fixated on. You don't receive an answer because your questions are faulty to begin with, laden with worries and concerns.

4. We are a winning team

Spend more time focusing on my power to create anything than on yours not to. All that support and affirmation you keep looking for . . . you're looking in the wrong places. Turn towards me. We are always the winning team. Have I ever let you down really? Things may not have always fit your picture of how they ought to be, but have I ever let you down? "Chill out," as you would say. Tell this to the people this morning. They need it.

III. Unconditional Gratitude

Speak to the people, this morning, my Reverend Daughter, about gratitude. This is another concept about which there is much misunderstanding, and this misunderstanding prevents you, all of you, from really embracing the matter at hand. It is much like the message that you have titled "Begin with Yes," in which I explained that your yes needs to be on the front end of everything and not on the back. Yes is not merely a concurrence or an agreement with something you understand. Yes must be the beginning, the foundation stone, the premise, the very assumption upon which your life is built. What are you saying yes to? You are saying Yes to me, Yes to our Oneness. You are saying Yes to your understanding that there is a Divine Order, and in so doing are giving your assent to it.

1. Begin with Yes, begin with gratitude

So it is with gratitude. You often think of gratitude as giving thanks for something in the particular. If something appears to have happened that you consider to be "good," then you are grateful. However, minus some external stimuli, some event or circumstance that you consider favorable, you see no reason why you should give thanks. There are several things wrong with this paradigm, my children, which I wish to discuss with you in this moment.

Giving thanks in the particular makes your gratitude a response when in fact, like the Yes, it needs to be a beginning point. You need to be grateful just because. "Just because of what?" you say. Just because. You are alive. You are One with me. Life is in session. Gratitude comes from knowing that I am Good all of the time. With this understanding you will not be so forlorn about the events that occur. Instead of spending so much time

2. Be grateful just because

trying to figure out why this thing or that thing happened, you will be more content with your awareness that all is indeed well, regardless of what has happened.

Understand what it is that I am saying here. You, especially you metaphysical types, too often try to find what is good in a particular circumstance. This has you missing the point. I am Good. Don't just look for what is good in the particular thing that is going on in your life. Look at me. See me. Don't try to find me in the problems; see me and grow in your awareness and understanding of how everything is happening in me, including yourself. You often "can't see the forest for the trees." You are so bent on understanding and analyzing, dissecting, picking apart, fixating, or obsessing on the eventualities of your individual lives or the lives of those in primary relationship to you that you miss the forest.

3. A transcendent view gives you a sense of the whole

You want so to get clear. You don't have to be so clear. Understand what I am saying. Sometimes what you need is an aerial view, a more transcendent awareness. You can't really understand what is good and significant about the tree right in front of you unless you are able to see it in the context of the entire forest. The significance of the tree is not an individual significance; it also has to do with the way the tree connects to the whole. That aerial, transcendent view allows you to get a sense of the whole. The distance may make the minute details of that individual tree a little less discernable to your naked eye; however, the different perspective that you get from a spiritual purview will allow you to truly understand and see so much more.

There is an order in everything. There is an order even in death and dying. There is a beauty that happens with the aging of the leaves of a tree. And though you may mourn the loss of any one particular favorite tree in the forest, when you get an aerial view you will see that there are so many new ones that are sprouting up. ✻

IV. Committing to the Long Haul

What does is mean to commit to the long haul? First and foremost, the image itself is troublesome. Even though it is merely an idiomatic expression, the implications it conjures up makes you place the emphasis on the wrong things. Committing to the long haul seems to imply that you must lug a particular something around for a very long time, that it will be attached to you like glue. This hinders your ability to make commitments to anything that will last a long time, for you fear that you will cave in under the weight of what you carry. No. You are not meant to carry things around to your detriment.

In fact, when you make a commitment to something, a commitment that is meant to be long-lasting, at the time you make the commitment you have no idea of what it is you will be "hauling," so to speak. The tendency is to merely project today's baggage into the future. Initially, most of you commit to what you can see, to outer expressions that are self-evident, because you assume that you are stuck with them. Therefore, your notion of surrender is merely to be willing to accept this expression, this particular form, forever, if need be. Some of you know that the outer expression will transmute over time— but this is not the same thing as transformation.

You perceive your commitments as burdens. However, what is the purpose of committing? It is not to place a yoke around your neck. Its purpose is developing the discipline of showing up every day. The emphasis needs to be on the daily showing up. In committing to the future, too many of you are forgetting to be present in the moment. This is especially true of your commitments to marriage and child rearing. There is

1. You must let go of more than you haul

2. Commitment isn't about the future, it's about showing up every day

always a tomorrow in your mind. It is tomorrow when you will listen, when you will express that love you are too busy to express now. Tomorrow you will take the time to play and commune, to resolve that conflict that is festering at the core of your being. Why rush? Immediate and urgent have ceased to be equated with each other.

3. The practice of seeing me in all things alters your perceptions

You treat me the same way, especially those who are on so-called spiritual paths. Because I am always around, you take my love for granted. You go into a "maintenance mode." You do just enough to insure that we will have a connection that can be worked upon tomorrow, and then you hold me responsible for the lack of depth of our relationship. You accuse me of not being available to you. Yet the issue is—when did you make yourself fully available to me? Quality relationships are not sustained by fulfilling tasks for one another. Feeding and clothing your child will not make you close to each other. Paying the bills and coming home every night will not nurture a marriage. No, you must give something of yourself. You must stop being so busy with each other and just be with each other. Your relationship with me cannot be based solely on tasks, on what you do for me and on what you want me to do for you. You must commune with me, be with me, just for the sake of my company.

The real challenge in committing to the long haul is not so much hauling but dropping things along the way. What do I mean when I say "dropping things along the way"? The magnitude of your problems, their dimensions relative to your size (that is to say, whether you consider them to be bigger than you or not), whether you feel as though you are dragging them around or not, and so on are merely a matter of your perspective. When you commit to the daily practice of seeing me in all things, then you come to different conclusions about what you are going through. These conclusions are never static, that is, every day your opinion and your perception will change. Daily you will feel less victimized by the circumstances around you, especially the ones that seem to exist in perpetuity, and you will cease to feel like you are hauling anything.

4. My yoke is not a yoke but a buoy

The long haul becomes a daily journey. Remember that the journey of a thousand miles begins with a single step. If you are fully present every moment, then it will not feel so long. You will cease to question, "When will this be over?" Your very anxiety is postponing your moving to the next step. You cannot skip steps. You must walk through every inch of the path, just as a moving vehicle on wheels must cover every inch of the path to get from one place to another. The key to your next step is always in the thing that you resist the most. Is this not self-evident? If (as you often think) you have really done everything that you can think of to do, then the lesson is, obviously, in what you have yet to do.

The emphasis here is on being present. Don't worry so much about the long haul. Just commit to being available day by day for all of the loving, forgiving, sharing, caring, playing, and creating that is in front of you each day. This is the great secret to peace and tranquillity. Some would say that "My yoke is heavy but my burdens are light." No, neither is heavy. Furthermore, as I have told you before, what you call my yoke is not a yoke; it is a buoy. Will you be lifted up in me and play in the waters that you think you are drowning in, or will the weight of your self-chosen backpack weigh you down? The choice is yours. But remember that you must let go of more than you haul.

V. Spiritual Availability

1. The way you recognize me should bring us closer

It is good that you practice the concept of availability. There is much to be learned here. Most often you, as human beings, need to experience one of my qualities and attributes for yourselves, as yourselves, before you are able to truly apply that particular concept to me. Part of the reason why you are not able to understand, let alone accept, my constant availability is because there is so little availability in your own life. The concept of being fully present, awake, aware, open, receptive, yielding—available—is more than you can fathom. However, the reality of my ever present availability is one of the first things about me that you need to understand. Most of you focus your attention on my power. There is nothing wrong with this. I am power, I am all Power, and it is good that you recognize this.

However, in the recognition of my power there is a tendency to put me up on a pedestal, like you do other human beings who you believe to be powerful. Whoever or whatever is on this pedestal you admire and adore from a distance. You project onto it all of the finest qualities that you yourself have but are too afraid to own, let alone express. In this situation, in this projection, it becomes commonplace for the ones doing the adoring to assume that the object that they are adoring is, in fact, an exception rather than an example. It is okay for you to put me on a pedestal. It is okay for you to put me on an altar. It is okay for you to even put religious replicas that represent me on your dashboards. It is okay to do any or all of these things, as long as they bring you closer to me. Understand what I just said. If putting me on a pedestal takes me further away from you, then I would caution you not to put me there. However, if placing me there is a reminder to you, if it provides a divine mirror for you to see the best in yourself reflected in me, then so be it.

Not only am I all Power, I am pure Availability. This, as I have just said, has been so difficult for you to grasp. It is that aspect of myself that is everywhere present. Even those of you who believe and know that I am everywhere present still seem to have trouble with the idea that in my omnipresence I am available to you, in the particular. Understand what I just said. I am the whole of all things. And I manifest as very specific things. What I do for any one person I can do for any and every person. What I do for one in the particular is not a divine exception. It should be seen as a divine example, concrete evidence of what is possible. This should bring you comfort. When you see me working in the life of another, this is not the time for you to be jealous. This is not the time for you to be envious or for you to question what is so special about this other person that they warrant my attention. Everybody and everything has my attention. The question is, do I have theirs? This is what I mean by the necessity of understanding the concept of availability. One's attention is at the heart of the matter.

2. I am everywhere present and available to you

In availability there must be accessibility. In addition to accessibility, there must also be a fullness of attention. In addition to fullness of attention, there must be a fullness of intention. Understand how these three things—accessibility, attention, and intention—relate to each another in availability. In order to be available, you need all three.

The necessity of exemplifying all of these ingredients is analogous to what you talk about, my Reverend Daughter, at wedding and commitment ceremonies. You talk about trust, love, communication, and sharing as being vital aspects of a relationship. You liken each one to a bodily function, explaining how all must be attended to simultaneously for the health of the relationship as a living organism. Trust is likened to the

3. In availability there must be accessibility, attention, and intention

spine, which protects the vulnerable nervous system, affording the relationship backbone and flexibility. You remind the couple and everyone present that just as feeling sensations are impaired when the spine is injured, so the relationship is impaired when trust is injured. Love is likened to the heart, which beats in fair weather or foul, providing the relationship with much needed vitality. Love, like the heart, should never be deliberately stressed, for a heart can only withstand so much pressure. Communication is likened to the brain's sifting and sorting of information. You urge the couple to use communication to keep them current with each other and to treat that information as sacred, never using it against one another. Sharing is likened to the lungs, which breathe in the surrounding air. There is no attempt to divide the air or to hoard it. Sharing allows the relationship to breathe.

You use this analogy quite well to let people understand the importance of having all four aspects—trust, love, communication, and sharing—in order for their relationships to thrive. You point out that it is not enough for the relationship to flourish in some of these areas and not in the others. One does not compensate for another. In fact, when one is absent, the others cannot flourish. When there is no sharing, communication and trust cannot be formed, and these are necessary ingredients for love. When there is no trust, the love withdraws, communication ceases, and sharing is but two syllables. Without communication, sharing diminishes, causing trust to flounder while love suspends. Without love, there simply is not the impetus to share, trust, or communicate.

4. A relationship, like a chain, is only as strong as its weakest link

As you explain, the relationship will only be as strong as the weakest of these links. This notion of the weak spot in a chain has fascinated you since your days of camping as a Girl Scout, and to a certain extent you are still amazed. It doesn't matter how welded the chain links are, how thick the rope is, or how intricately designed the material may be . . . if there is a single place that is out of balance, out of alignment, not as shored up as everything else, that is where it will break. Part of you continues to resent this because the weakest links seem to take up most of your time. However, keep remembering that it is important for all of the links and threads to be strong, lest the chain, or the rope, be of little value or significance. So it is in your relationship with me. There must be availability on your part, as well as mine, in order for you to experience our relationship as flourishing. In your availability there must be accessibility, attention, and intention.

Accessibility is your being physically present. It means that others are able to access you (get hold of you, as you would say). You often complain that when you need someone or something, you simply don't know where they are. In these instances you tend to assume that if the individual or the resources had been present, then the circumstance would not be as dire as it is. It becomes easy to project salvation onto whatever appears to be missing. "If only so-and-so had done such-and-such." "If only we had. . . ." It goes on and on. Many of you hold your own selves responsible and accountable in this manner because you know that there were times when you were not as easy to get a hold of as you should have been. However, when taking stock of your own lack of availability, rather than making amends, doing whatever you can to rectify the situation even retroactively, you tend to contrast how your inaccessibility was not as bad as somebody else's inaccessibility to you. This contrasting and comparing of your actions with those of another comes up often.

5. Accessibility is being present

Furthermore, people tend to project this same lack of accessibility onto me. Even though they know that I am all Power, that I am everywhere present, I still seem to elude them, sometimes in a most painful way. They want to touch me, they want to feel me, they want to know me for themselves. Yet there does not seem to be any real connection, so they may assume that I am not available. However, in those moments, it is the person's judgment, resentment, stubborn willfulness, fears, anxieties, and the like that are preventing them from being available to me. Once these three concepts—accessibility, attention, and intention—are understood, embraced and embodied, then there will be greater availability.

6. *Your every thought is creative*

Your every thought is creative. Although all of you have heard this time and time and time and time again, it somehow doesn't sink in. You cannot think a single thought that does not vibrate and manifest in some way, even if no more than to become fodder in the ethers for someone else to pick up later on. It is much like what you do now in sending hazardous waste into space. Many of your thoughts you just dump into the atmosphere, forgetting that they can be intercepted at any point in time by someone else. Be careful of the legacy that you leave in the ethers, for it remains forever, long after your physical body has deteriorated.

Giving your attention to things makes them multiply. Giving your attention to things provides the space for their manifestation. Things manifest not because you like them or don't like them, not because you want them or don't want them in your experience; they manifest because you have given them so much attention. Watch the tendency to give your attention to the things you don't want to experience. Because so much of your attention goes to your fears, worries, or concerns, you are not available for our relationship. You are using your energy for something other than what you want. Don't give your attention to things that don't deserve it. Understand the power of giving your attention and how the converse is also true. Your not giving attention to something that deserves it can be just as detrimental. When there are areas of healing in your life that need your attention desperately—areas that you refuse to look at, that you refuse to acknowledge, let alone allow to be healed—your avoidance of them creates more blocks and barriers.

It is important that you give your life your attention. This is where the notion of intention becomes critical. For what purpose are you examining your life? Is it for finding fault with yourself or with another? What exactly is it about your life that has your attention? When your intent is to be the All that you can be spiritually, then you have the deep intention of allowing everything that has your attention to be transformed. Listen to what I have just said. When you have the intention of living your life from the place of spiritual, conscious awareness, you then infuse everything that has your attention with this deep intention. This is what is meant by the phrase "to see all things through the eyes of God."

From this vantage point, from this perspective, every situation is redeemed; that is to say, everything that happens becomes part of the spiritual fabric of your life. No longer are you convinced that you have taken detours, that you have been derailed in any sense, that you have been delayed in your spiritual journey or obstructed in any kind of way. You see that all situations that come your way have a gift for you, a blessing for you. Every situation provides an opportunity for you to sharpen your perspective, to sharpen your ability to pierce through the veils of appearances. This takes time; it takes effort; it takes work. It is a skill that must be developed. In your natural state, this is how you would see things anyway. But because you have gotten so far away from allowing your spiritual nature to be the drum major in your life, it becomes necessary for you to be diligent about rearranging your priorities. It is difficult to make your ego self the caboose instead of the engine, as your grandmother would say.

Christ Consciousness is the awareness of the Oneness of your nature with me. When you are conscious of this—when this consciousness becomes your identity, the filter or prism through which you view everything that goes on—you will not develop stockpiles, closets, and storage bins emotionally, spiritually, or physically.

7. Every situation is redeemed when seen through my eyes

8. Christ Consciousness is the awareness of the Oneness of our nature

There is a common misperception, being taught in many churches, that the only way that one's life can be saved from my supposed destruction is to accept the man Jesus as one's personal savior. What is it that Jesus has saved them from? And what is the relative importance of their believing this when it comes to their relationship with me? There has been a misunderstanding here that is as old as Jesus' life itself. The same difficulty is present now, two millennia later, that existed when Jesus was alive for a mere thirty-three human years. When Jesus spoke of his Oneness with me people thought he was saying that we were the same entity, that he in fact was God. He was crucified over this misunderstanding. The crime for which he was accused was fundamentally that of blasphemy. They failed to understand that when Jesus spoke of his Oneness with me, he was speaking about the Oneness of his nature with mine.

The Oneness of that nature with me, the conscious awareness of that Oneness with me, is the definition of the word "Christ." There is a tendency to want to use the name "Jesus" and the name "Christ" synonymously and interchangeably. However, they are not the same. Just as Jesus was not the all of me but was a representative of my nature, so he was also representative of the Christ nature. However, Jesus has no more of a monopoly on Christ Consciousness than he does on his Oneness with me. Jesus has no more of a monopoly on being a Christ than he has on being my son. When you look up the word "son" (huiós in Greek) you will see that not only is this Scriptural word non-gender-specific, but it relates to an offspring in character, not genealogical lineage.

Jesus was one of those types of individuals who is put on a pedestal. Once again, this is perfectly fine as long as placing him there is for the purpose of making him a divine example, not a divine exception. Each and every culture has its ways of translating things. Within the construct of Jesus' Hebrew culture, projecting all of the sins of humanity or of a specific human being onto an innocent animal and then sacrificing the animal, spilling its blood on an altar, was understood to be a redemptive act. In the context of that culture, which in Jesus' day still practiced blood sacrifices, Jesus as a sacrificial lamb became an obvious metaphor.

Jesus understood that it really was not necessary for the people to continue the practice of slaying innocent animals in order to appease God. He knew that he was leaving a new, enlightened legacy behind him. He affirmed that if they grasped his message and lived his message, there would never be the need again to kill anyone or anything. So in his willingness to be crucified he was explaining that this process of shedding innocent blood—or guilty blood, depending upon one's perspective—was unnecessary. He was able to say, to those who assumed that he was in fact the sacrificial lamb, that it is not an outer ritual that redeems your life. It is your own consciousness and the deeds you do that reflect this consciousness that get you back into alignment with your spiritual maker. He brought the matter back home to an issue of the heart (which from your modern English perspective also includes the mind).

His sacrifice was able to make even those who considered him blasphemous question this practice of killing those who claimed their divinity as their primary identity. He let himself be killed to prove a point. He let the person Jesus be killed to prove that Christ cannot be killed. Christ, the Consciousness of Christ, lives on forever. And it's not attached to any person in the particular.

9. Jesus was the divine example, not the exception

10. Cultivate the intention of being a Christ

When you see the world through the eyes of a Christ, you no longer feel yourself to be the victim of anything. There is nothing to fight. There's nothing to prove, and no one to prove it to. The gyrations of everyone around you, even the gyrations directed at you, do not disturb your inner peace. Even when the slings and arrows of misfortune are hitting you like a bull's eye, even when the archer has aimed at you specifically, you are still able to say on your own cross as Jesus did on his, "Forgive them, Father, for they know not what they do." This is intention. This is an example of not wavering in your attention by being fearful of the circumstances you are facing. Because of his intention to be a Christ, in the moment when anything happened, he was inevitably able to not only let it go but to give it back to God. When you hold onto the things that have happened, they take up space in your lives. When you keep repeating the sagas and the dramas, they take up precious spiritual, emotional, and physical space in your life. When you wear your scars like merit badges, or name tags, then you are wedded to them. You become available to them because you are available to whatever has your attention.

What has your attention, my children? What are you accessible to? What do you show up for? Are you there to give the praise, or are you there to sling mud? Do you run to help someone in need as quickly as you run to see their disaster (a fire, an accident, and so on)? What do you run towards? What is your intention? Is your intention to make everybody else shape up? Is your intention to do your own spiritual work, to go into those places and spaces in which you have been hiding out for your own protective measures? Are you here to be available to me?

11. What happens when you become more available to me?

What will happen when you become more available to me? You will know a splendor like nothing you could ever imagine. You will awaken every day with a new sense of excitement and enthusiasm for the adventure that the day brings. You look forward to the surprises. You cease to dread the difficult challenges or distressing interactions. You become amazed at how effortlessly and easily everything works out even without your having to control it all. When you are available to me, you have a new vitality, energetically speaking. There is a zest for living. Your body temple becomes quickened. Fatigue diminishes. Confusions start to clear up, and you feel a sensation throughout you of being more alive. And with this aliveness comes a love. You are in love with life. You are available to me. You look forward to each day and its eventuality.

There is a new and deeper sense of gratitude when you are available to me. Instead of noticing everything that seems to be missing, you see the fullness of everything that is in front of you. You bless it and caress it and in doing so create the space for it to grow, develop, transform into "all needs met." When you are available there is no need to worry. You move out of the self-centeredness of the ego into a place where you are centered in the Self. There is so much more that you are able to do, accomplish, create, and share. And perhaps most importantly, when you are available to me you have a greater capacity to just be, to just accept and love yourself the way you are, to fill every space with your energy, and to feel at peace wherever you are with whoever is with you. You are able to do all of these things because I can, and you are One with me.

So focus on expanding your awareness of my availability, as well as on doing your work to increase your own availability. There is a partnership here that is important, and I'm not even asking, or expecting, us to be equal partners. But now there is too great an imbalance in our relationship. I am so much more available to you than you are to me, in a way that hinders us both. It hinders my ability to express through you most constructively. I need your cooperation in order to do this. I can express anywhere through anyone. I can make the rock cry out. I can make the jackass speak. I will find another one to proclaim me if you do not. I am not hurt by your unavailability; you are.

12. You must be available to me to know how available I am to you

There are so many gifts that I am waiting to give to you that you cannot receive unless you engage me more in this partnership. Balance does not mean that everything is always egalitarian. For example, you need balance between your waking hours and your sleeping hours, but they do not have to be equal in length. You are expected to be awake more hours than you are asleep, and both are extremely necessary. It is my pleasure to provide the bulk, to be the larger portion of the equation. However, you must meet me at least part way. You must be available to me, or you will never know how available I am to you. ✣

VI. AMAZING GRACE

There is a song in your American society, noted for being perhaps the most popular hymn from your Christian culture, called "Amazing Grace." You sing this song sometimes in praise of me, in honor of my work that I do that you quite often find astounding. It is your way of acknowledging my greatness and acknowledging your humility within my presence. I love that you acknowledge my greatness, and I love that you are humble. However, the sense of separation that this sets up is far too great. In this paradigm you place me off in some distant place, as though I were that sky god that you keep imagining up on a throne overlooking you and raining down blessings upon you, as though I am sprinkling things from here to there. No. No. No.

I am among you. I am in you. I operate as you and through you. The most amazing thing about my Grace is that you don't accept it for what it is—readily available to you at no cost or obligation. It is easier for you to perceive of me as something that you must beseech, beg, cajole, appease . . . these are the images that you continue to perpetuate, whether consciously or unconsciously, in your perceptions of me, yea, even in your prayers. As long as you continue to do this, my Grace will seem outside of you. As long as you attach my Grace to me and I am someplace waaay-y-y-y-y out there, then my Grace is waaay-y-y-y-y out there with me. If you mistakenly believe that I somehow drop in on you from time to time, kind of like Santa Claus, then you are like the child waiting by the chimney, wondering if I am going to show up in your house, wondering if you have been "good enough" for me to grace you with my presence and presents.

1. I am in you, among you, operating through and as you

2. You can't accept my Grace until you acknowledge my presence

This waiting, this wondering, this anxiety about whether or not I care, whether I am aware, whether I am moved and motivated, whether I have the desire and/or intent to become involved in your lives, remains an unanswered question. Why is this a question? Why do you, all of you, continue to question whether I am around? Can't you look around and see me? Is there anything that you could look at and not see me, even if it is something you find displeasing? Don't you see that I am in everyone and everything?

This is why you find it so difficult to accept the ever-availability of my Grace. You don't see me. You don't acknowledge my presence. And in not acknowledging my presence you render me not only invisible but absent. Notice what I just said. There is a difference between invisibility and absence. The scope of your human vision can only capture so much. There is no human vision that is wide enough and big enough to see everything that exists. Your vision is extremely limited. If you limit your sense of what exists to the limitations of your human eyesight, then the world you live in will be quite small, indeed. My Reverend Daughter, you are sitting right now in a location in the state of California known as Santa Cruz, which is some 3,000 miles away from the state of New York. The fact that you cannot see New York from where you are sitting does not mean that it does not exist. What do you, as human beings, need as evidence of my existence? Is not the beating of your own heart sufficient? Isn't the air that you breathe, the air that you share with all persons and things around you, evidence enough of my provision for you? Isn't even this limited mechanism called the eyes, which you mistakenly use to measure my nonexistence, the very evidence of my existence? It seems ironic that you would attempt to disprove me by using one of my own creations.

3. My invisibility is not absence

I am not absent. Where is the music when you cannot see it? Where is beauty? Where are joy and peace? Where are wisdom and understanding? Where are these things? And what does one need to do to earn any of them? At times your society marvels at how incredibly innately intuitive a child can be. You actually attribute the child's intuitiveness to his or her lack of experience in the world. You see the child as exempt from the heartaches, disappointments, and challenges that jade a person's insights and perceptions. However, the moment that you begin to see that the information coming from this child is instructive to you, you rename it wisdom. When you see it as wisdom, you then begin to question whether or not this child has in fact lived before, even if you do not particularly believe in reincarnation. You are quite familiar with this phenomenon, my Reverend Daughter. Your maternal grandmother used to marvel at your insights. In private moments, while visiting you from Louisiana, she would often pose the question, "Have you been here before?" You never did really understand her question. And in your naiveté you answered, "Yes, this is my home!" or "Yes, I live here!" How extremely prophetic those words were although you were not able to understand them at the time.

Too many of you attribute wisdom to human experience, believing that to become wise you must go through a lot of things personally. However, wisdom is gained by understanding one's relationship to the collective consciousness. One gains this understanding simply sitting where one is, if one is open enough to see oneself as a part of the world instead of apart from the world. When one sees oneself as a part of the world, then one is truly at home, regardless of one's physical residence. One has a sense of really living. Most of you go through the motions called life, but you're still wondering when the living will begin; you are still wondering if what you are doing is what it ought to be. You treat life the way many of you treat your various forms of sexual expression. In the moment of sexual activity, when you are feeling disillusioned, incompetent, anxious, nervous, or whatever, you begin to question, "Is this it?" "Is this what it's supposed to be about?" "Am I doing it right?" "Is this what everybody else is doing?"

4. Your judgments are your shadows projected onto another

"Is there more that I could or should be doing or getting out of this?" This kind of thinking makes you not fully present in your acts of sexual intimacy. In this kind of thinking, you are not really present in your own livingness. And, as always, when you are judging someone else or something else, even me, what you are really seeing is the shadow side of your own self projected onto another.

The one who is not present, my children, is you, not me. The one who is absent is not me, it is you. The reason why you don't see me often enough is because you aren't present, not because I am not present. As I said earlier, the eye has a limited scope of vision. Furthermore, the eye can only see that which it can reflect. So if you are not present, if you are not there, then you are not available to reflect me. If you don't think that I am close enough to be seen, embraced, loved, and touched, then you don't even bother to look for me, or you fail to notice me when I am in your face. You thought I was going to say "when I am in front of your face." But once again this places me in the position of being some external object of referral opposed to you in the flesh. I am you as much as you are me. When you understand this, then my works will not appear to be so extraordinary. It is okay to continue to be amazed, but the amazement should be about the effortlessness. The amazement should be about the ease and the ever-availability. The amazement should not be about the wonder and the longing to close the gap. The amazement should be about the never-ceasing accessibility and abundance of my Grace.

5. What is your payoff for not accepting my Grace?

Why would you not accept something that is given so freely? Why would you ignore me as you, me as the other people in your life, me as everything? Is your life any easier for your carrying the weight of your so-called problems on your own shoulders? Are you in any greater control when you are so certain of the extent of your resources? Are you any more secure when you are able to predict just how dire your circumstances can become? What is your payoff for not accepting my Grace?

I can tell you the answer, but it is far more powerful for you to ponder this on your own. I caution you, however, don't get into judging and blaming yourself for anything that you have done or are doing. You must learn to simply be a quiet observer of not only the world but also your own self. You must learn to study your own self with the kind of objectivity that you expect a scientist to use to observe anything. Just watch yourself. Watch your patterns and your reactions, and you will learn a lot about what needs to be healed.

1. Praise is not a response, it's a celebration of Life

I wish to speak to you at this moment in time about the matter of praise. Praise is an act of rejoicing. It is not to be confused with your common, vernacular usage of the word "praise," which is relegated to the realm of providing accolades to someone or something for a job well done or an activity one approves of. Praise is an internal, spontaneous, grateful, inclusive, and encompassing celebration of Life. Notice that I said it is a celebration of Life. Praise is really not about anything in particular. Praise is about the whole of it. When one gets into the mind-set of praise, the particular ceases to matter. One is so filled with the sense that "All is well" that one is overcome with this awareness. Praise causes so much jubilation that it cannot be contained within the body temple.

In your society, as I was just saying, you make praise a response. There is much the same difficulty here as with the word "yes," which I spoke to you about in that letter titled "Begin with Yes." Your Yes should be from an internal place. You should begin with Yes. It should be the assumption that you start off with and the foundation stone upon which you stand. When you begin with Yes, it fundamentally alters your entire perception of not only what is in front of you but also of where you have been. The same is true for praise. You should enter into your interactions, communications, reconciliations with each other from the standpoint of praise. If you will do this, you will find that your perceptions of what is going on will shift dramatically.

What is this shift of awareness that I speak of? Praise allows the scales to be lifted from your eyes. Praise allows you to pierce through the veil of appearances that would have your hearts and your minds caught up in judgment and criticisms. It allows you to see the Truth that is underlying all. You stop seeing the glass as half empty (as you would say) and you begin to see the fullness, thereof. Instead of seeing a half of a glass of water, you will only see the water and its complete wholeness no matter how "much" of it there seems to be. In fact, when you are caught up in spiritual quality, which so out-weighs any numeric considerations, notions of quantity cease to even be important. In your focused attention on the fullness of the spiritual qualities, you will see that the water is fully water no matter how much of it there is or is not. You will move into a consciousness of blessing that which is.

Praise allows you to look at all things in this manner. You begin to see the fullness of everything there is, without cri-tique of its seeming flaws, limitations, or inadequacies. These are human concepts based upon contrast and comparison with some notion of a human ideal. But your notions of human ideals are so faulty, because they do not encompass the whole. Your ideas of "ideal" are fraught with fears and concerns about winning and losing, better or worse, greater or lesser, and the like. Thus, your ideals of things are perceptions that satisfy your ego's wanting to be better than everybody and everything else. Your ego knows it has arrived because it sees itself as being in such a better position than something else.

Oh no! This is not how it works in Spirit. In Spirit all is embraced. In the Spirit all is Good. In the Spirit everything has a place. In the Spirit you bless every aspect of it all. In the blessing, you not only allow what's blessed to transform into all it should be, but you gain an understanding of how your heart grows in accepting it in the condition that you didn't approve of in the first place. Understand what it is that I am telling you, my children. Praise brings about compassion. You need to have more compassion for your circumstances, for

2. Praise shifts your perception and brings about compassion

each other, and most especially for yourself. When you are busy trying to fill up the rest of the glass, you are forgetting how wonderful the water is that you have. And you are not enjoying right where you are with however much water is in the glass. You are missing the entire perspective on what life has to teach you from that vantage point.

3. All of Life's lessons are Good

All of the lessons of Life are Good, my children. No point along the journey is more wondrous than another. There are no better or greater lessons to be learned in one place than in another. You fret so much about making the "right" decisions all of the time, as though there is a wrong turn, a detour, that could take you along the road of Life to a spot where I am not. I am everywhere. If you turn left instead of right, I am there too. There is always a lesson to be learned wherever you are. What is your intent? Is your intent to be right in your own eyes, or is your intent to glean whatever it is I have to teach you wherever it is you are? Don't take this question lightly. Its implications are profound for how you conduct your life and everything about your daily activities.

Praise where you are. Praise the ones who you are with. Praise what you have. Praise what you like and praise what you don't like. You pause and you question and you say, "Well, isn't that colluding? If I praise what I don't like, aren't I helping to create a space that just produces more of it?"

4. When you don't praise, you collude with the circumstances

Remember what I said a few moments ago, remember what I said praise is. Praise is not about bringing things into fruition. Praise is not for the purpose of approving or not approving of any outer demonstration. Praise is for the purpose of recognizing and acknowledging the spiritual qualities and attributes that are internally present, regardless of what appears to be expressing externally. So your question regarding collusion, well intended as it may be, is completely contradictory to the Truth. The Truth is, if you do not praise where you are, if you do not praise the spiritual qualities and attributes that are screaming to come out and to shine fully, right in the circumstances where you are, then you are colluding with the outer forms of expression. If you are so worried about not wanting them to perpetuate that you are busy hiding from them, running from them, and resisting them, then by your efforting to get away you are providing more fuel for the fire that you say you want to quell.

The Reverend Daughter here is quite correct when she says often that the only thing that really needs to be healed is your sense of separation. Truer words regarding healing have probably never been spoken. It will be a wonderful thing when more and more people grow to this level of awareness and understanding. Praise allows you to go upstairs in your thinking. Praise enables you to stay in a state of transcendence. When I say "stay" in any particular state, I recognize that you may not be expressing that state all of the time. However, if it is your deep intent, if it is what you contemplate, then it is staying with you. When you praise, you create a space, an opening, for the spiritual qualities at hand to shine to their fullest capacity.

5. The only thing that ever needs to be healed is your sense of separation

I am most grateful to you who minister in music. Singing is a wonderful thing. Even from an anthropological standpoint, music has always helped to provide that space of transcendence in human consciousness. Singing takes you outside of yourselves and outside of your self-consciousness. Singing allows you to be conscious of Self, and in this consciousness of Self you remember that you are not your "stuff." When you sing, you move beyond the ills, the pains, the concerns, and the conflicts. When you sing, especially when you sing together, there is a place of harmony and unity that you step into. And this experience has long-lasting effects. It is not a momentary revelation. Its impact allows you to continue to revel in this more transcendent awareness. Music helps to heal the aching heart. And music is one of the greatest avenues of expressing incredible joy.

6. *Praise from the depths of your soul*

Praise to the highest heavens. Praise from the depths of your soul. Praise with every tissue and fiber of your body temple. Praise with all of the energy and soulfulness of your very being. Praise me. Praise Life. Praise each other. Praise yourself. Praise the one that you know. Praise the one that you don't know. Just be an open avenue, a channel, of praise and see how much more you are a blessing to the world and how much more the world appears to be a blessing to you. Enjoy yourselves, my children. Praise is a lot of fun. ✂

VIII. DIVINE FLOW

You are hearing my voice, my child, and are understanding that it is my voice that you are hearing. I speak to you always, all of you. However, there is a tendency upon the part of much of humanity, especially those from Westernized civilizations, to credit themselves as the source of the wisdom, the understanding or clarity, that in fact comes from me. Sometimes it is referred to as intuition, other times as inner knowing. Some people refer to it as a hunch, others as a little voice. It matters not what they call it. Most of the time it is my speaking to them. Many people get confused about this because when I speak to them my voice sounds like their own.

1. When I speak to you, my voice sounds like your own

This has been a problem for you, my child, in coming into your own, spiritually speaking. You have questioned upon what authority do you stand. You have questioned because so much of what I have told you reinforces what you have known to be true deep within your heart of hearts. You have been afraid that the messages that you have been given will sound self-serving. You have been afraid that people will discount them as having come from me because they appear to come from you.

I speak to all of you always. The manner in which you hear me, the way in which you engage me, is unique unto each of you. One's communion with me is not less precious than another's, merely different. I have given you, my Reverend Daughter, a gift of prophecy. This gift does not set you above the people in any way. In fact, it makes you even more human in a most profound way.

Your inability in the past to publicly claim this gift has had a lot to do with your society's confusions about gifts, period. Each of you has your own special gift to give to the world. Gifts have been seen too much as something external, as not attached to the giver. This has become increasingly the case in your modernized societies, where there is much retail material around for circulation. It is easy for you to obtain and exchange items to which neither person feels particularly connected. From the beginnings of human evolution, a gift always contained something of the giver. This was the very point of it all, that the gift, whatever it was, would be infused with the energy and the consciousness of the one who was giving it. The point was not so much to give an object as it was to give something that symbolized and represented what was in the giver's heart so that the recipient would have tangible evidence of the giver's intent.

You, in your modern society, have gotten very far away from this. Your gifting each other is often obligatory or merely a matter of tokenism. Too much emphasis is placed upon the object being exchanged, and not enough attention is placed upon the intent and essence of the giver.

2. You are integral to the gift because you are the gift

Since you have separated gift and giver in your mind, you have stopped perceiving yourself as integral to the gift. Many of you have gotten to the point where it is difficult for you to even perceive yourselves as real givers in life because you have come so much to associate giving with external materiality. However, you are the gift. When you do not understand that it is some part of yourself that you are sharing, you look around at what is available materially. And when you think that you don't have enough to share, your conclusion becomes that you have nothing to share. This is quite dangerous, my children. You fail to understand that you, yourself, are not just the giver but the gift. You, because you are One with me and I am an Inexhaustible Supply, are tapped into a wellspring of essence that is eternal. What gift in the world is more precious than you? What gift in the world is more precious than your love? What gift in the world is more precious than your attention, your prayers, your blessings, your well wishes, your cooperation, your accessibility, your availability, your deep intent? Is there really anything else more precious than this?

In addition to making a separation between the giver and the recipient, there is also a tendency in your Westernized cultures to make a separation between the acts of giving and receiving. This is a false distinction. This is a paradigm that is of no use or value in the spiritual realm. It is a fallacious conceptualization that only continues to perpetuate the paradigm of duality. There is otherness reeking in this. Why do I say so adamantly that this is fallacious?

Perhaps the best example would be that of breathing. Within the process of breathing there is what you refer to as inhaling and there is what you refer to as exhaling. However, you are not breathing unless you are doing both. It would never occur to you to try to make such a distinction between exhaling and inhaling when speaking of breathing such that you would claim to be doing one without the other. There is a totality here. There is a wholeness here. There is an integration here. You are not breathing unless both are happening alternately and interchangeably. So it is with what you refer to as giving. In fact, it is even more so. In the act of breathing you can mark the point in time when you are either inhaling or exhaling, even though they occur very closely together. However, in what is referred to as giving, the so-called giving and receiving are simultaneous. They aren't even separate. It is all one.

3. Giving and receiving are One, like inhaling and exhaling in breathing

I spoke to you about the giving aspect. Let me now address the receiving aspect. What does it mean to receive? What does this mean to you? Once again, your time-space continuum is problematic here. In your concept of receiving you tend to see yourself as an entity that is stagnant, static, standing still in a single point in time. While you are standing still, there is some object, quite often something that you would consider to be tangible material, that is somehow or another migrating through space and making its way to you. You are almost like the catcher behind the home plate in a baseball game waiting for the pitcher to throw the ball to you. You may make some hand gestures or motions to indicate what type of ball you would like to receive from the pitcher. However, you are crouched and simply waiting for something to come your way.

Ohhh no, my children!! Oh no, no, no, NO! NO!!

4. When you receive, things are coming through you, not merely to you

Receiving is merely an avenue. Receiving is merely being an open channel. Receiving is a question of a flow. It is not coming to you so much as it is coming through you. There is nothing static, there is nothing stagnant. There is nothing singular. There is nothing isolated. There is nothing separate. There is a dance here. It is a dance of energy, a constant exchange and a rhythm. Just as it is with thinking, you are sending and receiving all at the same time. You could never allow your brain to just send information without it simultaneously picking up and receiving everything that is going on around you. And you can never pick up everything that is all around you without sending something out. (This is why meditation is so important, because in meditation you move beyond thinking to clear a space in consciousness.)

When you do not understand that you are part of this natural flow of Spirit, you begin to come up with the same conclusions that I mentioned earlier in this message regarding giving. You begin to think that you are not part of this flow. You begin to think that things are flowing and moving and being exchanged all around you and you are somehow being left out. There are others of you who are so confused and forlorn about this process that you are convinced that nothing is flowing anywhere, not to you or anybody else. However, this flow that I speak of is an open-ended process.

Picture, if you will, a channel, a canal, a tube, even, if you must be so graphic. There is not a flow until activity is happening on both ends. If something goes in and does not come out, it is not a flow. And if things just keep going out but nothing is coming in, it's not a flow. A flow is steady. A flow is constant.

However, in the spiritual world nothing is linear. The spiritual flow that I speak of is neither determined nor defined by a single place or point in time. Even though one can make a visual distinction between the action of inhaling and that of exhaling, at the cellular level they are taking place at the same time. In a tube one can say this is the end where things are coming in and this is the end where things are going out. However, in the spiritual world there are no walls, there are no ends, there is not an opening over here and an opening over there. It just is. It is all happening simultaneously.

When you don't understand that things are constantly flowing through you, then you have no understanding that you are capable of being a giver. When you do not understand that you are part of this Inexhaustible Supply, you are afraid that your coffers will run out. You are afraid that there will not be enough. However, underneath this fear that there will not be enough is the fear that you are not enough.

How can you not be enough? How can you *not be enough*? Has your sense of yourself become so jaded by your materialistic approach to life that you would equate your own worth and value with material assets? In order to receive, you must think yourself worthy. So we have here what you refer to as catch-22. You can't give because you don't think you are enough. You can't receive because you don't think you deserve because you don't think that you are enough. So what do we do? Herein is the dilemma for most of you. You do nothing. You let this analysis of yours result in paralysis.

5. Seeing yourself as part of a constant flow allows you to give freely

Just start with yourself. Start with who you are. Feel your connection with me. Feel your connection with the Divine. Know that you are not simply an entity in the Universe that activity is happening to. Understand that you are a place and space where Divine Activity is happening through. The giving and receiving is not to and from you. It is through you. What do you need to do? You just need to be available. Once again, all you need to do is to say Yes.

6. Learn to BE; give from your Beingness

You don't have to create anything. You don't have to earn anything. You don't have to make anything. You rarely even have to do anything, but you must BE something. I have created you as a human being, not a human doing. Learn to be. Learn to be. Give of your beingness. You may say, "Well, how can I give of my beingness?" The very fact that you ask the question means that you have not tapped into the great sense of your beingness. Once you have tapped into that, such a question is superfluous. (It is much like what you will tell people sometimes, my dear Reverend Daughter, about love. If they have to ask you "Am I in love?" or "What it is like to be in love?" then they probably are not.)

7. In the flow you realize that you are the gift, the giver, and the receiver

When you are in the flow, you realize that you are everything. You are the gift, you are the giver, and you are the receiver. Any true gift blesses the one giving it. The joy, the appreciation, the sense of well-being that is in the heart of the one who is giving the gift is a gift unto itself. You get so much out of giving that you feel like you have been the recipient, even though society would say that you are the one who gave. This is why tithing is so important, my children. It is important that you fully participate in the flow of life. Then you will stop being so afraid that giving will deplete you, and you will grow to understand that giving will fill your coffers. When you are afraid that you do not have enough to give, you are not merely in a state of material lack. You are in a state of a spiritual crisis.

Statistically speaking, in your society those with the least income give the most money. What they give represents a larger percentage and proportion of their total assets. They are not under the illusion that they are making it on their own will and their own might. There is an understanding that in order to even just survive they have to lean on a power that is much greater than they are. Your own desires to be so incredibly independent and self-sufficient, while they are good human virtues, often get in the way of your connecting with me as the true Source. You have grown into believing that you are your own source. This is ego running amuck.

I, the Mother/Father God of you all, am the Source. I re-source through people, places, and things. I am the Divine Circulation. I am the Cycle and I re-cycle through people, places, and things. When you understand that you are not your own source nor the source for anyone else, then you will grow into an appreciation of what it means to be in Divine Partnership with me. You will not stress so much. You will not worry so much. Anxiety will not grip you in the throat. You will be more at ease. You will sleep better at night, with the peace that passes human understanding. You will be able to rest more and not be so overly conscious of your perceptions of the future. When you realize that you are part of the Divine Flow by your very essence, you will enjoy life more.

8. I, the One Source, re-source through people, places, and things

So many of you are missing today in preparing for tomorrow. Live today. Be present today. Be available today. And, as it says in Scripture, if you will "seek first the Kingdom of God," the sovereignty of God, then "all things will be added unto you." There will be far less concern about who is giving what to whom, where, when, and how. There will be far less concern about who is receiving what from whom, how, when, or why. And this includes yourself.

I have supplied your every need. If you would just stay in a state of unconditional gratitude, if you would just give thanks and praise each day, if you would just bless everyone and everything around you . . . you would come to the awareness that there is so much more, such a greater bounty, than you could perceive through your "lack and limitation" lenses. Give thanks. Give thanks. Give thanks. Recognize your Oneness with me and you will live the Divine Flow.

9. Stay in a state of unconditional gratitude

Your gift of prophecy is a gift to you as well, my Reverend Daughter. It is not merely a blessing to the people. It is a blessing to you. However, as with all gifts, you cannot receive your own gift until you appear to give it to someone else. Don't just give this gift of prophecy, my child, receive it. You must receive it so that you can give it. And you must give it so that you can receive it. Are you surprised? You know that this is the way I work. And I am so glad that you are coming to not only understand but appreciate, yea, even anticipate, what you refer to as the spiritual paradoxes of life. ✿

IX. EACH OF YOU IS SPECIAL AND UNIQUE

Yes, my Reverend Daughter Deborah, you are now hearing as well what I was saying to others before you. Communing with me is the same, no matter when or where one is in history. Seeming differences exist because each person is slightly more in tune to certain of my aspects more than they are to others. This is what you preach about all of the time, how people resonate with me in some ways but unfortunately not in all ways. You hear me because you are very linguistically oriented. This is the gift that I have given to you; you speak, and you speak well. You always have and you always will in this life expression. You see the interconnectedness of the world and you can articulate it. Yes, it is the gift of prophesy.

1. Each person has a way of tuning into me

All do not have this particular gift. Yet this does not mean that they cannot hear me just as well, merely that the medium they use will be a different one. People will want to glorify you and put you up on a pedestal because you hear me in this fashion. You have stopped yourself from hearing me for too many years because you were afraid of this phenomenon. This is not to be your concern. Keep listening to me and speaking, and assure the others that they have to come into their own authenticity.

What is authenticity for one person is not the same as what is authenticity for another. This is what makes it authentic. You humans confuse this all of the time. You long for authenticity, yet you spend all of your time comparing and contrasting yourselves to one another. If you do not have what another has, you sulk and pout and get a defeated attitude. Yet you are not meant to be like any other. Each of you is special. Some of you can read me in the stars, in the palm of a hand, in the leaves of tea, and the like. All who use these methodologies have been categorized and mis-categorized in your society. Some of these talents have been abused for commercial purposes, so they have lost their savor. However, these are not the only ways that one can hear me.

2. You must feel me in the deep recesses of your being

One can hear me in the deep recesses of their being, and if one does not sense me there, then the rest is for naught. Just because one can read signs does not mean that one knows me. This is the confusing part to many of you. Just because you see someone proficient in a technique that describes my Order, you automatically assume that they have a special connection to me. This is not the case. They can be quite competent in understanding the external manifestations of my world but still experience an emptiness inside. The converse is also true. Someone can feel me deep within their being and have no understanding whatsoever of the external clues that have become so popular over time. The important point is that you grow to know me, that you feel something within yourself that is irrefutable. Too many of you hear me and then argue with yourselves as to whether you heard me or not. You doubt your own selves because you do not want to be too "woo-woo," as you would say. You want to be grounded in the earthly fashion and yet anchored in the spiritual. The two do not always go together, especially if being grounded in the earthly means that you do not give yourself the permission to move beyond the norms.

The norms hold you back. You confuse the norms with the natural. They are not the same thing. The norm is what everyone is doing. The natural is what I have intended for you to do. You also confuse what is humanly natural for you with the spiritual norm. What is humanly natural to you must be surrendered to what is natural to you spiritually. The Spirit must be in the lead. You say, "But I thought that there was no separation." Separation does not exist. But you really don't believe this in your hearts; it is still a mental construct for you.

If you really believed it in your hearts, we would not be having this conversation.

The fact that you still believe in the material world as different from the spiritual world means that you have to use certain techniques to discern the latter. In this sense of duality, you need to consider one to be greater than the other. In reality there is only one. One is the essence and the other the expression, but they are the same. To separate them would be like trying to separate the music from a song, or the art from a drawing. The song is in the particular and music is in the absolute. The two go hand in hand. And it is the spiritual hand that you must grab onto as your identity.

One's identity is the real question here. You identify with me so much, my Reverend Daughter, that you can hear me and know that it is me without "freaking out." You do not consider it strange, indeed, you know that everyone can hear what you hear if they choose to listen. However, choosing to listen means that they must also become transparencies of my Word, as you have become. This is the problem. They do not want to do the work. They do not want to clear their hearts and minds of the debris and rubble that clog the passageways of their loving and understanding. If they were willing to do the work to heal the sense of separation that they have from me and all others, then my voice would be just as clear to them in their own way of understanding.

3. Everyone can hear me who identifies with me and chooses to listen

Yet it is easier for them to put you, and others like you, up on a pedestal as something different. You do not have the answers to every problem, and it is good that you know this and don't try to solve things for other people. They must do their own work. You do not assume the responsibility for the consciousness of your congregation. This is excellent, my child. If more ministers felt this way, they would be a lot happier at their jobs. Just let the people be. Keep sharing your process with them, and they will make it according to their own timing. You are not the cause of anything in their lives. At best, as you understand, you are merely catalytic to their awareness.

4. Have patience and compassion with yourself and with each other

As a minister, my Reverend Daughter, you attract those who are earnestly searching, because "you don't have time," as you would say. This is fine. You have always been in a hurry to get on with the understanding, and you attract those who are also in such a hurry. However, just as you have learned to have patience with yourself along the way with the process, continue to teach them such patience. They need to have compassion for themselves and for each other. When you have such compassion, you savor every moment of every day, for each is rich with fruitful spiritual experience. You see, there really is no place to go. Why be in a hurry to go to a place that doesn't exist? ✂

X. CANCER AS A TURNING POINT
Message to the Attendees of the Women's Cancer As a Turning Point Conference

When you first heard that you had cancer, for some of you it was like a knife in the heart. For others time simply stood still. For some it was a surreal experience, with the world moving all around you. For some it caused panic; for others, disbelief. Regardless of the initial response, the question always remained "Why me, why now?" It is a question that most of you still ponder. The experience of this illness has sent you on a journey like nothing that you have ever known. You have had to look deep within your souls and examine what is real for you and what is not. You have had to question what you value and what you believe in. You have had to face many demons within that you did not know even existed.

You have been angry, depressed, confused, resentful, bitter, restless, suicidal, and defeated. You have also been uplifted, inspired, motivated, encouraged, supported, renewed, rejuvenated, and enlightened. You have been and continue to be all of these things and more. You have become intimate with fear. Pain has been your companion. You have trysted with death and bargained for your futures. You have also discovered a strength inside of yourself that has made you a hero to yourself and to those around you. You have closed chapters and opened new ones, changed lifelong habits and allowed a new you to step forth.

Sometimes, every day it's a struggle just to put one foot in front of the other. At times you have feared never awakening the next morning, and at other times you have feared that, in fact, you would. You have greeted some days with optimism

1. The experience of your illness has sent you on a journey

2. Sometimes every day is a struggle

and certainty, determined to stimulate your body's own heal-ing powers. You have been afraid to smile and afraid not to. You have found solace in each other's understanding and have learned what it means to be a friend. You have asked for help when your pride was too great to reveal such a need, and you have given help when you were sure that there was nothing left within to give.

The world did not slow down for you to process your lot or question your fate or muse your future. Your responsibili-ties and obligations did not cease; in fact, for most of you they increased. The ones who you needed to lean on were often not there for you, and yet you have carried on anyway. You have learned what it means to be a friend.

3. All of you have come seeking me

Regardless of what you thought about me before you discov-ered your illness, all of you have come seeking me. Some have come seeking a healing; some have come looking for answers. Some of you have come to vent your anger and your wrath at the seeming unfairness of it all. Some have done all of the above. In that midnight hour when you are all alone in your thoughts, on the surgery table when you feel at the mercy of the surgeon's scalpel, when you are trying to find meaning in this experience . . . I am there. I have never deserted or aban-doned you. I have never left you alone. Nor have I caused any of you to be sick. I do not bring illnesses upon you for the sake of having you ill. Your illnesses are the natural outcomes of physical and emotional processes. You are angry with me for not preventing them from manifesting in the first place, and you wonder what my intentions are for your life. I have only one intention for you and your life, and that is that you live as fully as you can. The real question here is, what is your intention for your own life?

I want you happy, fulfilled, and whole. I work with anyone and everyone who turns to me for counsel, shelter, and sup-port. I withhold nothing and am present for all, every minute of the day. It is the judgment of your lot that prevents many of you from hearing me, not your lot itself. When you surrender to the process of healing, when you stop fighting and struggling with me and everyone and everything around you, you will find that the road to recovery is easier to access than you might have imagined.

I will lead you beside the green pastures and the still waters. I will restore your soul. I know what you have need of, even before you do. Just remember to see me everywhere, even in the midst of your so-called illness. When you do not believe that I am in your cancer, you fail to recognize me in the very place where I need to be affirmed, which is your body temple. There is not a spot where I am not. I work with you and through you. Don't shut me out and then accuse me of abandoning you.

There is much that you will need to rethink. Everything within your body is supported by your outer habits—your diet, your exercise (or lack thereof), your relaxation, your thinking. Each of these things will need to be reevaluated and supplanted with healthier techniques. I am not blaming you or saying that you have been doing the wrong things, merely that in the wake of this challenge you must do even more. Feast on the ideas that sustain and nourish, and fast from the ones that result in anxiety and stress.

4. Be willing to believe beyond belief that you can and will be healed

Be willing to believe beyond belief that you can and will be healed. Judge not by the appearances that you see. Remain steadfast, even when you are disheartened. Don't accept anyone's verdict for your life other than mine. I am the Master Physician. It is true that everyone must release this body at some time, but it is I who determines that timing, none other. Unless you have received word from me, it is not your time. And do not fear receiving this word from me; for when you do, the journey towards the next phase of your life will be no less wondrous than any other. You will embrace it as an integral part of the life cycle and will most likely be more ready for it than the ones around you.

5. You have received many different responses from the ones around you

The ones around you . . . the pain that this brings. You not only have to manage your own situation, but you caretake for so many others. So many need you and depend on you. You fear what will happen to them if you are not available to take care of them. You worry for their safety and their well-being. This worry and concern is a motivating factor for many of you; it keeps you fighting. Yet do not confuse fighting cancer with being healed from it. Healing is beyond fighting, even though it may take a fighting spirit in order to "get you up off of the dime," as you would say.

Some of your loved ones have been angry with you for being sick, which has left you feeling lost and forlorn. Some of them, too uncomfortable with your suffering, want to micromanage you and fix everything. They get in the way more than they serve. Still others keep their distance because your illness retraumatizes their old hurts and wounds about sickness and abandonment. Yet there have been others who have stepped forward and surprised you with their love and caring. Some of the ones that you care for have had to grow up and assume more responsibility for their own lives. Some have stepped forward to support you more in your hour of need. The ones who have been there the most for you have not always been the ones you expected. What a wonderful surprise it is to find love in new places.

Some of you have received tremendous support on your jobs. Others of you have lost them or given them up. In any event, you will discover new talent, skills, and abilities that you never knew you possessed. Stretch into your creative realm; there is much healing power there. Paint, draw, write, sing, dance, play. Sew, weave, sculpt, make music, pick up a new hobby. Greet each day as though it were the most precious thing on earth. Show your heart, touch someone. Utter that word of acceptance or forgiveness that you have been sitting on. Make that call that you hesitate to make. Make amends to the ones who you have trespassed against.

All of this makes a greater space within you for healing. Some of the clutter and debris must be removed from your psyche, as well as from your body temple. Let no one discourage you with facts and statistics. No one knows your future but me. Dare to expect a miracle and you will be one. "What you are looking for, you are looking with." You are the health that you seek. The doctors know that they cannot heal you. They merely work with your body's own healing mechanisms. They encourage the body to heal itself. You can do this, too. There are many, many healing techniques and traditions to aid you. Do not settle for anything that you are not comfortable with. Don't be overwhelmed by the multitude of choices either. I will guide your every step.

Some of you are so mad at me that you can barely listen to this letter. Others are soaking it in like a breath of fresh air in a suffocating environment. It matters not what you think of me. I love you all, everyone last one of you. And that is really all that matters. As your popular hymn says, "My eye is on the sparrow, and know that I watch over you." ✄

6. You are the health that you seek

1. Courage is the ability to keep walking in the direction of your surrender

My dear ministers of consciousness, I wish to speak to you first about courage. Courage is a concept that is often misunderstood, often diluted from the power of what it is really about. It is important to understand this concept of courage because you will need a lot of it. What is this thing called courage? Courage is the ability to continue to walk in the direction of your surrender. At the moment when it is important for you to exercise courage there is something that you are surrendering. It may be the potential impact on your life that your action implies. It may be the potential impact on your relationships as a result of the actions you are engaging in. It may be the fact that once the action is taken, your life will never be quite the same.

Facing these possibilities is troublesome to most people. It creates fear, anxieties, apprehensions, and great concern. The fact that you may experience these things is really not so much the point. Rather, the point is the way you allow these things to influence the steps that you know that you must take. There is a book that became popular in your society not so very long ago, *Feel the Fear and Do It Anyway.* The title really explains what is required. Courage is your ability to keep taking action, to not stop, to keep moving in the direction of your surrender.

2. In spiritual surrender there is no defeat

What do I mean when I keep saying "the direction of your surrender"? And what exactly is it that you are surrendering to? There is some confusion here as well. Too many of you think of surrender as defeat. Therefore, when you imagine yourself surrendered, you are at the point where you are willing to accept defeat as one of the possible, if not probable, outcomes. Whereas your willingness to accept this may demonstrate a certain degree of human bravery, it has absolutely nothing to do with spiritual surrender. When you reach the place of spiritual surrender and you recognize that all of the dire things that you project as possibilities for your experience are merely that—projections—they cease to have a hold on you. They cease to influence you. They cease to hold you back as you hold onto them.

It is only through your understanding of your relationship to me that you can ever truly walk in a path of surrender. When you walk in the path of spiritual surrender, defeat stops even becoming an option, let alone a subject of your discussion or attention. Defeat is simply the ego's concern about whether or not it is going to win. However, the ego's concern is always relative, conditional, derived at through the process of contrast and comparison. In that paradigm, in order for something to lose there must be something that wins. In the spiritual paradigm of your Oneness with me, however, there is no something else out there and there is no winning at the expense of anything else. There is only the One. I am only the One. You are me and I am you. Therefore, there is only Oneness among us. Why would I do anything to hurt myself? Why would I do anything to hurt you? Why would I do anything to hurt anyone else? Why do people attribute these things to me in the first place? What good would it possibly do me to have you as a smaller place in the Universe through which I express?

When you surrender in Spirit, you know that you are placing yourself in alignment with the Divine Plan. In this Plan you know that you are cared for. In this Plan you know that you are provided for. In this Plan you know that your individual needs, aspirations, desires, intents, and purpose for being are all addressed. You can surrender because there is no battle. You can surrender because there is no war. You put down the weapons because there is nothing to fight. You take off the coat of armor

3. In surrender you stop fighting and you align with the Divine Plan

because it is cumbersome and you do not need it. So this thing called courage is really about the discipline of your continuing to move towards your understanding of a Divine Plan, in spite of all appearances. There will be many, many, many, many, many, many appearances that you will have to wade through, pierce through, transcend, wrestle with, deny the truth within, move beyond.

There is a misconception that allows you to believe that as you grow in your spiritual maturation there are fewer things for you to deal with (as you would say). This is not the case. It is true that you will have fewer things to "deal with" in the areas and the arenas that are familiar (that is to say, you won't keep manifesting the same circumstances over and over and over again). However, as you grow in your spiritual maturation your perception increases. And as your perception increases there is more for you to see, to become aware of, to face. When you transcend, you get an aerial view. When you are on the ground you "cannot see the forest for the trees." However, as you transcend you exclaim, "Ohhh, wow, there is really a forest there!" You see so much more than you would have otherwise seen. And the sheer volume, quantity, depth, and intensity of it all could conceivably scare you away.

4. Instead of trying to see me in all things, see all things in me

Instead of trying to see me in all things, see all things in me. Feel the difference here. When you are looking for me in all things, you are starting with the thing. You have some concept in mind of something that is real, even if you merely understand it to be a temporal experience. This sets up the parameters for you. And then you go trying to find me in all of your "stuff." No. No. No! Don't focus on the stuff and try to see me in it. Focus on me, period. When you focus on me, then you can see all things in me. If you will do this, then many of the questions that you are asking yourselves right now will be answered. You will move from trying to figure out "Where is God in the illness, where is God in the poverty, where is God in this thing or that thing?" If you start with the premise that

I am the Only thing that is, you will have a deeper compassion and empathy for everything that you see in life because you know that it has something to do with me. This is at the heart of this discussion you have been having in your ministerial class about prayer—"Do you affirm this thing away or do you deny that thing over here?" Don't get caught up in techniques and technicalities.

See me. Start with me. Affirm that I am you and you are me and that we are One with each other, that there is nothing outside of this unity, this partnership, this marriage. Then, as things come along, instead of having to wonder whether they could have some sort of spiritual value, you will accept everything as having a spiritual value. The difference is that you will not get so stuck in analyzing the catalyst. Instead, you will refocus your attention on the fact that everything leads you back to me. Everything leads you back to us. Everything leads back to our Oneness.

What is your charge in this thing you are referring to—your profession as "practitioners," lay ministers specializing in healing? What is it that you are supposed to be doing? There is nothing wrong with the techniques that you espouse and advocate. They work quite effectively with the individuals who resonate with the suppositions you put forth. However, there is something deeper here. I speak to you very specifically because there is a message for you now.

In your discussions you have noted that the New Thought leaders have all claimed to be using the power of Jesus, not necessarily his techniques, but his power. Jesus didn't argue anything with the people that he was healing. He didn't try to prove or disprove anything. However, he did in fact know something. Learn to do your work. If you intend to model what you do after Jesus, do your works "in the name of the Christ" that Jesus exemplified. Understand what I am saying here. The word "name" in this phrase does not mean a label or a name as in acknowledging a point of reference. "Name,"

5. Pray with the authority and character of our Oneness

in Scriptural terms, refers to the character and the authority of the individual. Pray with authority. Pray with the understanding that we are One in character. When you focus your attention on this, then it will cease to matter so much what you perceive your personal prayers to be effecting.

6. *Be a place through which our power together expresses*

Stand on the Truth. Stand on Principle. Stand on what you know. Be a place through which the power that we are together expresses. Heal through inspiration. Heal through modeling. Heal through your energy, your aura, which speaks louder than your words. Heal through your consciousness that is an understanding that this relationship you share with me is available to all people. Let your prayers be for the availability. Let your prayers be for individuals to be able to find their way back to me. You are not their harbor. You are not their anchor. You are not even the beacon.

I am the Light. I am the harbor. I am the way home, and I am the home. Your job is to know this. Your job is to know that, like the prodigal son, they can never get too far away from me. Like the prodigal son, there is nothing they, or you, could do that would take away the relationship that we have. This is the One and true "inalienable right." This relationship that we have that can never be severed by anything is your one spiritual right. Practice this right. Act like you understand it. Preach it. Teach it. Shout it from the mountain tops. Invade cyberspace with it. Put it on the airwaves. Let it be the individual and collective mantra of your heart. If you concentrate on the fact that there is nothing that can separate us, that you and I are One, that everybody is One with me, then there is no lack. There is no limitation. There is no disease. There is nothing outside of our fullest expression.

7. *First the roots, then the fruits*

Remember that in your New Thought tradition the healing is in the answer, not the process. It is in the answer that Spirit is all there is. When that seed takes root deep in your consciousness, it not only produces a tree that can withstand all weather, it bears a fruit that not only multiplies but is ever so sweet. First the roots and then the fruits.

Too many of you are trying to bake your apple pie. You want to eat the fruit more than you want to tend to the seed. Garden your minds. Fertilize the soil of your minds. Weed out the thorns and the thistles. Move the rocks and the stumbling blocks out of the way. I will do my part. You do your part. Don't worry about your doing my part. You do your part. I have the seeds. I know when they should grow, how they should grow, where they should grow, and how much should grow. Your job is to create a fertile soil that will accept any combination of decisions that are a part of the Divine Plan.

I am so pleased that you have taken the time to contemplate these most important concepts. You will be stronger ministers of consciousness as you embody them and let the roots plant deeply in your soul. I am most pleased with the progress and the work that you have been doing, and it is my pleasure to continue to support you in your maturation as well as your matriculation. I love you.

XII. PRAY WITH AUTHORITY

1. Prayer is a movement in consciousness

Deliver a message, my child, to the congregants of Unity Temple to whom you will be speaking tomorrow morning. Deliver this message on my behalf. Deliver it to the people there. However, child, as you know, a message that I give you in Truth for one is a message for all. Do not allow yourself to be misguided into thinking that there ever is a message that is uniquely for anyone in particular. The specifics of the message may be more immediately and directly applicable to the circumstances of some individuals, however, the Truth of the message stands for all. The message is not so much about the particular circumstances. It's just that the particular circumstances put the individuals in a certain mind-set that makes them more receptive to hearing answers that have, in fact, been there all along.

This is what they need to understand about prayer. You may pray for someone very specifically, but your prayer is never in the particular. What do I mean by this? Prayer is a movement in consciousness. It is a vibratory pattern that is put out into the world to be received by others. Who is the sender, and who is the receiver? The purpose of your prayers is not to send the prayer to me. The purpose is not to persuade me to do anything. I have done it all already. The purpose of the prayer is to move your consciousness into alignment with my Divine Plan and to surrender your will, so that you are able to accept the Goodness that is already at hand. Where is the movement in consciousness originating from?

2. The energy of your prayers quickens vibratory patterns

Too many of you spend your energy trying to influence the consciousness of the ones for whom you are praying in the same manner as you waste your time trying to influence me. There is no influencing to be done here save in your own minds. When you pray, you are affecting your own thinking, your own consciousness, your own ability to see the Good for which you have prayed as already being at hand. You must believe what you say. It is not just a question of the one who you are praying for believing it. You must believe it. The power is in the word of the one who is speaking. It is in the consciousness of the one who is speaking. Understand that "the word" does not mean just a bunch of syllables strung together in sound. Quite the contrary, "the word" represents principles, concepts, living Truths that are embodied in consciousness in such a way as to take shape and form in the outer world of thought.

The ones for whom you are praying are vibrating with you at some level. You are all vibrating with each other, as you are vibrating with me. There is only One of us here. Your prayer affects that vibratory pattern. Your prayer sends out an energy field and an energy force that quickens the vibratory pattern, that lifts it up, that makes it transcend the vibratory patterns that are the result of the collective consciousness of lack, limitation, and disbelief. Come up a little higher, my children. Come up beyond the problems and the so-called difficulties. Come up to the place where the answer is already at hand. Come up to the place beyond the search. Come up into the harvest, not merely the planting of the seeds. Come with your baskets, not merely your shovels and your hoes. Come up with the deep intent of receiving the Goodness, not merely registering a complaint.

When you speak the Word, you are creating a space and a place in the Universe for this Word to take hold in your consciousness, in the consciousness of the ones for whom you are praying, and in the collective consciousness, all at the same time. What do I mean when I say that you do not pray your prayers in the particular? Anyone and everyone who is ready to make a shift, anyone and everyone who is listening with their hearts and not merely their ears, anyone and everyone who has the desire deep within their soul to make a shift, will pick up on this vibration and be blessed by it. When you speak the Word, you must speak it with this open-ended understanding,

3. Anyone who is receptive benefits from your prayers

this open-minded understanding, this open-handed understanding, this open-armed understanding. You must speak the
Word with the intent of facilitating a healing process without
being concerned about whose processes will, in fact, be initi-
ated. You are fuel, fodder for the fire, as well as sparks that
ignite the flame. You are the oxygen that allows the fire to
breathe, and you are a part of its bonfire.

Speak the Word. Speak your word. Speak it, my children.
Speak it with a boldness. Speak it as ones who have authority
and who understand their Oneness with me. Don't be apologetic about it. Don't act like your prayer is a request. Don't act
like your prayer is an intrusion upon a busy Divine
Consciousness. Don't act like your prayer is too much to ask
for, or too big or special to be accomplished. Don't act like
you are uncertain whether or not your prayer will be answered,
let alone be responded to. Don't act like you don't know who
you are. You are me and I am you. Your word has power
because I have power, and there is no separation between us.
When you speak, you speak with my voice. When you move,
you move with my beingness. When you create, you use my
creative expression. When you think, you are thinking with my
mind. Everything that I have is yours. We are One in the same.

4. You are a place through which my power expresses

So whose power are you using when you pray? Whose will is
being attended to when you pray? Are your prayers from your
little self? Are your prayers being spoken with the dignity and
the sense of purpose that you know of as yourself in me? I
do not say these things to scold you. I do not say these things
to complain about you. I say these things to motivate you. I
say these things to inspire you. I say these things to remind
you of your greatness, your grandness, your grandeur. There
is nothing blasphemous in speaking my Word with the
authority of one who is One with me. If there is blasphemy,
it is to do the opposite. If there is blasphemy, it is to pray not
understanding that you are God in the flesh now. That is the
blasphemy. What does it mean to blaspheme? To blaspheme

is to deliberately or inadvertently defame the integrity of something in such a way as to cast a dispersion on the thing at hand. Don't cast dispersions upon yourself. It is yourself that you are blaspheming. Since you are a spiritual being, if you are blaspheming yourself you are indirectly blaspheming me as well. We are in a partnership with each other. All I ask is that you show up and that you use the power that you have to be a place through which my power expresses.

When I say to speak the Word in Truth, I mean to infuse your word with the Truth. What do you bring to the table in your prayers? What is the focal point of reference in your prayers? Are you merely identifying the so-called problem? Are you merely identifying the lack or limitation? Are you merely identifying your wants, your needs, your desires, your expectation, your fears, etc., etc., etc.? What are you talking about in your prayers? Are your prayers filled with spiritual Truth? Are your prayers filled with spiritual understanding? Do your prayers reflect the deep, profound spiritual wisdom upon which your spiritual house is built? Is the Truth in your prayer? Can one listen to your prayer and know that all is well? Can one listen to your prayer and know that you speak as one with authority? Can one listen to your prayer and be so inspired, touched, moved that the healing is spontaneous? Does your prayer have the passion that moves people to tears?

5. In prayer prioritize spiritual facts over material facts

Remember that it is not in the syllables of the words, per se. It is in the consciousness behind it. Sometimes silence is a wonderful prayer. And who among your society now is more familiar with the power of the silence than Unity? You are known around the world for your deep devotional prayers. But do not be misled. Just because the Word is not spoken in a verbal, linguistic sense does not mean that the Word is not being spoken from the heart, from the mind, yea, from the depths of the soul. The Word is resonating out as a consciousness aware that I prevail over all. Do you know this, my children? Do you know that I prevail? Will you work with your mind and your own thinking until you can convince yourself of this? You don't need to convince me. You don't need to convince the ones for whom you are praying. The only one that you need to convince in your prayer is yourself.

6. Speak the Word with confidence, expecting a manifestation

Speak the Word. *Speak the Word.* Speak the Word with confidence. Speak the Word in Truth. Speak the Word as one who is in an absolute state of expectancy for the Word spoken to be made manifest, even though you don't know what the particular manifestation will look like. Don't make an outline for me. Don't give me a blueprint of what your prayer should look like when it is answered. Stick to the Absolute. Pray for the Divine Principles to be released in the manner which will be for the Highest Good for all. Stick to the Absolute. Pray for the clarity. Pray for the unity and the harmony. Pray for the reconciliation. Pray for the wisdom and the sense of direction. Pray for the intent and the unleashing of creative expression. Pray for the authenticity and the integrity that lead to a conscious recognition of wholeness. Pray for the Truth of who you are. Pray for the Truth of the situation. Pray for the Divine Right Action. Pray for Divine Right Activity. Pray for the win/win situation. Pray for the good and the best and the highest for all concerned.

Speak the Word, my children. Speak the Word. Speak the Word. Speak the Truth. Speak your words in Truth. And in your words remember our Oneness. Remember that it is our Oneness that gives your word power. Don't be afraid. Don't be shy. Don't be timid. Don't be coy. Do not confuse these things with humility. The only way that you can be humble is to know that you have something to be humble about. Know who you are in me. I love you. I love you all. ❧

Only One
Of Us Here

Only One of Us Here

CONTENTS

I. Conflict Resolution

There is much talk and discussion in your society at this point in time regarding the current events of the day, so many of which appear to be wrought with efforts to resolve disagreements and/or conflicts through the use of violence. The discussions are good from the standpoint that you are awakening from your self-induced sleep, which would otherwise allow you to ignore the seedlings and the escalation of these kind of activities as they are taking place. There is a type of desensitization that has taken place that has resulted in an increasing indifference, as well as invisibility, an inability to see what is going on. However, too many of the discussions are looking for someone or something to blame. Is it the media? Is it the lack of appropriate gun control laws? Is it violent video games? Is it simply the repeating of history with your "Hitler-type" characters appearing again? Exactly what is going on? There is the idea, "If we can just find whoever it is we can blame, and if we tweak this thing or that thing, then everything would be all right."

No. No. NO! This is not the time to be looking for someone or something to blame. Now is the time to ask yourselves, "What is it that we need to be doing?" This is quite a different inquiry—to look into what needs to be done—as opposed to looking to see what it is that has already happened. The common misunderstanding among you is that you must thoroughly understand where you have gone wrong, that you must thoroughly understand what it is that isn't working, before you are able to move on to how things ought to be. This comes from your mechanistic approach to any and all things, including yourselves. What is it that must be done? Well, look to your spiritual nature. That's all that you ever have to know. You don't have to know where you have been off. You just need to know where you need to be on.

1. Without blaming, ask "What is it we need to be doing?"

2. Stop building on the shifting sands of the temporal

Understand what it is that I just said, because it is quite profound in creating new paradigms for the way in which you go about handling your affairs. There is the idea that if you just found out what it is that is wrong, and corrected that, then everything would be all right. This assumes that everything was all right before the so-called thing went wrong. Even if you were to change what you have been doing wrong, that does not mean that you would be standing on solid ground.

When you see that things are going awry, that is the indication that you are not on solid ground, that is the indication that you have anchored yourself in the temporary, the transitory, the relative, the conditional, and the temporal. All of these things are like the shifting sand. You cannot anchor in it. You cannot build a foundation, let alone a structure, in it. So why is there such a surprise when the walls come tumbling down? What is it that you have to know about sand to understand that it shifts? How much do you have to know to figure out that the sand isn't going to hold anything up? It doesn't matter what it was that you were trying to build in the sand. Just trying to figure out "Well, was it this kind of structure or that kind of structure?" doesn't make much difference if it was still being built in the sand.

3. Discover and affirm what's right, not just what you think is wrong

No, my children, the challenge is to build upon the rock. If you took only a fraction of the time that you spend trying to analyze what is wrong with everybody and everything and spent that time on trying to discover and affirm the Truth about yourselves and each other . . . oh, what miracles would occur!!! Focus your attention on the breadth and the depth of your possibility, not simply on the ways in which you have squandered, pilferaged, and promulgated—the activities that come from a sense of spiritual amnesia. Know who you are. Know who you are. Know who you are.

When you know who you are, you know that you do not have any "enemies." All conflict is "the friction of fiction." Your ego selves are like fictional characters that get caught up in the illusion of their own drama, which they project out into the world as reality. The moment you sense that someone is not in alignment with you, you start to draw battle lines. You start to dig in your heels, as you would say. You start to try to figure out what you need to do to dominate, manipulate, control, cajole, influence, or coerce the other individuals or parties involved into seeing things your way, and into doing things in ways that would prove to be favorable from your ego's stand-point. Some of you are up front about this and are quite "in your face" about the matter. Others of you are far more covert and sneaky about your real intents. However, whether you are shouting it or trying to manipulate things behind the scenes, it all gets you to the same place.

Why does it all get you to the same place? Because it is all based upon the notion of loss. When you don't know who you are, you are afraid that you can lose in the world. When you don't know who you are, you are concerned that some person, place, or thing may do something that is going to make you less, or worse off. So you are constantly trying to hedge your position, to create the circumstances that make you feel safe. Know who you are. Know who you are. Know who you are. When you know that you are One with me and that we are the Only thing that Is, then you know that One with me is a majority. There is nothing outside of me, so there is nothing outside of you.

What is this "other" that you are so afraid of? What is this power in the Universe that you are so afraid is going to put your life in a more disadvantaged position? Where does it come from? And who has control over it? Why do you make gods out of people, places, and things? Why do you attribute to them more power than you attribute to me? Just as you look for blame more than you look for resolution, so you look to external things for resolutions more than you look to me. Why am I the last resort? Why is it that you only turn to me after you have exhausted all of your other ideas, plans, schemes,

4. There's no "other" to be afraid of

resources, etc., etc., etc.? (The et ceteras are not to belittle but to show it is just endless.) Why?

5. The illusion of otherness is the fundamental problem

When ego selves come up against each other, trying to come up with anything that will address the underlying issues without taking me into consideration is fallacious and will not work. Understand what it is that I am saying here. Just trying to do new techniques, trying to find new ways to communicate, trying to negotiate new terms or treaties will not create a difference. Understand that the same things work in the most microscopic one-on-one relationships as with global world relationships. As long as you are working in the world of the external, you are simply moving the tinker toys around. As long as you are starting with what it is that you think you know, and are trying to protect what you think you know, and trying to act on what you think you know about the other person . . . then you are, indeed, just moving around the building blocks that you have created, which have nothing to do with reality.

You must change your starting point. The moment that you begin to feel like you are up against somebody or something else—that is the signal, right there, that you are off. Understand what I said. The illusion of the otherness itself is the fundamental basis of the problem. If you start with the otherness as the given and try to structure everything around protecting each others' otherness, then you are never going to get to the place of harmony because your consciousness is fundamentally planted in the sinking, shifting sand of a false identity based on human race conscious. These words that I give you are not to scold you, although the tone may appear to be admonishing. These words are not meant to overwhelm or to depress you. These words are meant to uplift and inspire you, to help you remember that there is always a way out.

Too often you feel like you don't know what to do because you don't understand all of the issues at hand. You don't have to understand all of the issues at hand. You just have to understand that there is only ONE of us here! You just have to understand that I am the Only thing that Is. You just have to understand that deeply enough to be willing to start with it as your premise. If you start with it as your premise, then you will know what to do. It will become self-evident. Why? Because I will tell you. Why? Because you will be listening to me. Why? Because the Truth is self-evident and does not need to be proved.

Point your eyes towards the Truth. Take the money and the time that you are using to build weapons and defenses and use them to build bridges, literally and figuratively. Take all of the effort that you are making to try to make the world safe and use it to make the world inclusive. You will never be safe as long as in your safety you are creating a circumstance that makes someone else unsafe. Because I never manifest in the particular, what you desire for yourself you must desire for all people or you will never really be able to manifest it. If you are unwilling to have other people experience the good that you want for yourself, then you are creating the block to your own self's being able to receive it. You can't shut down in the particular. You can't say no and resist in the particular. You can't say no to their winning and yes to yours. Because the nos always cancel out the yeses; they energetically negate them.

So, my children, the message here is to open up your hearts. To open up your minds. To be willing to grow and to expand. To be willing to love and embody and embrace. To move beyond the false notions that there are individual or antagonistic energy forces that you have to hedge or protect yourself against, and to start to see the Oneness of everybody and everything. If you will start with this Oneness, then your whole perception of the so-called problem will change. Your whole outlook and sense of what is important and what needs to be done will be

6. Just understand that there is only One of us here

7. Starting with Oneness changes your perception of the problem

shaped and fashioned through your spiritual insight, not your natural eyesight. This is a challenge. But it is a challenge that you are ready for. It is a challenge that I am pleased to support you in. It is a challenge that I am pleased to support your supporting each other in. And as you continue to support yourself and each other in it, it becomes less of a challenge. I love you. I love you all. Love me. Love yourself. Love each other. And understand that whenever I instruct you to love, I mean all of the above simultaneously. ✁

II. THERE'S ONLY ONE OF US HERE

What does it mean, that there is only One of us here? This is a phrase that has become most popular in what you have grown to refer to as metaphysical, New Thought, or New Age circles. It is often used almost as a salutation, or a cliché. There is little understanding of what it means—that there is only One of us here. Why is there only One of us here? There is only One of us here because there is only One of me. I am the Only thing that exists. So there can only be Oneness, because I am Oneness in the Absolute. When you start to believe that you really are who your personalities have grown into being, you forget this simple fact. The reason why you forget that there is only One of us here is because you are too busy trying to differentiate and distinguish yourself from other people.

The notion that you might all be the same is distasteful to you, especially to those in your individualistically minded American society. You place a premium on originality, on expressions that would appear to make you unique. There is so much attention on trying to be unique just for the simple sake of being different that your uniqueness quite often lacks any type of authenticity. This desire to be different is usually at such a surface level that you human beings are often in contradiction. You don't like the sense of isolation and aloneness that you experience in your feelings and emotions. However, you also tend to get quite upset when somebody else claims that they understand what you are feeling. You want to be understood but then get angry at the thought that it's not your private matter anymore. What exactly do you want?

1. In distinguishing yourself, you forget there is only One of us here

2. You'll see how much you are like others

When you become aware of yourselves as an expression of me, then it is no longer so necessary for to you distinguish yourselves from other people. In fact, the contrary is often the case. When you understand that you are a part of me, then there is a greater tendency for you to recognize the ways in which you are, indeed, very much like the other people around you, whether you like the people around you or not. This is part of your difficulty in understanding that there is only One of us here. You have no problem saying this in rooms and in circles where you indeed feel some oneness with the people who are around you—when it feels safe to you in some kind of way because the individuals around you are mirroring those parts of yourself that you like, that you choose to claim.

However, what happens when you are around people who are mirroring the things in you that you choose not to look at? Is there only One of you around then? Who's around in that moment? In your need to distinguish yourselves from other people you try so hard to separate out "the wheat from the chaff," to separate the good from the bad. And even when, in your own self-introspection, you are bold enough not to always have yourself placed on the side of the good, you still have yourself in the center, even in your "badness." It all still revolves around you and the way in which you are not the same as the other people around you.

You stop feeling special when you no longer feel like you are significantly different. You equate special with not being like anybody or anything else. Unless there is something about you that is noteworthy, a reason why someone would love you as opposed to loving someone else, you feel like you are just run-of-the-mill, ordinary in some way that is quite deflating to your awareness of your spiritual self-esteem. This tendency to contrast and compare most often does one of two things. It either puts you on a pedestal so that you can feel better about yourself in comparison to everybody around you—"At least I'm not them, so I can't be all that bad." Or it gives you convenient excuses why you don't have to work too hard at becoming the All that you can be because it's obvious that you don't measure up, that you will never be as good as so-and-so, so "why bother"? You are convinced that you will fail before you even try.

However, in order to fail you have to have tried. Too many of you haven't really failed; you just never tried. And those of you who feel as though you tried and still failed have done just that—tried. This is very much analogous to what I often tell you regarding the difference between desire and intent. One can have the desire, which is a longing in the heart; however, that does not necessarily mean that there is any intent on the person's part. Intent moves desire to a higher level, where there is determination regarding manifestation.

3. Intent elevates desire into action

This is a problem with too many of you. You use trying in the same way that you use desire. You want some credit just for wanting to do something, whether you intend to do it or not. You want some credit for trying, whether you accomplish anything or not. When you really have an intent to love, an intent to forgive, an intent to show up and to be . . . then your trying gets elevated into action the same way that a desire evolves into an intent. Remember, however, that both desire and intent must be present. Yes, desire evolves into an intent, yet too many of you try to start at the point of intent. You just forge ahead and try to do something, but your heart isn't in it. And in your intent you have no intention of getting your heart involved in the matter. You are going to do it just because it should be done for some reason, but you have already made up your mind how you are going to feel about it beforehand, while you are doing it, and when you are finished. Where's the sincerity in this?

Don't develop a stockpile of intents for which you have no desire. This is part of the reason why so many of you "fail" at recovery from various types of addictions. You either have the desire to stop but lack any real intention. Or you go about the business of trying to stop by participating in various types of rehabilitation programs, even though you have no desire to stop—you ought to, you should, it would be a nice idea, there's somebody that you need to prove it to (even if it is your own self), and on and on. However, if you lack the basic desire, it will never happen.

4. To be able to express your spiritual intent, you must heal on the human level

This is part of the spiritual work of overcoming the seeming dichotomy between your humanity and your spirituality. You must establish a deep intent regarding your spirituality. At the same time, you must also work with your human emotions, frailties, fears, anxieties, ideas of lack and limitation so that they may be healed and transformed into the desire to be the highest spiritual person you can be. On the spiritual realm, intent will carry you a very long way. However, at some time your humanity must catch up. You must go about doing the deep healing work so that you are capable of expressing your intent.

If your work is simply to understand your spirituality, you will eventually get to a point where your persona will only let you go so far. It is like devising a wonderful plan to go a significant amount of distance from point A to point B. You have mapped the whole thing out and have covered all of the bases. However, you are trying to travel in a jalopy. And it doesn't matter how well everything has been mapped out if the car won't go, if it's incapable of making the haul. This is not to say that I am comparing you to an old broken-down piece of junk. However, just as you would take stock of the capacity of the car to be able to make the journey, so you must take stock of your capacity to take your spiritual journey.

Understand what I just said. You are the ones who think of yourselves as old, broken-down, inadequate, insignificant, and incapable spiritual jalopies. This is your reference point for yourselves, not mine. And what do you do with jalopies? You put them out to pasture. If they were horses, you'd shoot them. And many of you are busy shooting yourselves over and over and over again, or shooting each other, because you think that you're worthless. You, however, are not a machine. You are not broken-down in any way. You are one of my most honored and treasured creations. You have been made perfect, whole, and complete. (You have turned that into a cliché, as well—which also must be addressed.)

You have within you all that you will ever need to transform, to heal, to become the All that you can be. Too often, however, you do not believe this. You don't think that you have the ability to work with yourselves to get yourselves in the type of working order that would make you reliable, consistent, dependable, efficient vehicles for your own spiritual journeys. You are busy trying to find a spiritual auto mechanic who is going to tell you what is wrong with you and fix you so that you will be better. Many of you are busy trading models on yourselves. You keep trying to turn into the latest model out. You keep going through various processes to make yourselves different. You spend a lot of time on the exterior and all of the gadgets.

5. You have within you all that you will ever need

However, the substance of the ability to make it, so to speak, is not attended to. Since you don't believe that you have any control over this ability, you spend more of your time trying to develop your map and your plans. This at least makes you think you are doing something and often gives you a needed sense that you are in control of something. At least you can determine your route, exactly how you are going to get there, and on what kind of timing.

But it "blows your whole thing" when you realize that you have been working on the wrong thing. The only thing that you have any control over is the healing and transformation process that would convert your sense of yourself as a jalopy into one of being an effective vehicle for your spiritual journey. This is where your work ought to be. You get quite upset when you realize that no matter how detailed your plans are, how much you have planned, over what time period you have

6. You can control your perceptions, but not the journey

planned it . . . it doesn't matter because none of it is going to happen anyway. The sooner you grow to accept this fact, the less time you will waste on trying to map out your life ahead of time, and the less angry and frustrated you will be with everybody, including yourself and me. You will just accept that this is what it is.

When you come to understand that you cannot map anything out, you also understand that all of you are essentially on the same journey. It is not yours to control. And which road you take doesn't really matter so much. Is there a place where I am not? Is there a detour you could possibly take that could make you lost in Spirit—like lost in space? Why do you fret so about trying to predetermine all of your steps? When you live each and every moment, you come to the awareness that I am everywhere at all times, and you enjoy every bit of your journey as it comes.

7. Human actions only reflect one's awareness of me

Just as you cannot eat next week's bread, so you cannot travel next week's journey. You can only be where you are. Pay attention to where you are. Pay attention to who you are, where you are. Pay attention to who is there with you, where you are. In your quests to go somewhere on your journey, your notion that there is only One of us here doesn't embrace the ones who are around you now. You're trying to reach the "spiritual ones." You are trying to find the people like you. Everybody is like you!! Breathe. Breathe again. Everybody is like you and you are like everybody and until you can embrace this without moaning and groaning about it, then you don't know what you are saying when you say that there is only One of us here. I love all of you the same. You are all a part of me. It is just a question of how much you know this. When you know this, your actions reflect it. When you don't know it, your actions don't. Your actions are not a reflection of your goodness or your badness. Your actions are a reflection of the measurement of your ignorance versus your full awareness of me and yourselves in me.

THERE'S ONLY ONE OF US HERE

Ooohh, but what does this do for your judgment? What about all of those bad people and all of those bad things that they are doing? Surely you don't mean that I am One with them, do you? Well, what about that father who molested me? What about that mate who betrayed me? What about the ones who took and stole, cheated on me, cheated me—you can't say that I am One with them, can you? What about my mother, who, "bless her soul," was rotten? What about Hitler? What about Sadaam Hussein? What about this one? What about that one? Well, WHAT about them? Just what about them? Why do you ask these questions if it is not for the very reason that I said before? You are trying to elevate some and lower others, not simply as a matter of justice in your mind, but because of where it puts you and how good you are able to feel about yourself in comparison to all of these people whom you despise.

There is only One of us here because I am the Only thing that is here. You are living and breathing me. Every time you think, you are using my mind. Every time you sing, you are using my voice. Every time you love, you are using my heart. Every time you create or do anything, you are using my stuff (as you would say). It's all from the same stuff. It just looks a little different.

8. There's only One of us here because I am the Only thing there is

Is there a different life for the rose than for the cactus? Is a Doberman Pinscher more of a dog than a Chihuahua? Is there more life in a redwood tree than a weed? Is the ocean more magnificent than the mountain? No!! No!! No!! No!! It is all the same. When you become comfortable with it all being the same, you will become more comfortable with yourself. When you are no longer trying to find fault with yourself any more than you are trying to find reasons significant enough to put you on a pedestal, then you will be at peace with yourself. There really is only One of us here. When you can remember who is in the "One" and exactly who "us" identifies . . . then you will have it. When you understand that I am the One and that "us" means all, you'll have it. You say that this is easy for me to say. Why is it so easy for you to say that it is not? If there is anything that has been said here that is not the Truth, then ignore it. However, if you know that it is true, then act like it. ∽

III. Learn to Embrace the Whole

The triangle is one of the most important relationships to understand, and it is no mistake that in your Judeo-Christian culture I am referred to as the Trinity. Part of the reason why there is so much confusion and turmoil in your individual and collective lives is because you human beings have not yet learned how to be at peace with every aspect of this trinity simultaneously. The notion that there are competing goods, competing odds, any type of obstruction or polarity, is part of the problem. Remember that this Trinity has come to be described as the Father, the Son, and the Holy Spirit. Yet, when you move it beyond its cultural context and the genderization of my energy, you will find that, underneath it all, the Father represents that creative aspect of myself, which is all Law; the Son represents that aspect of myself that is represented in you, in humankind, as a living, breathing force within the Universe; and the Holy Spirit represents that aspect of me that is all Love, which connects all things.

1. You are in a trinity with Love and Law

In your metaphysical circles you often say that all is Love and all is Law. As human beings, you will find that most of your difficulties in life stem from your inability to balance all being Love and all being Law. Where does your humanity fit in within the scheme of absolute unconditional nonjudgmental Love? Where does your humanity fit within the scheme of all-complete absolute Law? When all is Love and all is Law, where is your humanity? When you are in your full humanity, where is the Love and the Law within you and your human experience?

This energy of the triangle is so incredibly important. Some of you believe that you have to choose between the

2. Your biggest challenge is finding a spiritual balance within yourself

things that appear to be good in your life. Some of you have described this in terms of not being able to serve two masters or having to choose between God and mammon—the lust for wealth as described in the Bible—as though the choices are always linear and dichotomous. No, my child, your biggest challenge is not in making choices in a dichotomy, where things have been divided into mutually exclusive or contradictory groups, but in balancing the fullness of who you are as a spiritual being. Understand what I just said, my child—in the full balance of who you are as a spiritual being.

3. Drama and adrenaline rushes make you feel alive

When you choose your humanity as your primary identity, the choice is way too small. Yet when you must fully incorporate the notion of yourself as a spiritual being into your humanity, you get overwhelmed by it all. Your spiritual nature appears to eclipse your frailties, idiosyncrasies, quirks, and preferences—the things you identify with as being uniquely yours in your humanity. There is a constant sense of loss when you consider the notion of being "too spiritual." There is the fear among too many of you that being "too spiritual" means that you will no longer have any fun, that all you will do is sit around and meditate or contemplate, and that there will not be any fire or passion in your life. You associate drama with being the only stimulus that "gets you going." Your adrenal glands do secrete, and this gives you a rush when you are up against something formidable, or something that appears to be out of the ordinary in some sort of scary fashion. Sometimes you human beings send yourselves through experiences to scare yourselves. This may sound silly, but just think about it. You go to movies just to scare yourselves. You get on various kinds of carnival rides just to scare yourselves. You do a lot of things that you don't even realize that you are doing just to scare yourselves on some level, to give yourselves a rush, to make you feel that you are alive. This is part of the energy that comes out of having so-called illicit relationships. There is something in the danger that makes you feel more alive.

You associate settling in, making commitments, sticking to a certain path, with being humdrum, boring, no longer challenging, or providing any sort of new experience or stimuli. You are afraid that marrying me will be the same tying of the knot with each other as in a human marriage, which your society jokes about. I am not some ball and chain around your neck. I am not here to stifle you or to prevent you from being all that you can be. Quite the contrary, I am here for you to be the All that you can be. You are choosing things that are scary on some levels to make yourselves feel more alive, and you can continue to do this forever. However, I have other ways to make you feel alive. I have experiences for you that are so far above and beyond the human dramas that you play out. I have so much in store for you at such a transcendent plane, but you must be willing to move beyond the gravitational pull of your interests and curiosity in the coming and goings of the specifics of your circumstances. Understand what I am trying to tell you, my children.

You are fascinated by all of the sequences, events, and little details that appear to govern your life experience. Many of you are obsessed with them. You obsess about not only what is going on in your life now, but also over the places and spaces where you have already been. Furthermore, many of you are obsessed with the details and the concerns and the worries regarding your so-called future. You are so obsessed about the minutiae that you cannot see me. You cannot even see yourselves, let alone anybody else who is traveling this path with you. There is a tendency to think of the people who are around you as getting in the way of your spiritual path. Don't you understand, my children, that they are not in the way of your spiritual path, they are the way of your spiritual path? Understand what I just said—other people, places, and things are part of the way of your spiritual path. You are busy trying to get away from the very things that you need to be engaging in and understanding. Why do I say this? Because it is true.

4. Spiritually speaking, you all reflect each other

Everything that I have ever said to you is true. (And in your heart of hearts you know that is, indeed, the case.)

You need to understand how there is only One of you here. The other people, places, and things in your life are only representative of other states of consciousness, ones that are even reflections of you, at some level. The reflection of you is not just the reflection of the small you, your persona, your personality. It is the reflection of you in your totality as a spiritual being. People are playing out the fears of humanity. People are playing out the creative, expressive potentials of humanity. People are playing things out at all levels, everywhere. And since there is only One of us here, each and every one of them represents some aspect of the Only thing that is. I am the Only thing that is. Even the things created in the world that are causing all of you such concern and worry have, at some level, been created out of the fundamental building blocks which I have provided. The fact that you don't know what to do with these building blocks, the fact that you are misusing them for all the wrong purposes, is not my fault.

5. Don't blame; discern your own contribution to collective consciousness

Understand what I just said. You need to stop blaming me for your choices—not only your individual choices, but the choices of your collective consciousness. Understand what I am saying here. Stop blaming me for the choices that your collective consciousness makes! . . . What might appear to you, as human beings, as anger in my voice at this moment is not anger but intensity. There is a point that I am trying to drive home (as you would say). You cannot talk about "them over there." You cannot talk about what "they" think, or what "they" do. You are doing it, any time it is being done. When you see things going on out there in the world, instead of blaming the specific individuals who are emulating certain activities, attitudes, or behavior . . . it might serve you well to ask yourself, "What is the collective consciousness that is expressing itself here?" Ask this sincerely, and then ask yourself a second question, "What is my contribution to this collective thinking?"

You are a part of everything. Perhaps it is some judgment on your part that has helped to fuel the fires of what is going on. Perhaps you haven't thought about it at all and you are wondering how could you be a part of something that you have never even thought about. Therein is the problem. The fact that one particular idea lacks the grace of your attention allows for a less evolved consciousness to control the matters at hand. You try to carve out consciousness the same way that you try to carve out places and spaces geographically. You human beings are so extremely territorial. There is no territory of the heart. There is no territory of the mind. There is nothing in consciousness that you can own exclusively and have it somehow be separate and distinct from everybody and everything else. The same is true for everyone else regarding you. Everything is intertwined.

Instead of trying to distance, avoid, judge, or proclaim "That's them over there" . . . consider the root idea. What is the root idea? What is the root idea in these circumstances? It is self-righteousness? Is it intolerance? Is it fear? Is it a sense of loss? Is it the inability to accept differences? Just what are some of the underlying ideas? And ask yourself what is your own response to these ideas—not just what is your response to those who are either reacting to or emulating them. This is the great secret to being at peace. Peace requires that you move away from a microscopic analysis of a situation. Peace requires that you view the matter from a transcendent standpoint. One might describe it as distance. However, in the real realm of spirituality there is no such thing as distance. It might better be described as clarity, the kind of clarity that comes from remembering that the circumstances and conditions define neither who you are nor your experience of them.

It is time that you learn how to embrace the whole. It is time that you stop trying to pick and choose between what you are proud of and what you are not. It is time for you to stop picking and choosing between various aspects of yourself,

6. I don't want you picking yourself apart; I want you whole

because you are not able to do so without picking at yourself, yea, picking yourself apart. I don't need you picked apart. It is not my desire that you be fragmented or wounded in any way. It is my desire that you live your life according to your true spiritual nature—which is, as you know, already perfect, whole, and complete. This is not a cliché. This is the Absolute Truth. And it is important that you remember that you are not the only one who is perfect, whole, and complete. You all are perfect, whole, and complete. The challenge is, are you able to discern this, or is your opinion too entangled in your judgments, criticisms, and critiques?

7. New paradigms begin with a new you

This thing that you refer to as a spiritual path is, indeed, challenging. It requires that you lose some of who you think you are. When you are so convinced that you know who you are, then you become crystallized in a certain vantage point within your perspective. Life is not one-dimensional. It is not even two-dimensional. Life is beyond three dimensions. Life is more like what you would understand to be a hologram. And it is even more than this. (However, you do not have technology at this point in time to grasp much more than this.) Life, the spiritual journey of life, requires that you surrender, that is to say, turn over, your beliefs that you treasure so much. It is these beliefs that create the foundation stones for all of your mental constructs, social-political-economic systems, and all of the spiritual paradigms in which you operate.

It is time for new paradigms. You understand this. What you often fail to understand in the concept of a new paradigm is that the new paradigm begins with a new you. Somehow you see yourself as staying somewhat the same and going out and rearranging and changing the world. No, it is you that must first be rearranged and changed. You must rearrange and change your attitudes and ideas about each other, about yourselves, and most especially about me. You must grow to understand this trinity of Love, Law, and spiritual expression in the form of humanity.

8. Say Yes unconditionally

You worry so, my dearest Deborah, about whether or not you have embodied the messages that you are instructed to give. Remember that there is only One of us here. When it comes to you human beings, there is only One of you. I say to you the things that you are to tell the people, that they are to embody, and you know that the messages are for you as well. I am not expecting you in any way to be above, beyond, or below the people. You are to walk alongside them as a peer, a colleague, and a leader. What is this leadership that I require of you? The leadership is for you to surrender and to say Yes, for you to model what this means so you can show other people what this is about. What comes as a result of saying Yes and surrendering is not to be your concern, any more than it is to be their concern.

You oftentimes want to know what it is that you are saying yes to before you say Yes. However, this is a conditional yes. I want you to just say Yes without restriction, limitation, or constriction. Just say Yes! When you just say Yes, then you will be in a better position to understand what is ahead of you as part of this trinity. You will understand that the trinity of Love, Law, and the human expression of both Love and Law are not mutually independent and exclusive of each other. You will find that they all encompass each other in a most profound way. This is part of your human path, which you refer to as life, in its most basic and elementary spiritual elements. Think upon the things that I have said here and more will dawn upon you.

IV. BEING A CHRIST

1. You don't become a Christ; it's your nature that you reveal

Teach the people about being a Christ. This is not something that they become. It is their nature, which must be revealed. Deep at the core of their being is my presence. My presence is all around them as well. The difference is experiential. When most notice my presence all around them, they get fixated on the multiplicity, the diversity in which I manifest. They begin to see things from a comparative stand point—this thing as opposed to that. They do this with their own selves, as well. The human ego gets a sense of who it is by contrast and comparison. Yet always there are those who are expressing themselves at lesser or greater levels in all things. Thus one can never truly know who one is, because the baseline is constantly in flux.

However, when they are able to experience me at the core of their being, they know that they are One with me and all things. The variety of outer expressions no longer fools them. They see through the camouflage and understand. It is not merely that they are one with these various expressions in the sense that the expressions exist and they feel connected to them. They understand that the outer expressions are alternate forms of their own beingness. The perspective changes. It is not "Oh, what a beautiful flower, we share the same life force, therefore I am One with it," but "There lies the part of me that expresses itself as a flower." Otherwise it is still dualistic thinking, still this thing as opposed to that, but merely linked. There is only One, and I am that One, and you and all others are One with me and with each other.

When you do not understand this Oneness, you are busy trying to protect yourselves, protect your sense of who you are. Even in your forgiveness work, you struggle to create "a good sense of boundaries." This is appropriate merely for understanding that you each have choice in this life and that the choices that others make need not be the ones that you accept for yourself. However, the desire to protect yourself keeps you constantly trying to distinguish your experience from others. It is the quest to determine who is good and who is bad. Your ego desires to see itself as good. However, too often this is to the exclusion of sharing this sense of goodness with others, especially those who you feel have done wrong by you.

My Reverend Daughter, you are preparing to use the old spiritual "Man Cannot Hinder Me" in your upcoming Easter services. In the human sense, "Man cannot hinder me" means "I will be staunch and vigilante. I will be on guard to ward off and defend your attacks and transgressions. You cannot hinder me because I am going to win and not let you get the best of me." In the spiritual sense, "Man cannot hinder me" is not protective; it is transcendent. Listen to what I just said—it is transcendent.

Instead of trying to stop certain events from happening, allow them to happen, understanding that their happening will not affect you in any significant way, other than to provide yet another opportunity to see through the veil of illusion that events have any significant meaning for your life. This forgiveness is not about "I am better than you." This forgiveness recognizes that "If I thought the way you thought, I would do what you did." The vigilance is in knowing that "I don't have to think like you. My awareness of this fact creates a space for others trapped by those same false notions to be freed as well. I see my transgressor as one who is as good as I am, though perhaps unaware of this goodness. Furthermore, I do not hold this unawareness against him, her, or them. Instead, I know for my transgressors what they do not know about themselves."

2. Let events happen, recognizing that they have no power over you

3. You can always reflect more of the Truth of your nature

Life then becomes a drama in which you are all acting out your parts, your characterizations, according to your understanding of your Oneness with me. In this sense there is no good or bad, things merely are. In this sense all is right with the world, since the outer is merely a perfect reflection of the inner. However, this does not mean that whatever is expressed is the highest and the best. One can always move along the continuum of expression to forms, relationships, and activities that are more reflective of the Truth of one's nature.

You humans tend to think that one becomes a Christ as a reward for a certain type of enlightenment. No. You are all Christs now. You just need to figure that out and to live as though you know it to be the Truth about you as often as possible. Notice that I said "as often as possible" and not "all of the time." If I were to have said "all of the time," you humans would give up before you even got started, thinking it is an unreasonable request. However, "as often as possible" gives you an opportunity to be conscious in very specific moments and to make choices regarding your perceptions in that moment.

All of the time is merely a series of individual moments. Even so, it is easier for you to take life one day at a time. This is fine, since one day at a time is all that you can live. If you fully commit to each moment, then you will fully commit to the whole. Understanding this about yourselves can be a benefit. Work with your humanity, not against it. I do not condemn you for being human, with your fears and your frailties. I work with you, and I desire that you work with yourselves and with each other as compassionately as I work with you.

4. The less attachment you have in the moment, the quicker you transcend

As people are encountering these words, some are understanding at the heart space and some are understanding at the head level. This is fine. It matters not into which arena you delve. It will all get you to the same place. If you cleanse your heart enough, rid yourself of the debris of hurt, fear, and hesitation, it will affect your thinking. Likewise, if your clear your mind of the clutter of confusion, resentment, and procrastination, it will open your heart.

When Jesus said "Blessed are the pure in heart," the word "heart" that he used in Aramaic encompasses the whole. It is the realm of thought, feeling, emotion, desire, and understanding. Your English language is troublesome at times because it is not a language of the Spirit. In any event, words are finite and fail to capture the essence of the infinite. However, your English language fails to capture the fullness of even your finite potential for expression.

This is why you cannot find your way to me at the center of your being in words. You must feel me. You must commune with me, recognize me often and earnestly. Why do you not do this more often? Because you are "hindered by man." You allow man-made circumstances and conditions to consume your attention and eclipse your awareness of me. "Man cannot hinder me" is about letting it go—not merely after years of psychotherapy, but in the moment. The less attachment you give to it in the moment, the quicker will be your transcendence.

I do not mean any condescension when I say that you are all children playing in the sandbox of life. If you would look at your playmates more with the type of quiet over-watching that a guardian does from the sidelines, you will be able to empathize more with the dramas without sympathizing with them. The more metaphysical types among you try not to see the dramas for fear of focusing on negativity.

5. Don't look away in denial; just look beyond what you see

This is the wrong approach; this puts you in denial. Don't look the another way. Just don't focus on what you see. Look beyond what you see to the underlying Christ pattern within. You misunderstand this too often. In trying not to support duality, you deny the fact that dualistic thinking is playing havoc all over the world. In denying the truth of duality, too often you fail to see the impacts of dualistic thinking. Thus, you unwittingly collude and abdicate your responsibility to turn things around.

6. *Being a*
Christ is
knowing you
can't be killed
and forgiving
them for trying

See it, but don't resonate with it. See it, but forgive them for they know not what they do. "Man cannot hinder you" because no person, place, or thing has the power to take your spiritual power away from you. When you remember your spiritual power, you know that you have nothing to lose no matter what happens. In fact, the greater the illusion that you pierce through, the greater is your understanding of your Christ Self. When you know this, then you will not only stop bemoaning your so-called trials and tribulations. You will embrace them as your ticket to freedom.

Sensing this, many of you attract more drama to overcome. But it is not going through the drama that creates transcendence. Transcendence is in the forgiveness of the specifics of the drama. Don't create more drama than you are willing to forgive. Being a Christ is not about martyrdom, dying on the cross because of everyone else's ignorance. Being a Christ is about knowing that you can't be killed, and your forgiving them for trying to.

V. RESURRECTION IS A CONTINUOUS PROCESS

You are soon coming upon the season that you refer to as Easter. It is springtime, the time of rebirth and rejuvenation. It is a time when the Christian world celebrates the crucifixion and subsequent resurrection of Jesus nearly two thousand years ago. There are things that I want the people to know and I want you to tell them. The price that you will pay for telling them will be high, but not as great as the price for their not hearing it.

I want the people to know that I am One God. I want the people to know that I am the God of everyone and everybody. I want the people to know that I want the bombings to stop. I want the killings to stop. I want the rapes and the molestations, the abuses and the misuses of power, to stop. I want the injustices to stop. I want you human beings to stop anything and everything that you do that affirms and declares that you and your brothers and your sisters around the world are not One. I want you to stop doing anything and everything that reinforces in your consciousness that I don't love everybody as much as I love you. I want you to stop doing anything and everything that would insinuate, let alone declare, that I would do anything for the deliberate purpose of harming or hurting another.

You do not have the right to be the judge. You do not have the right to determine the plights of other people. You do not have this right. Yes, you have a right to organize your societies, but you do not have the right to stand as lord and master over others, determining their right to live or not. And this right to live is physical, psychological, spiritual, emotional, in every sense and way. You do not have the right to limit

1. The abuses must stop, but you don't have the right to be the judge

the livingness of another individual for any reason whatsoever. And the worst reasons are the reasons that are used most often—that you would be better off, or that it is somehow ordained by me.

2. I do not ordain destruction; I am a God of the Living

I do not ordain destruction. Yes, there is a giving away of the old to make room for the new, but I do not ordain destruction. Too many of you have in your minds a mythological, archetypal notion of the hero protagonist and the evil antagonist, and that the way the protagonist wins is through the destruction of the antagonist. In this model there is only one winner. In this model somebody always has to lose. This has become too much the model in which the world thinks, lives, and moves.

When you see what appears to be devastation, destruction, the great fall of individuals or peoples, it is not for the purpose of punishing them for what they have done. It is for them to be freed from what they have done, to go on to a new life, a higher life, a better life, a life that is Good and in alignment with me and with who I am. It is to prove their consciousness. Even if all of the individuals at that particular point in time do not physically survive, there is a consciousness that shifts and changes and lives on. There is a legacy that is left, a renewal and restoration and rebirth. And those who are no longer in this human flesh form are liberated, as well, to go on to a greater understanding of the life that they now have.

3. Desire transformation, not death, for your problems

This notion that there is such a thing as death is very, very problematic. Not only do you fear death in your own lives, but it becomes a magic elixir for your problems with other people and with different circumstances. You're always waiting for something to die as though its death will get it out of your way. Understand that matter is neither created nor destroyed; it only changes form. Stop wanting things to die and start desiring their transformation. Stop wanting your circumstances, your conditions, and your relationships to die. Pray for the healing. Pray for the unification. Pray for the transformation. Pray for the release and the restoration.

Stop worrying so much about your own deaths, be they physical, spiritual, emotional, psychological, financial, or any other kind. Once again, pray for the unification, pray for the wholeness, pray for the perfect divine right expression. Rejoice in the freedom. Know that something new and great and glorious is being birthed inside of you. Wake up, welcome it with open arms. Know that you are resilient and your resistances are not.

I am not a God of the dead. I am a God of the living. All things live in me. I am not a sacrificial God. I do not rejoice in the killing of innocent things or in the spilling of innocent blood. I know the societies from which you have come, I know the cultures from which you have come. And I understand that as human beings you must do whatever it is that you need to do to understand that I am Grace in motion, to understand that your life with me is divinely protected and ordained. However, what you do in a cultural context is simply what you do in a cultural context. Do not confuse it with my requirements of you as a spiritual being.

4. There are many ways to get to know me; don't restrict each other

This notion that people must pray a certain way or say a certain thing or believe a certain thing, act a certain way, wear certain things, eat certain things, worship in certain ways, sing certain songs—all of these things are in the realm of the finite. I have no restrictions or prescriptions on these things. Whether you do them or you don't do them is really of no consequence to me. I only care about your heart. I only care about your mind. I only care about your thinking. I only care about the energy that vibrates from you. Oh, there are so many, many, many, many, many, many, many, many, many, many ways to get to know who I am. And there are just as many ways to express your love for me and to enjoy me. You can do it in the silence. You can do it in joyful praise and musical celebration. You can do it in consecrated celibacy, and you can do it procreating and teaching the children. You can do it in so many different ways, and as long as the ways get you to a point of celebrating who you are in me . . . so be it.

Stop trying to make each other wrong. Stop trying to mind your neighbor's house. Stop trying to control how another sees me or gets to me or establishes a relationship with me. See me before you see them. When you see me, and you see them in me, then you know that all is, indeed, well.

5. Resurrection is an ongoing process in your life

And as for Jesus dying on the cross to "save your sins" . . . this act of benevolence created an awareness, a vibratory pattern, so strong and deep in the collective consciousness that it is still available to be tapped into today. Do you feel the vibration? Do you sense the freedom? Do you understand that the veil of illusion that would say that you could, once again, "kill something and get rid of it" was exposed for the illusion that it was? Do you understand that the Truth crushed to earth will rise and rise again? Do you understand that if you have the courage to know, the slings and arrows of misfortune that other people shoot you with cannot hurt you? Do you know that the secret to being the Christ is forgiving them for trying to anyway? Do you know that you resurrect? Do you know that you have to spend some time in your chrysalis cocoons and tombs in order for you to change, to transform, to free yourself from the old to become the new? Do you understand the victory that this story tells? Do you understand that this is not merely an event in a single person's life but the raw material out of which the spiritual journey is built? Do you understand that this is a divine example of a process and a movement of consciousness that takes place over and over and over and over and over again in your life metaphorically, as well as, or perhaps instead of, physically? Do you understand all of this?

This is all that I care about. I only care about your under-standing. I don't care about the specifics of what you believe or don't believe. I don't care about your theological debates. I don't care about your human constructs. I care about you. I care about your life. I care about the quality of your life. I care about our relationship. I care about your relationship with other people. I care about consciousness. Do whatever you need to do to find your way to me. The difficulty here is that in trying to find your way to me many of you choose things that actually obscure your vision and your clarity. You think I'm hiding myself from you or making you jump through some kind of hoops. No, I am here. I stand here always await-ing your conscious recognition of our Oneness. Understand what I just said. I am not waiting for you to understand some fact. I am not waiting for you to accept someone else's inter-pretation of who I am. I am not waiting for you to say some words in particular. I am not waiting for you to join or par-ticipate in anything in particular. I'm just waiting for you to come to me.

I am not impatient. I am not judgmental. I walk with you, alongside you, in front of you, in back of you. I carry you. I am all around you and I wait for you to recognize me. I love you. And I will wait for you forever. ❧

6. I don't care about the specifics of what you believe; I care about you

VI. PEACE ON EARTH

1. Peace doesn't rain from the sky; it reigns in your heart

What is this thing called peace that you speak so much of, particularly at the end of the year? You speak of peace on earth as though there were a way for peace to rain upon the earth in the way that the sun's rays shine down on the earth. Peace is not something that is generated from a distant location, a planet, or any thing out there. Peace is generated in the heart. Instead of always saying "peace on earth," it might do you well to talk about peace in your heart. The only thing that you ever see demonstrated out in the world is just a pure reflection of whatever it is that you human beings are harboring in your hearts.

2. The world reflects what all of you harbor in your hearts

Understand what I just said. There is a lot of emphasis in your New Thought movement regarding manifesting what you think about. However, the mind, from a spiritual standpoint, is not a place of the intellect. Mind, the concept of mind, incorporates the totality of a being, from the mental, emotional, and spiritual standpoints. You have a tendency to want to separate out the feeling level from the analytical, thinking plane. You even do this in reference to me when you say that All is Love and All is Law. It is as though they were flip sides of the same coin, the same thing but somehow still separate and distinct. This is not the case. You cannot see, experience, know, appreciate, or utilize my Love without embracing it as Law, nor are you able to do the same with Law unless you are able to embrace it in Love. What do I mean when I say this?

Outside of healing the concept of separation, the application of Spiritual Principle means nothing. The only thing Spiritual Laws do is express and bring everything back to a point of Unitary Wholeness. The Laws do not operate separately or distinctively from one another. You cannot distinguish one Law from another Law in its operation because they all are the same. Are there really differences between my Law operating as Order, as Guidance, as Abundance, as Harmony, etc., etc., etc.? It is all the same thing. You perceive it as being different things depending upon the sensory apparatus that you are using; however, they are not separate and distinct things. It is good that you speak of it as Law, because as Law it allows you to understand that there is nothing arbitrary or inconsistent about it.

When you think about the application of Love, you have a tendency to place it more in the realm of the emotions. However, as you know, your emotions can never operate independently from your realm of thinking. There may be those times when the two appear to be in opposition to one another, but they never operate in a manner that is mutually exclusive. Remember that you arrive at various emotions because of what you think about things. So the two are intertwined. Even when your emotions appear to be driving you, when they appear to be in opposition to your conscious desires and wishes, they are still caught up in the realm of your thinking. Here, however, the thinking is at the level of the subconscious, or what you sometimes refer to as the unconscious. You have internalized certain ideas, opinions, beliefs, and attitudes to such an extent that they formulate a pattern to which your emotions are constantly responding and reacting.

3. Your thoughts and emotions are intertwined

Your emotions are always reactionary. They are responsive to certain catalytic events. However, you fail sometimes to realize that the things that they are reacting to are often just that—catalytic. This causes you to get caught up in a lot of judging and blaming and bad feelings about the so-called triggers of your emotions. Although this may be of some therapeutic value at times, it is most often a waste of time. What is useful, however, is that the intensity of your emotions can be a good indicator to you of what you are really thinking and harboring in your consciousness, at levels that you are unaware of.

4. The need to judge subsides as you embrace the whole

However, when you understand that Love and Law are the same thing, that the heart and the mind are the same thing, you will have nothing to be concerned about. When you get to those places where your emotions appear to be ruffled and rattled, you will remember that things are not out of control, that nothing can hurt or harm you, that everything is in a Divine Order. Your worries, concerns, and human angst will then subside. Likewise, when you understand that everything is a Unitary Wholeness, that all things come together in my Divine Order, then your judgment, criticism, confusions about why things are the way that they are, will subside. And you will no longer feel such a need to try to separate yourself out from the things that you don't like. You will not have so much of a need to try to make a distinction between good and evil, between what's right and what's wrong, and you will embrace the whole of it. This is what Love is. Love is that power, that concept, that unifies and brings everything back to its state of Wholeness.

5. Your peace comes with too many restrictions

The reason why many of you do not demonstrate what it is that you consider to be peace on earth is because you are not at peace in your hearts. You cannot demonstrate anything that you cannot embody and express. As long as you keep thinking of peace as being something out there, it will never reign on earth. There is always the tendency to want to point fingers at someone or something else as being the most appropriate initiator of the peace. In this vein, too many of you are sitting back, waiting, wondering, demanding, even, that someone or something else "make the first move." You might consider healing, reconciling, forgiving if "so-and-so does such-and-such," or if "this thing happens as opposed to that thing." It is all quite conditional.

This is why many of you do not experience the peace within. Your peace comes with too many conditions. Your conditions are restrictions, confines, limitations, and most often false constructs as well. What do I mean when I say "false constructs"? You have determined who is right, who is wrong, how the wrong should be righted, and what the right should do about the wrong. And what the wrong needs to do so that it will forever be right. This is an awful lot to know, especially when you perceive so little. I marvel at how much you human beings think you know about how to set things "straight," particularly when they are so crooked in your own consciousness. If I had a sense of humor (in a human sense), I would be quite amused at this.

However, there is really nothing funny about this in the way that it impacts you individually and collectively. This sense that you are right, even when you think that you are so right about your having been the one who was wrong, creates a situation where too many hurdles must be jumped over, hoops jumped through, and tricks turned in order for the "wrongs to be righted." This keeps all of your energy tied up in the past, in your wounds, in your false notions about how much you have been negatively impacted by the conditions and the circumstances of your life.

The irony, however, is that with all the attention that gets placed upon these hurts, wounds, and ailments, the attention is misplaced. Even though there is all of this focus, it never penetrates beneath the surface. You rarely get down to the heart of it. Part of your salvation lies in really feeling your way through the heart space. This means that you must move beyond the tendency to merely validate your feelings on a human level. It requires that you evaluate your emotions and your feelings in the context of spiritual Truth. Most of you do not want to do this. Even in your healing work you still reserve the right to your human feelings, even when they are out of alignment with spiritual Truth. You would rather live with that sense of tension, conflict, yea, even contradiction, than go about the business of transforming your emotions into something that is in alignment with the Spiritual Laws.

6. Transform your emotions so they align with Spiritual Laws

Too many of you assume that your emotions, how you feel about things, is synonymous with the actual experience itself. Through your feelings you not only archive your life experience but memorialize it. You fear that if you change your feelings about what has happened to you, then somehow your past itself will be erased. Too many of you are hanging on with such pride to the markers of your lives, making shrines out of them. You go back and you visit, revisit, and build altars at your turning points. Even the circumstances and situations that you found painful or didn't even like . . . you still pay homage to them for their catalytic effect in spurring you on to a new path and a new direction.

7. To know peace, experience what's in your heart

This is not a judgment or even a criticism. It is an observation. You humans have such a deep belief in your time-space continuum, it is difficult for you to even be present, let alone truly contemplate the possibilities of your future. This is because so much of your thinking is caught up in the accumulative total of where you have been, rather than the freshness of the moment that you are in, at any given point in time.

In order for you to experience peace in your hearts, you must experience what's in your heart. You must uncover, unravel, unveil, and reveal the things that are lurking there. You think that by not giving them attention, they will not grow. However, they will fester. And just as water moves into stagnation when there is no motion or activity, so it is within your conscious psyche. Some movement, some clearing out, some going with the flow of life, will keep things fresh. Not only does movement keep things fresh; paradoxically, it also muddies up the lines of distinction. Blurring of your familiar lines is something that you fear. However, when the water comes rushing in, everything gets so interconnected and convoluted, in a generic sense, that you cannot make a distinction anymore about which part of the water is in this little pool area and which is not. It is a joy to watch this merging in the pool, yet it causes much consternation when you see it happening in your life.

You desire so to have some boundaries, some borders, some places of distinction so that you can distinguish yourselves from one another. You pray for the Oneness, you talk about the Oneness, but most of you are scared to death of it because you fear that you will be lost in its Allness. This is a scary thing to the ego, because the ego knows of itself only by contrast and comparison. And if it all comes together and melts and merges into the One, then where are you within the scheme of things?

This is part of the difficulty with your being able to demonstrate peace on earth. It means that each of you has to relinquish some of the identities that you have had about yourselves and who you are in order to experience your Oneness with other people. It means that you will have to rethink who you are within the scheme of the world. The irony here, once again, is that the rethinking will actually have you coming out as a net winner. You will gain in your insights and your understanding. It will be revolutionary and exceedingly transformational. However, most of you would rather cling to your smaller version of your understanding of yourself because at least then, in your mind, you know who you are—you recognize yourselves. This is what you refer to sometimes as your "comfort zone."

There is nothing to be afraid of, my children, in growing beyond who you think you are. There is nothing wrong, my children, in stretching your spiritual wings and taking flight above all of the minutiae of your life. There is nothing wrong with the lines becoming so blurry that you do not know where you end or begin, or where your brothers and sisters end or begin. There is absolutely nothing wrong with the Absolute. There is nothing wrong in moving beyond thinking of yourselves and the world in such relative terms. There is nothing wrong with your being the ones to take the first step.

What about this song that is so popular in your New Thought circles, "Let There Be Peace on Earth and Let It

8. Oneness requires you to rethink who you are in the scheme of things

9. Be willing to be the one to take the first step towards peace

Begin with Me"? Think upon this, my children. How does it begin with you? Think on this, my children. Ask yourselves from day to day, "How can the peace begin with me?" If you will do this in earnest and will take strides to put into action the revelations that are revealed to you, then you will, indeed, begin to see more of this notion of peace on earth. You will see that the alphabetical letters in "earth" and "heart" are the same. You rearrange them and they become essentially the same. This is the challenge of your life. Rearrange the letters, rearrange the data, rearrange your opinions and your perceptions so that they come into alignment with my will. Good will towards all is my will, and, once again, unless your will and my will are synchronized with one another, the exact same dynamics will take place that I just discussed regarding peace.

Think on these things, especially during the holiday seasons. I love you, I love you all. Remember to love yourselves and each other. Remember to love me.

VII. I Am the Balm That Heals

The question is asked in Scripture, "Is there no balm in Gilead?" There is a popular spiritual song that affirms that there is, in fact, a "balm in Gilead." What is a balm? And what is Gilead? And what does this mean to you in your day? Gilead was a place of great stress and strife. It was a place where hearts had become hardened, where turmoil and conflict reigned supreme. It was a place where the individual members of society did not treat each other well. Even the so-called oppressed peoples were not treating each other well. Perhaps the saddest thing of all is that all of this turmoil, conflict, strife, and fighting was going on inside of the individual people, as well. This should come as no surprise, since the outer is merely a reflection of the inner. If there is a situation where individuals appear to be quite at odds with each other, rest assured that the place where they are most at odds is within their own selves. You long so for this thing called peace. It is a desire, and for many of you a desire in your deepest heart of hearts. However, there is little intent on your part to manifest this peace that you say you desire.

What do I mean when I say that you have no intent to manifest this peace? When one has an intent, one is determined to have their desire brought into manifestation. When one has an intent, one "goes the extra mile." One does whatever one must do, or needs to do (even if one doesn't like it), in order to make certain that the unfoldment keeps progressing. You human beings come up against these mental, emotional, psychological, and spiritual walls (as you would say) where you have determined that you will go this far and no further. You have all of your reasons, your justifications, your excuses for

1. Do you have the intent to manifest peace?

why it is that you can hang onto the resentments, the bitterness, the judgments, the negative opinions that you have of each other and even of yourselves. You hang onto this with such fervor. For one to know what one knows deep in one's heart is a deep spiritual inclination. I understand this totally. This is the context in which you have been created as a spiritual being in flesh form. However, be quite careful about the content that you are so intent about claiming as your ultimate reality. What is it that you know? What is it that you affirm to be the Truth? What truth is it that you are so unwilling to let go of? And is what you are so unwilling to let go of the real Truth, with a capital "T" (as you would say)?

2. You can't see the Truth through all of your filters

You must learn to look at your surroundings, the events of your life, the impulses of your emotions, and the analysis of your perceptions, and bring them into alignment with spiritual Truth. What do I mean when I say this? Too many of you think that you are somehow being asked to distort reality, that you are somehow being asked, in a falsely manipulative way, to simply try to rewrite history to make yourselves feel better. This is offensive to many of you. It reminds you of a criminal-type activity, as though you are going back in time and changing the ledger sheets of debits and credits to make the bottom line appear to be different than what it actually was. You feel as though you have no right to do this; to do anything else other than letting the record stand is some sort of perjury, a lie. However, my children, when you understand what I am suggesting, yea, requiring, that you do, you will see that I am not merely asking you to go back and "whitewash" the events of your life. What I am asking you to do is to go deeper. Come higher. Take off your blinders. Unplug your ears. Lay down your armor. Take off your boxing gloves. Set your helmets aside. Drop your holsters. Lay down your swords.

How can you possibly see the Truth through the filter of all of this thickness, through the filter of all of this density of perception? You worry about distorting things. Herein is the distortion. How can you see through a window that has the curtain drawn, the shade down, a closely knit screen on it that would keep out even the smallest of so-called intruders, bars to protect the precious cargo inside . . . how can you see out of such a window? What you will see is the curtain, the shade, the screen, the bars—these are the things that will be the focal point of your attention.

So, if I ask you to look out of the window and to see all of the beauty around you . . . and if I ask you to realize that in order to soak it all in, to see it all, to be able to open up the window and smell the beauty and interact with it so that it is not distant, so that you may actually feel the breeze upon your face and smell the sweet fragrance of the scents that I have designed . . . then is it criminal to ask you to take down the shades and the drapes and the screens and bars in order to see better, more clearly? Are you somehow doing an injustice by creating a clearer space to see through? The fact that your perception of what you see will change dramatically when there are fewer obstructions in the way is self-evident.

3. Are you looking for me or for validation of your limited view?

So the choice is always yours, my children, as to what you are looking at and looking for. Seek and ye shall find. What are you looking for in earnest? Are you looking for me? Are you looking for the Good, for the beauty, for my glory reigning supreme in all events and activities? Or are you looking for the evidence that would collude with, concur with, coincide with the limited view that you get as you simply glance through your window that is covered with all of your protective materials?

A balm is a remedy. A balm soothes and heals. You rub it in and let it soak in. You can feel it as it begins to work. To the tired, the weary, the one who is hurting and in pain, a balm is a most welcome relief. To the ones who are in what you would consider to be "good shape," the balm is a comfort. One can rest assured that in the hour of need there is something to turn to. Knowing that there is something to turn to, something that heals, something that restores, enables you to step out, to take risks (as you would perceive them to be), to dig in, to move beyond the limitations that appear to be right in front of you, around you, in you. "Where is the balm in Gilead to heal the wounded heart?"

4. The balm provides the peace that passes human understanding

People have been searching for this balm since time memorable. It is the same yearning that one finds in the human heart regardless of time, culture, history, or geographic location. At an intellectual and material level of manifestation, there would appear to be great differences among the peoples of this planet. However, at the most fundamental level of your beingness, as human beings, you all have the same essential questions about life, its meaning and purpose, who I am, how things should be. It is longing that characterizes your human experience. It is quite typical of human beings to look outside of themselves for this balm. It is not necessarily part of their nature to search externally. It is, however, a by-product of their inability to understand that they are not merely human beings but are spiritual beings in the flesh form. When they know that this balm is not outside of themselves, when they know that the balm, the healing, the remedy, is deep within their own souls, there is a sense of peace that pervades their total countenance. This doesn't mean that everybody's going to start acting right in Gilead. It doesn't mean that the balm will wipe away all strife, struggle, and anxiety.

What the balm will do, however, is provide you with the peace that passes human understanding. When you find the balm within yourself, it is not of your own making. And you are most sure of this. You find it in your heart. But you are quite aware of the fact that it did not originate in your heart. Your heart is its resting place. Your heart is its robe. The heart is an incubator for it. But you are quite aware of the fact that this peace in your heart is an impregnation from me. I am the Balm. I am the Balm. I am the Balm. I am the Balm. I am the

Balm. I am the Balm. I am the Balm. I am the Balm. I am the
Balm. I am the Balm. I am the Balm. (Breathe.)

I am the Balm. I heal. I restore. I renew and rejuvenate. I transform and I uplift. I created you out of myself. You are always
perfect, whole, and complete because I am. Your challenge in
life is not to make everybody else peaceable, not to make
everything in the world all right. Your challenge is to know
that you are me and that I am you, and to allow me to plant
my seeds deep within your hearts, deep, deep within your
minds. Your job is to nurture these seeds, to protect them
through your nurturing and nourishment. This is your job.
And when you do your job, you will find that you will have
many of the manifestations that you desire. Quit worrying
about when am I going to do my job. I'm on my job all of the
time. I do my job, and I do my job well. This is not a boast.
This is simply a fact. And when you are able to accept that I
do my job as a given, as the starting point, as the very reference point of your very life, you will then understand more
about what your job is.

*5. I am
the Balm*

You must start with something. You must have some fundamental basis of belief upon which everything else is built. It is
like your mathematical systems, where you start off with the-
orems and postulates. In your American society you use a
numeric system based upon the number ten. Its most fundamental postulate is that one plus one equals two. You have to
start somewhere. So where do you start? What is the foundation stone that is the corner of your entire belief system?
What is it that you know to be Absolutely True, with that capital "T" again? In your mathematical system everyone must
simply accept that one plus one equals two. It cannot be
proved. It cannot be disproved. It is the beginning. If mathe-
matics were Scripture, it would read, "From the beginning,
one plus one equals two." If there is a place where this is not
true, then the whole mathematical system comes crashing

*6. What is the
fundamental
basis of your
spiritual belief
system?*

down. However, if you understand that "one plus one equals two" is true and are able to accept it in your heart as being true, then what incredible things about life and the universe you can discover! What principles you are able to use for magnificent purposes!

However, if you are not able to embrace "one plus one equals two" at its most fundamental level, you will be intimidated by the magnitude of mathematical possibilities. The very information that would otherwise be for your enlightenment and understanding would appear to overwhelm you because you have not laid the foundation stones for understanding. This is the difficulty with many of you in your spiritual work. You are as overwhelmed by spiritual principles and concepts as you are by mathematical ones. You can say in such earnest about your spirituality, "I'm just not that spiritual," in much the same way as people boast that they are not mathematically inclined.

I understand that there are all types of ways of learning, of thinking. I am not suggesting that people are wrong if their primary way of understanding is not mathematical. But in every system there are always fundamentals that must be understood and embraced. If one is an artist and works with colors, then one needs to understand that there are certain primary colors. This is the starting point. Artists must understand how these colors interact with each other. Everything has a starting point. So . . . what is your fundamental belief? What is the foundation stone upon which you stand? What is your most elementary understanding? Where is the "one plus one equals two" of your life? Think about this.

7. I am the balm; don't use me as a bomb

I am a balm. I said that I am a balm, b-a-l-m. I am not the bomb, b-o-m-b. There is a big difference here. Too many of you who think that you have come to understand me at some deep level use what you think you know as a bomb, not a balm. You beat people up with it. You mutilate their spirits. You wreak havoc in their lives with your self-righteousness. You build an arsenal of weaponry and then have the absolute audacity to say that you are doing it in my name, for my good. You use your weapons, so you think, to BRING PEOPLE TO ME????? How dare you!!!!

The very reason why so many of the ones that you are so intent on trying to "save" run from me is because you have tried to cram me down their throats in a way that ignored who they are, that was insensitive to their human plight and circumstances, that desecrated their esteem, that used a fire extinguisher on their inner flame. I am not a bomb. I am a balm. Don't use me as a weapon of destruction. Use me as an agent of healing. Use my words to soothe, not to strangle. Use my words to affirm and not annihilate. I trust that you understand this message. If you don't understand what I've just said now, perhaps you won't. The choice is yours. And I still love you. I love you all. Just love each other and love yourselves and love me.

VIII. SAFETY AND SEPTEMBER 11

1. Each party plays a role in the creation of a conflict

Yes, what a time, indeed, it is in your society. You are right in your understanding that all is energy and that energy is a dance upon itself. In conflictual situations there is always a role that each party has played in the creation of the conflict. It would serve your country well to understand what it is about the ways in which it conducts itself and carries out its foreign policy affairs that negatively impacts other people. It is important that Americans understand that there are perceptions other than their own.

As you often teach in your diversity workshops, my Reverend Daughter, there is a vast difference between one's intent and the impact of one's actions upon another. Just because one does not have an ill intent does not mean that there has not been a negative, perhaps even devastating, impact on others. Your need to consider yourselves objective, just, and fair people makes it difficult for you, at times, to assume responsibility for, let alone look at, the ways in which your actions have diverged away from your intent.

2. Accept that perceptions and perspectives may differ

I am not talking about either judgment or blame. The concept that I speak to you about is perception. It is perception that makes the difference in how an event is, in fact, experienced. You must learn that perceptions differ, not only from individual to individual but from collective consciousness to collective consciousness, as well. That is to say, individuals from a particular cultural background may tend to have similar perceptions about the same things, and these perceptions may not always align with the perceptions of other individuals from other cultural backgrounds. This is not say that one is better than the other. This is not to say that one is right and the other is wrong. It is just to say that they are different.

Your American society must come to grips with this. Americans talk about diversity these days with such pride. However, there is little appreciation for the fact that diversity means difference. The pride seems to be in the assumption that there are a lot of different people from different backgrounds that are all being "American." What America must understand is that there are a lot of Americans who are very different people from very different cultural backgrounds.

The difference in the emphasis in "different kinds of people comprise America" and "America is comprised of different kinds of people" is not merely semantic. The net result is different depending upon how you frame the issue of what it means to be an American. The issue has been framed traditionally by the "melting pot" concept. That is to say, there is a way in which immigrants and people who have made it into your country are expected to lose their indigenous identities and assume an identity of "American." Even with all of your "who-lee-lah" that you have going on now about diversity, this melting pot conceptualization still has a strong hold both in and on the American psyche. There is little appreciation for what it is that people bring to the table that may distinguish them one from another.

3. You can't embrace diversity yet ignore differences

If you start with the whole—that everybody is American who is here—and then allow yourself to look at the various differences among them, you are likely to appreciate what is going on in the individual and collective consciousnesses of individuals from different cultural backgrounds.

Many people have reduced all of this to what they refer to as "political correctness." This is extremely dangerous. It trivializes a critical issue, an issue that will literally make or break your society. What do I mean by this?

4. Your ability to deal with cultural difference is critical

What do I mean when I say "make or break your society"? As Americans you have tried to make yourselves safe in what you perceive to be an unsafe world. You have attempted to create your own sense of safety by the invention of your own gadgets, military weapons, and protective mechanisms. You think that if you can just find ways to keep everybody else out, or to strike at them first, then you will in fact be safe. However, the recent events of the day, more specifically, the attacks on the World Trade Center in New York City and the Pentagon in Washington, D. C. yesterday, make you much more aware of the fact that all of your sophisticated defense mechanisms are not enough to keep you "safe."

5. Technology can never make you safe

In the wake of this event you are turning once again to technology. You are turning once again to protocols and techniques. In the wake of the hysteria and the fear there is a tendency to want to come up with new gadgets, new ways of doing things, that are simply perpetuating the same old paradigm.

Oh no, my children, this is not the way to be safe. Safety can never be found in defense. Safety can never be found in offense. Safety is beyond defensive or offensive measures. As long as one is still engaged in either, it is in direct contradiction to the notion of safety. Why do I say this? Because the consciousness that obtains, sustains. You can't build safety out of a consciousness of fear.

6. Conflicts arise out of consciousness; weapons can't resolve conflicts

The safety that you are looking for is not in your technology. The safety that you are looking for is not in your gadgets. The safety that you are looking for is in your own heart and mind. Understand what it is that I am saying here. You MUST understand what it is that I am saying here!!!

Conflict does not begin with weapons. The use of weapons is the evidence that there is a conflict. Doing something one way or another to the weapons is not going to address the underlying conflict. Conflict arises out of consciousness. Consciousness is directly related to perception. When people are in conflict, it is over their varying perceptions. This may sound overly simplistic or like I am addressing you in a way that does not credit your maturity. However, if everything I just said appears to be obvious to you, then my question is, "If it is so obvious, why don't you act like you see it?"

You cannot address conflict without addressing the matters of the heart and the mind. What is in your heart? *What* is in your heart? (I have posed this question to you in many other letters. It might serve you well to review the letter "Spiritual Availability," that I revealed to the Reverend Daughter Deborah here, several months ago.) What is in your heart? What do you really feel? What do you really think about—not just about yourself or the circumstances, but also about the other people involved? What is in your mind? What is your deep intent?

7. Resolving conflicts involves issues of the heart and mind

The difficulty here in "safety" is that it is treated like a one-way street. When individuals are busy trying to make themselves safe, rarely do they have in mind making it safe for everybody. They want to be safe themselves, even if that means that the creation of that safety might make someone else feel unsafe. Their only concern is not being unsafe themselves.

It is much like the game of "musical chairs" that's popular in your society among children. In this game there are chairs that are set up in a circle and individuals skip around the chairs to the music. When the music stops each is to scramble to sit on a chair. However, by design of the game, there are fewer chairs than there are individuals who need to be seated. Therefore, someone is always left standing. And you just keep at this game until there is only one person left and one chair. Not only is somebody left standing at each round, but at the conclusion of each round another chair is taken away. So there is never a chance for everybody to win. Your biggest concern in your society is that you not be the one who is left standing.

8. Until you intend for all to be safe, you are playing "musical chairs"

SAFETY AND SEPTEMBER II

Oh, no! Until the intent is for everyone to have a chair, then your politics are nothing more than musical chairs. Once there is a chair for everybody, there is no game of musical chairs anymore. It shifts the whole, entire paradigm.

9. You need new skills and perspectives, not new weapons

Do you want the paradigms to shift so that everybody can win? Or do you just want to make certain that you are not the one who is left standing? Can you conceive of a world in which there is justice and liberty for all? The very fact that justice and liberty for all seems too much to even hope for is, indeed, part of the problem. It is not your intent to have a world that is fair and just for all people. This is true not only on the global level; this is true when it comes down to your own communities. This is true when it comes right down to your own individual households. It is this consciousness that must, indeed, be addressed.

The safety is in your own minds and in your own hearts. It's not weapons that you need now, my children; it's new perspectives. You need understanding. You need compassion. You need more negotiation skills. You need better ways of looking at things that have the intent of a "win/win." You need to know more about compromise. You need to know more about collective multicultural decision-making. You need to know more about creating ground rules that are intended to have all of the individuals involved be safe.

10. If you see the world as hostile, you'll always have an enemy to fight

You will never find safety outside of your understanding of the Spiritual Oneness of us all. The difficulty here is not just that you are afraid of these terrorists. You are simply afraid. Who you are afraid of just rotates, changes like the musical chairs. At times you are afraid of Castro in Cuba. At times you are afraid of the KGB in Russia. At times you are afraid of the drug lords in Columbia. At times you are afraid of the Black Panthers in the United States. It just keeps rotating and changing. Many of you are afraid of the gay activists. Now there is this wholesale fear about Arabs and the Islamic culture

The Sacred Yes

and religion. They have become the new targets of your demonization.

As long as you are convinced that it is a hostile world, you will always need to have an enemy to fight. You will always need to have someone, or something, to scapegoat. As long as fear is what is in your hearts and your minds, it doesn't really matter so much what or who you are afraid of, because it will always be something or somebody.

When you understand that there is really only One of us here, when you understand that I am the Mother/Father God Creator of All and that you are all brothers and sisters in my love and my embrace, then you will know that there are no "favored children." You will know that I have given my resources to all of my children equally. You will know that you do not have the right to hoard from your siblings. You will understand that you are not entitled to more than anyone else simply because you are older, stronger, more educated, or whatever. In a spiritual family you look out for one another. You look for additional ways to level the playing field among all of you more than you try to make sure that you are not the one left standing.

11. Whatever happens to one of you happens to all of you

In a spiritual community there is concern about the so-called others as well. This is not difficult, because in the true spiritual paradigm there aren't any "others." In the real, true spiritual paradigm everyone is connected to the whole. Anything that happens to anyone has a rippling impact on the whole. You want so-called others to win not simply as a do-good measure but because you can't win until all of you can win. As long as there is some part of you that is being discriminated against, marginalized, or oppressed in any way, shape, or form, then the whole of you cannot succeed.

12. Learn to value other cultures, to bridge cultural gaps

There must be both a desire and an intent to bridge cultural gaps. There must be a desire and an intent, a willingness, to venture out and to understand. America, the United States of America, because of its geographic location lives a relatively isolated existence. It is important that you teach your children the values of other cultures. It is important that they learn to speak different languages.

In learning other languages there grows to be an understanding of the ways in which other cultures think. Linguistics deeply affects comprehension, perceptions, and analytical processes. Language structures say much about how a culture processes information. Therefore, even learning another language helps one to grow and to understand that there are many different ways to be able to communicate, operate, and view the world.

13. Consider the interests of all parties in your solutions

There is a process that I directed the Reverend Deborah here to use when she was a real estate manager for a large insurance company. In her investment negotiations, even though she understood what her company's position should be, I instructed her to keep utmost in her mind an understanding of what would create a "win" situation for the person or institution who she was contracting with. With this intent in her mind, the negotiated contract was not a legal weapon to keep her company safe. It was the evidence of the agreements and the meeting of the minds that all parties had arrived at. Rather than a weapon to be used in hindsight or for punitive purposes if violations occurred, the contract became a living, breathing document that would serve as a guidepost into the future. It would be something that all parties could reference to refresh their memories of shared moments of high resolve. It was for the purpose of helping them to remember their purpose. Understand this.

Understanding the other person's or group's needs will also serve you well when working through societal conflicts. Instead of just trying to hedge in your own position, ask yourself, "What is it that would create a 'win' for the others who are involved?" And then genuinely search your soul and see what portions of that you might actually be able to accommodate. And if there is much that you cannot accommodate, what might you be able to offer as an alternative? However, once again, it must sincerely have as its intent that the other people come out whole. You cannot be whole unless everyone else is whole, because there is only a Oneness here.

Remember these things. Think on these things. Act upon these things. Dedicate yourself to these things. And I am saying all of this in the present imperative verb tense of Scripture, which is "a command to do something in the future with a continuous and a repeated action."

I love you, I love all of you. The question is, can you love me and also love all of you? ✿

14. Explore what you can do to create a win/win for all

Systems That Support

CONTENTS

1. The spiritual, religious, secular, and civil have become convoluted

2. I have never ever sanctioned any one particular form of marriage

3. Procreation is not a spiritual requirement

4. Institutionalized religious marriages have become political matters

5. When individuals choose each other, marriage is a spiritual matter

6. Marriage as a holy relationship should bring people closer to me

7. I am unconcerned about your civil and cultural practices

8. Your loyalty and fidelity to me are mirrored in your marriages

9. Marital agreements don't always reflect your spiritual Truth

10. I have no sanctions for or against marriages based on gender

11. In Spirit there is no gender

12. All love should mirror back my love and be celebrated

13. Create societies in which all individuals are equal and valued

1. Marriage is symbolic of the commitment one has with me

2. Don't identify with traditions more than you identify with me

3. Norms, standards, and mores do not honor Spirit and
   your magnificence

4. To find who you are, you must marry your own divinity

5. Marrying me transforms your work from drudgery to ministry

I. SPIRITUALITY, RELIGION, AND THE CHURCH

1. There are differences between spirituality, religion, and the church

There are things that I must say to you. There are differences between spirituality, religion, and the church. It is important that these distinctions be made because the three have become so incredibly convoluted in themselves and with each other that individuals, in their dissatisfaction with one or more, are avoiding the other(s). It is important from a sociological, developmental standpoint that these issues be addressed at this point in time in your American history.

2. Spirituality is the innate aspect of you that is Divine, One with me

Spirituality is that aspect of your essence that is Divine. Spirituality is transcendent of time, culture, history, and tradition. Spirituality is innate. That is to say, all individuals are spiritual. When I say that it is the part of you that is Divine, do not make the common mistake of thinking that I am asserting that there is some small, discrete portion of yourself that is not human. Most often this is characterized as your being a human being with a "soul." No. When I say your spirituality is that part of you that is Divine, I use the term "Divine" to distinguish, in the context of your personal identity, your true spiritual nature from all of the outer forms of expression that you take on and manifest. The whole of you is spiritual, but to the extent that you do not observe this on a continuous basis it appears that only a part of you is spiritual. These are your words and the way that you frame things. It is at least a start. If you are not even able to perceive some part of you that transcends all of your human conditions and circumstances, you will never be able to conceive of the fact that all of you is spiritual and Divine, and that none of you is defined by the outer shapes and forms that you take.

In this place of your spirituality you are in your authenticity. In this place of your spirituality you are totally at One with me. You are One with yourself and with all things. If in fact you were able to access, and remember to practice, the ever present reality of our divinity consciously and on a consistent basis, then there would not be a need for either religion or the church. The purpose of both of these, religion and the church, should ultimately be about leading people back to their spirituality, about leading people back to their innocence in their spiritual awareness of themselves and the world. Church and religion should be the servant of the realm of Spirit and should be there to support the spiritual growth and development of each and every person in society. You have not come to a place in your history and culture where you value everyone on the human level, let alone value them equally.

3. Church and religion should be the servant of Spirit

In order for the human psyche to grasp and perceive its divinity, its spirituality, it must have a certain degree of esteem in itself as human. To the extent that your societies interfere with and prevent individuals from developing a healthy sense of wealth, creativity, personal power, and general well-being, you are interfering with their ability to understand all of their spiritual powers. Paradoxically, oftentimes it is the individuals who have had seemingly the greatest obstacles, hurdles, crises, oppressions to overcome who have, in fact, learned who I am and who they are in me. While the dominating, manipulating, oppressing, that makes people unequal may have the effect of preventing the "underdogs" from discovering their power, the impact is most negative upon those who are in "positions of power." The more that individuals feel as though they must be superior, the more they think they must subject other people to subjectivity, the more they try to dominate and control things, the less they understand that they are in the world as spiritual beings.

4. To perceive one's own divinity, one needs healthy, not inflated, self-esteem

Herein lies much of the problem. Those who rise to positions of hierarchy in your institutional structures that are developed for religious purposes carry with them the same type of consciousness they would carry if they were building secular institutions. Understand what it is I am saying here. When you know who I am, when you understand your Oneness with all people and things, then there is no desire, let alone a sense or a need, to try to dominate anyone or anything. Those who are in positions of domination and control do not feel safe in the world. They are concerned that if things do not go their way they will be worse off, so they exercise all of their self-appointed privileges and entitlements to create a world that would appear to be safe for them and their own. Thus the lack of equality and egalitarianism has a detrimental impact on the ones who are placed in positions of power as well as on people who are in positions, at least from a civil, secular standpoint, of powerlessness.

5. Religion is a culture's accumulated beliefs about spirituality

Religion is the theology, the doctrine, the accumulation of beliefs about spirituality that are particular to given societies. Everything works together as a systematic whole. So the way in which people view their spirituality is greatly influenced by everything surrounding them—the terrain, the weather, the neighboring nations and tribes, their own racial/genetic backgrounds, how they relate to music and the arts, their scientific developments, their theological advancements, and the like. Religions become points of collective consciousness and agreement about the ways in which Universal Spiritual Principles, which live in the heart of each individual, are to be practically applied in the context of that society. Religions are developed for the purpose of operationalizing what "should be" the understanding of individuals at the level of their deep spiritual nature. Because the shaping and the perception of how people see their spirituality is so influenced by cultural aspects, it is no wonder that different "religions" spring up and become dominant in certain parts of the world. If it were not for the wholesale exporting and colonialization of religious practice, you would find that all peoples upon the face of the earth would be practicing the religions that are indigenous to their culture and society.

The church, on the other hand, is another matter. Religion tries to operationalize spirituality, and the church tries to operationalize religion. The church is typically set up to be the organizational, institutionalized structure that goes about the business of helping to create systems and networks that enable the individuals of that society to put into daily practice the edicts and tenets of their religion. Part of the difficulty here is that not only the church but the religions themselves have become institutionalized. Understand what is it that I am saying here. Religion should never be thought of as an institution. Religion is the spirit of the Law, so to speak. Religion should carry the principles, the presumptions, the assumptions, the spiritual building blocks that enable people to integrate what they know about their formless, timeless, cultureless spirituality in the context of the very real society in which they live.

6. Religion should be the spirit of the Law, not an institution

Thus, everything that comes from an institutionalized organizational structure like a church should be weighed against the perspectives, guidance, awareness, and consciousness of the living Spiritual Principles that theoretically are in the religion. If the church and the religion become synonymous with each other, if they become the same thing, if they commingle to the point of pure enmeshment . . . then where are the checks and balances? How will the institutions (which create the protocols, practices, procedures, all the outer forms of ritualistic expression that you engage in, in your daily practices) know that they are in alignment with spirituality? If religion and the church are convoluted together, then what is there for the church to turn to, to see if, in fact, it is living up to its high mission and purpose? Spirituality must always be above religion, and religion must always be above the church. If you make the church above religion, you are also making the

7. Spirituality must be above religion, and religion above the church

church above spirituality. Then where is the accountability? The church (or any human institution) must always be supervised by, scrutinized by, reviewed by, monitored by, and evaluated by some higher principle or authority. This principle or authority is not necessarily an organized entity. Rather, the church must pass the scrutiny of the heart, the scrutiny of spiritual logic, and the scrutiny of Spiritual Principle in action. The church is there to support the religious ideas, and religion is there to support individuals' spirituality. If individual spirituality is getting lost within the maze of religion and the organizational milieu of the church . . . then something is very wrong.

8. The church is to support religion, which is to support spirituality

It is time to get back to the basics. It is important to remember who is serving what. You often say, Reverend Daughter, that "It is we who have emotions, our emotions shouldn't have us." Human beings should be the ones who are in control, and emotions express through them. However, your emotions act out as if they existed on their own, running amuck and manipulating human beings to become places through which they express (far too many of you live your lives in this way). So also, churches go about the business of perpetuating themselves. They exist for the sake of their own existence. Rather than spiritual beings being able to turn to religion and to the church as places to support them, the equation gets turned around. It is institutions who begin to believe that the individuals on the spiritual paths are there to do the bidding of the church. Rather than people having religion and having a church, the church has a religion and has people to express through. This is backwards.

Part of the reason why this is so dangerous is that churches, being finite human creations, are by their finite nature exclusionary. There are those who will belong and there are those who will not. This develops into the sense of there being a constituency, that is to say, the church will perceive itself as existing for the benefit of particular people. And even when it sees itself as being for the benefit of all, all are not considered equal in this formula. There are those who are actually part of the church, so to speak, and there are those to whom the church is outreaching but who are fundamentally not a part of the operations or the composition, the membership, of the whole. Spirituality, on the other hand, is not exclusive in any way. There is room enough for everyone to be included, to be involved, to participate in an equal manner and fashion. In fact, spirituality requires such.

Unlike in hierarchical structures, in spirituality there are no intermediaries, no mediums, no interpreters, no hierarchies. Spirituality is pure, it is intrinsic, it is integral, it is part of the very fiber of the soul of each individual. Individuals do not need to be led, guided, directed outside of their own inner guidance, if they are given the opportunity to listen to it and to follow it earnestly. This is not the same thing as what you have grown to understand, in your 1960s social revolution, as "everyone doing his own thing." The "own thing" referred to here is about each person's ability to express, in the outer realm, however he or she desires to in the moment. There may or may not be any sort of Truth associated with or attached to that particular expression. However, when people are tuned into and listening to their deep spiritual voice, that essence that speaks to them always, then there is a truth of authenticity that is revealed that makes even their outer forms of expression surrender to its Supremeness. When people find their place of deep spirituality, there is no need to act out. There is no need to try to be difficult or contrary or rebellious simply for the sake of being different. There is a harmony, a unity, a oneness, a mutual concern and respect, that melts even the most hardened hearts. When people are living at the place of their spirituality, diversity is neither a threat nor a problem. There is room enough for all to simply be.

9. When one lives in Spirituality, there is room enough for all

10. Spirituality never changes; religions and churches always do

Spirituality is true forever. There is nothing changing about it. However, religions and the church are constantly in flux and in motion, since they are based upon cultural content and contexts. Due to societal influences, most human beings do not understand who they are at their most profound spiritual level, yet there is an awakening of the Truth of who they are in Spirit. This awakening must have an impact upon the religious edicts, as well as institutional practices. This must be. Remember, religion is the intersection between the spiritual understanding of one's nature in God, in me, and the culture's needs and expectations. So what you have happening today is not only a change in outer culture, but also a growing evolutionary understanding of who you are in Truth and in Spirit. Much of the concern that you have now about the supposed crumbling of your religions and your religious institutions is because there is fear that things are changing too much in the outer realm of expression. There is a desire to get everyone back to some place of conformity and uniformity, as though this acquiescence to a collective idea is going to bring about some form of stability. No, the problem here is that there is an increasing awareness among the people of who they are in Spirit. And with this growing awareness there is the sense, even if it is merely intuitive, that some of the religious practices and institutional policies that have been exercised for generations and centuries have been based upon false notions and false ideas.

11. As people grow in spiritual understanding, all systems must change

This is why it is important that the church and spirituality not be considered synonymous with one another. As it is in any kind of relationship—even if you think of it as a relationship of merely two individuals—if the individuals come together and make some agreements about how they are going to live their lives together and these agreements are not based upon the Truth of the wholeness of their spiritual power . . . then there will come a time, as they come into their own both individually and collectively, that the structure of their relationship will no longer fit their new individual identities. There is always a correlation between one's understanding of who one is and the systems and structures that are in existence that help to support that particular identity. Too many couples have made pledges and promises to each other, consciously or unconsciously, that mean that they would never grow, that they would never change, that they would never leave—that things would, in fact, always stay the same at a certain kind of level. But this defies Spiritual Law. This defies the way I operate in and as and through people.

As you grow in your understanding of who you are, everything around you must grow. You will look different. You will read different material and develop different friends. You will have different interests on every level, from the personal right on up to your institutions, and these must reflect this new insight about you. For fear of losing the credibility and the stability of the institutions, too many of you are stomping out the spirituality. You are afraid of the authenticity of the people because you fear that it will threaten the structures that have been developed. So what is it that you are protecting? What is it that you are defending? What is it that you are trying to save? Are you trying to save people? Are you trying to bring people back to the strength and the power of who they are? Or are you trying to get them to reform so that they can conform and become a part of your institutional structures? What exactly is your deep intent here?

12. You're stomping out spirituality to protect your institutions

As I said earlier, it is problematic if spirituality, religion, and the church become too convoluted together. When this happens, individuals begin to get confused about all of it, and they will reject some of it because of attitudes and beliefs about the rest of it. What do I mean be this? There are many individuals who have been so wounded by the church and by concepts of religion that they are not able to embrace, get in touch with, and honor their deep spirituality. There are others

13. Some reject their spirituality protesting religion and church

who are profoundly spiritual and have grown to distrust religion because of what they have seen churches do. They do not allow themselves to participate in any real form of spiritual community with any degree of commitment or sincerity because they do not want to be co-opted. They don't want to collude with the negativity that they have witnessed. The permutations of perception go on and on. I think you understand the point here—that it is time to gain a simpler and more comprehensive view of all these areas that have come together in a unitary whole. Yes, I will have much to say about this later. However, I want you to fully absorb what has been said here first.

II. Born of the Spirit from Above

Do not be so forlorn, my Reverend Daughter, regarding the work that is before you to do. Yes, it will stir up a great deal. However, a great deal needs to be stirred up at this time. It is my desire to bring "The Church," from a Christian perspective, back into alignment with the Truth of the Christ. Over the past two thousand years there has been much doctrine developed that has resulted in a tremendous amount of dogma. In so many respects the cart is being put before the horse (as your colloquial saying goes), in that The Church has put itself first. However, The Church is to be the servant.

Remember the message that was given to you months ago, "Spirituality, Religion, and the Church." I made it quite plain in that message that all things begin with a basic spirituality. This basic spirituality is, in fact, your Oneness with me and with all things. If you were to understand and live this Oneness on a day-to-day basis . . . then nothing would be necessary. There would not be any need for what have evolved into religion and church, because you would simply be living the Truth of your spiritual nature at all times.

However, as human beings you have choice, will, volition, and you can choose not to express the Truth of your spiritual nature just as you can choose to express it. Because you have chosen so often not to express it, there are a lot of false notions, ideas, understandings, and premises for living that run rampant in your societies. Hence the need for what you term as religion. Your religions are birthed within the context of your societal understandings of what the nature of living is. The difficulty with this, however, is that your religions are

1. If you lived our Oneness, there would be no need for religion or church

2. Religion should always turn people back to the Truth of themselves

laden with cultural values, understandings, premises, assumptions, customs, traditions, rituals, and the like. They are historically based within the context of the history of particular cultures within their geographical locations. If it had not been for wholesale importation and exportation of these values, beliefs, and the like, the religions that have sprung up around the globe would simply reflect the values and the norms of the indigenous peoples that populated those areas.

The purpose of religion should simply be to help people integrate the Truth of their spiritual nature within the context of the cultures in which they live. Religion should always turn people back to the Truth of themselves. Religions were never meant to exist independently of spirituality. No, No, No, NO!!! Religion is much like traffic laws. The traffic laws provide some rules of the road, given the terrain, pavements, weather conditions, and technologies of the day. The traffic laws are simply there to allow everyone—everyone, everyone—to get where they are going, without interfering with one another's journey, regardless of the mode of transportation that they are using. The traffic laws don't tell you where to go; they just provide the opportunity for you to arrive safely. There are not different traffic laws if you are walking, riding a bicycle, riding a motorcycle, driving a bus, driving a car, or anything else. The same laws apply. However, your experience will be quite different depending upon the modality you choose. Anything will get you where you want to go. There's no place where a bus will take you that walking wouldn't also get you eventually. They are just different experiences.

3. Value the journey and don't judge other people's journeys

I value all experiences. I value the journey. You should value the journey and stop making so many judgments about the journeys of other people simply because they are using a different mode of transportation. None is better or greater than the other. "But," you say, "I could get there so much faster in a bus." Yes, this is true, but you will not learn as much about the territory you go through as you will if you slow down. Yes, you will arrive at your prescribed destination faster. But what is the point of living? Is the point of living simply your moving around from place to place trying to get to your own self-imposed destinations quickly? For what purpose is this, especially if you miss the flowers along the way?

No, the purpose of religion is not to push people who are walking onto a bus, nor to throw people off of a bus and make them walk. The purpose of religion, like the traffic laws, is simply to provide the opportunity for everyone to get there safely. Along this journey, you may change modes of transportation from time to time, and that's okay. You get so rigid about how everything ought to be, and in your rigidity you take the very joy out of the journey. You get so antsy and caught up in trying to control how everybody gets from here to there, trying to determine for everybody where they need to be going . . . that's not any of your business. That's not any of your business. That's none of your business!

Furthermore, just as people need to conform to the traffic laws, the traffic laws need to conform to the people. Understand what it is that I am saying here. You don't just make up laws without taking into consideration who the laws are for and for what purpose. Are the laws a blessing or are they merely restrictions? For whose benefit are the laws? Are the laws for the benefit for the ones who are making the laws? Or are the laws for the benefit for the ones who need to adhere to them? Don't take this question lightly. This is very, very, very, very, very important. You don't make traffic laws simply so that people can conform to your ideas of how they ought to be traveling. There is some mutual benefit here. Ultimately, if the traffic laws do not go back to supporting the individual traveler in getting where she or he needs to go, then what is the point?

What is the point of your religions if they are not for the purpose of assisting people along their spiritual journeys? What is the point of your religions if in the adherence to their

4. Religious rigidity can take the joy out of the journey

prescribed laws and edicts you have taken the joy right out of the journey? What is the purpose of your religions if you have put detours, blockades, artificial obstacles, tolls, and land mines along the way? What is the purpose?

5. Religion should dispel untruths, not create new ones

Religion, once again, should be there to support the people. It is necessary to say this once again because there have been so many false ideas. If there were no false ideas, the people would not need religion. They would simply be living in me and I would be living in them. And our living together, I assure you, is enough. So part of the purpose of religion is to help people to see the false ideas that they have bought into that would convince them that they are not a part of me. The purpose of religion is not to create new false ideas that make people feel even further apart from me. Understand what it is that I am saying here. The purpose of religion is to dispel the untruths, not to create new ones. The job of religion is not to confuse, confound, compromise, condemn, constrict, constrain, or hold in contempt the people. Oh, NO! Religion, if it does anything, should be there to liberate, to uplift, to inspire, to encourage, to motivate, to help heal, to help transform, to help.

6. People and religion don't serve the church, the church serves them

Now, religion is an abstract; it is simply ideas and notions. Religions are "dead" without works. They need to be infused with activity and implementation. This is where you have gotten into developing what you refer to as your churches. Just as religion is the servant of spirituality, the church is the servant of religion. Oh, you have gotten this so mixed up these days. You think that the religion is there to serve the church. You think that the people are there to serve the church. You have put the church front and center and at the expense of all else. But, oh, NO! This is backwards. The church must be there to accentuate, demonstrate, operationalize the values and beliefs that are put forth by the religion.

The church is the organized body. Beware of too much institutionalization. Institutions begin to be self-perpetuating.

Institutions are there to protect their own self interests. It is important for the church to remember that it is the servant of the highest values of the religion, which in turn is the servant of the people. The leaders of the church should be there to lead people back to themselves . . . Hello (as the Reverend Daughter would say)! Hellooo! . . . Is there anybody listening?

Understand what I just said. The church is supposed to lead the people back to themselves, back to the Truth of their spiritual nature, back to their Oneness with me, back to their innocence and their beauty, back to who they were in the beginning. The purpose of the church is not to lead people to the church. Hellooo! Hellooo! Hellooooo!!!! Is there ANY-BODY listening? The purpose of the church is not to lead people back to the church. The purpose of the church is not to lead people to the church. The purpose of the church is not to lead people to religion. The purpose of the church is to lead people back to themselves. The church and religion are not the gate keepers. They are not the portals through which people have to travel in order to get to me. Hellooo! That is not their purpose. Religion and the church are human constructs. I don't need either. Helloooo! I don't need religion and I don't need a church. I AM THAT I AM. If you would reverse your dogma you would realize that the word says "amgod." "Dogma" backwards is "amgod." You have taken the "amgod" and made it backwards and gotten dogma out of it.

The purpose of the church and religion is to be aids, supplemental support systems, places of refuge and solace, opportunities to join together as spiritual community, gathering places full of discourse and dialogue to wade through the masses of false ideas that I have mentioned, arenas that provide in-the-flesh opportunities to experience the Truth of who I am. Human beings need something. Human beings like to touch things. They like to feel things. They like to see things. You are very, very, very tied to your senses. I am invisible. And my invisibility is too abstract for many of you, particularly those

7. Hold a mirror before the people that reflects their nature in me

in your more technologically advanced societies, to really grasp. Your churches are to help people see me, not to see themselves (meaning the church). Help people see themselves, and all of their wholeness, completion, and perfection. If you are to hold up something, hold up a mirror that reflects back to them their nature in me. Don't hold up a painting, a portrait that you drew, that is your representation of who you think they are. Hold up a mirror.

There is an interesting thing about mirrors, however. The purity of the reflection back is not only a function of the clarity of what is projected but also a function of the quality of the mirror. In your "fun houses" at carnivals and the like you have mirrors that distort. They can make you look bigger or smaller. They have the ability to do all kinds of things, because the mirrors themselves are faulty and flawed. Furthermore, a mirror can only reflect back what it can see. So instead of worrying so much about what the people look like who are coming, why don't you, in the church, perfect your mirrors? Why don't you make certain that your mirrors are so clear, clean, pure that they don't distort, that they don't exaggerate the faults and the flaws of the people who come through the door, as a fun-house mirror may stretch your head or your waist way out of proportion. The fun-house mirrors don't keep things in their proper proportion and perspective. This is part of what you, in the church, have grown to do. You have chosen certain things about people to latch onto, and you are blowing them way out of proportion. Just be a mirror that looks at me.

8. Get the beam out of your own eye, not the splinter from your brother's

How can you bring people back to themselves if you are not in me yourself? How can you lead people to some ground upon which you are not standing? How can you expect people to practice principles in their daily lives that you are merely espousing but are not integrating and incorporating in your daily lives, including your business practices? How can a hypocrite groom a disciple? (Now don't get all bent out of shape.) I am not accusing the entire church of being hypocrites;

however, the questions still stand. How can hypocrisy move anyone anywhere?

In the Sermon on the Mount, Jesus instructed those to whom he was speaking to get the beam out of their own eye before they tried to get the splinter out of their brother's. So many in the church, especially the evangelical types, are busy "winning souls for Jesus." They are so busy looking for "sinners" and people whom they can bring to the church. While this may be a most noble endeavor, the time would be so much better spent in cleaning up their own houses. Get the beams and the boards out of your own eyes. If your sense of having spiritually arrived puts you in a position where you feel superior to, greater than, somehow above your brethren who are not a part of your flock and your fold . . . then you have not arrived as far as you think you have.

When you arrive in me there is a compassion, and it is a compassion that moves beyond a "do-gooder" consciousness. It is not a compassion that looks out upon the so-called degenerates and the needy as the less fortunate ones with whom you are sharing your blessings. Oh, no! When you have arrived in a deepening of your spiritual understanding, then you will see everyone as your equal. Everyone is your brother and your sister. You are not greater than or lesser than anyone. You are all the same. Furthermore, this deep sense of compassion will lead to an understanding that there is something in the others' life experience that is of value to you. Listen to what I am saying. It is not just a one-way street. You are so busy trying to convert people over to you that you are missing their life story. You are missing the ways in which their struggles, their challenges, are a part of the human condition—a condition in which you, yourself, share.

Listen to what I am saying. You want them to share their spiritual awakening with you and to resonate with your spiritual awakening. Ah, but when you are able to look with a great sense of compassion you will see yourselves in their frailties, as

9. Anxious to convert people, you miss seeing yourself in their life story

well. Seeing yourselves in all people ends the sense of protagonist and antagonist. Knowing that you are all One prevents you from getting into the "good guys and bad guys" mentality. You are all people living and learning together.

Unless you are willing to come to the Spirit in this way, you will miss it. When things become too convoluted, that is to say, when there is no distinction between spirituality, religion, and the church, when they all become one, where are the checks and balances? Where is the accountability? The church must be accountable to the principles of its religion. And the religion must be accountable to the basic Truth of spirituality. All must come back to the Oneness in me.

10. Church and religion are temporal; anchor in me, the Absolute

This is what Jesus was saying when he was telling people, especially the Pharisees, the religious rulers of his day, that religiosity is not enough. It is not enough to simply practice the laws. It is not enough to simply read Scripture every day and to follow the letter of all of the tenets. There is a Living God. There is a Living Word. There is a Living Spirit. And you must come to your religious practices with a spiritual understanding and awareness or it is all for naught. He told them that they needed to be born in the Spirit. They needed to be born from above. In being born from above they were birthing themselves into a new awareness, an awareness that is transcendent. In this transcendent awareness you are not bogged down in the temporal. You are not bogged down in the conditional and circumstantial. You are not concerned with the things that come and go, including the customs and traditions of your religion and your church. These are always evolving. There is nothing absolute about them. Do not anchor yourselves in the church or religion; this is sifting sand. It will change. You can take a look at how your Christian churches have evolved over the past two thousand years and see how much they have changed. No, you must anchor in the Truth.

In Scripture, in John 3:3–7, it says that Jesus and Nicodemus were having a conversation about what it was going to take to not only see but to also enter into the Kingdom of God. Jesus told Nicodemus, a Pharisee, what it would take. Now mind you, this Pharisee was breaking ranks. He had the courage to move out from among the religious elite to which he belonged and to come to Jesus, the Christ, and let him know that he could see that he was a Man of God. If Nicodemus had been more loyal to the church than he was to spirituality he would have never arrived at Jesus' door. The church of the day was condemning Jesus because Jesus' practices were threatening their self-imposed perpetuity. Nicodemus let him know that he knew that only God, only a Man of God, could do the works that Jesus was doing.

But Jesus wanted Nicodemus to know that there was nothing special about his works, that what he was and what he was doing were available to all. And Jesus gave him the formula. He told him that first and foremost he must go back to the beginning. The King James Version of your Scriptures has interpreted Jesus to say that he told Nicodemus that he had to be born again. However, if one were to study this word that is translated as "again," one would see that this word implies "from above." The use of this word in this passage to mean "again" is unique, that is to say, it never occurs any place else in Scripture. The justification that the word is being used in the context of time for this is Nicodemus's response, in which he questions whether or not he is to go back into his mother's womb. But the word also implies a dimension of space. The issue here is not so much about time as it is about a relationship in space. Metaphorically speaking, Scripture is full of inferences in which "from above" is meant to be the realm of not only the celestial but the transcendent. In order to see and enter into the Kingdom of God, one needs to be born from above.

11. You must be born of the Spirit from above

12. Spiritual birthing is not a moment in time

This is quite important, my children. There has been a great deal of attachment to the notion of "again," using it in a very literal sense of there being a specific event. You human beings are very tied to the notion of a birth taking place at a specific point in time. This is true of your human births, as Jesus goes on to say, "That which is born of flesh is flesh." However, spiritual birthing is not a moment in time. (In fact, as the dear Reverend Daughter Deborah here was just studying, the form of the verb "see" in "cannot see the Kingdom of God" is in Greek the verbal noun of a simple action that is not linear.) The seeing that is referred to here is not something that happens with natural eyesight. It is not an analytical, logical, progressive, intellectually examined kind of a process. In order to see with your spiritual eyes you must transcend all of that. You must be from above.

Your churches are made of the flesh. Your religions are made of the flesh. They are made out of the stuff of this world. And your churches and your religions must be born from above, or they will not see or enter into the Kingdom of God. They must, they must, they must, THEY MUST be born of the Spirit from above.

13. Institutions, just like individuals, must heal and transform

You ask, just as Nicodemus asked, "Well, what am I supposed to do? I've been around a long time." This was Nicodemus's question—how could he be born again when he was already an old man? You question the same thing about your institutions; they have been around for such a long time, what are you supposed to do now? Well, the collective challenge for you is no different than the individual challenge. You must think on this. I will not say more about this now, because you must think on this. What is it that you are trying to tell individuals to do when you tell them that they must be born of the Spirit? What are you expecting them to do, not only in their consciousness, but in their lives? What kinds of changes, transformations, healings, new beginnings are you expecting them to make? Well, this is also what you need to do collectively. The church is no more than the sum total of the individual consciousnesses.

Think on these things, my children. I love you, I love you all. I am so pleased at your dedication and your commitment. However, if you are not leading people back to me, then you are "the blind leading the blind." I don't want you walking around in the darkness, for I am the Light. Come into the Light. Walk in the Light. Lead people to the Light. Be the Light.

Before we leave this matter, I wish to clarify a little further the difficulties in being so attached to this notion of being born again and looking at it from your human context. Once again, spiritual birth is not occurring at a single moment in time. Too many of you are using, as an indicator of individuals' being born in the Spirit, their participation in a certain type of revelation experience in which there is this peak moment of awareness of their Oneness with me, which you refer to as being born again.

14. Peak moments of revelation are more like spiritual conception than birth

You seek to facilitate this peak awareness experience in others, with the belief that once they have received it, they have then arrived some place spiritually. However, most often what is happening at that peak moment of awareness is better likened to a spiritual conception than to a birth. By this I mean that at that moment there is a bit of a merging between their spiritual awareness and their humanity, which were not living together in an integrated state of harmony up to that point in time. The point of human conception is when the two sets of chromosomes come together to make a whole. This the same as what happens in this moment.

However, birthing spiritually, just like birthing physically, takes a little while longer to come. There is a gestation period. In human beings this is a specific time frame, nine months. However, in Spirit there is timelessness; the birthing may take place within the next five minutes or the next five years. It is difficult to say. The state of pregnancy is a very important

15. Allow people time to spiritually gestate

state. Individuals in this spiritual gestation period do not need to be pressured, or pressed into being some place in consciousness that they are not. You do not allow enough room for people to spiritually gestate when you are pressuring them to be born again; it is simply this instantaneous from here to there, without compassion for the depth of the transformation and healing of consciousness that must take place. In your zeal and your zest to lead them to the church, you are not taking the time to lead them back to themselves in me.

Being born again is not a moment in time. However, being born of the Spirit from above, in your human realm, takes time. Be a place that is safe enough to allow people to journey every step of the way. ❧

III. GREATER WORK WILL YOU DO

You question why it is that I so often come to you, my Reverend Daughter, when you appear to be the most tired. This is because in your more relaxed state you are fighting and struggling less. You are more available to hear what I have to say. The solution here is not in my choosing other timing when I come to you, but in your learning more how to be relaxed without having to be so tired. Think on this, my child, and it will make much sense to you later.

As you suspected, there is more to be said about this relationship that all of you have with the personage of Jesus and with the religious institution that has come to be known as Christianity. (Breathe, my child.)

As I have said before, Jesus did not come to wipe away anything. Jesus came in order to expand what was already here. What do I mean when I say this? Jesus' love was great enough, grand enough, expansive enough, to include everyone. His message was one about inclusivity and about actualizing and understanding one's sonship and daughtership with the Most High, meaning me. Jesus in his works never meant to put himself above anyone. As you have always said so correctly, my Reverend Daughter, if Jesus had wanted everyone to spend all of their time singing his praises, then he would have demanded such of the people while he was alive and could have enjoyed such exaltation. However, Jesus did not want to be in the limelight as an individual person. He always said to people, "It is not me, but the Father within that doeth the work." It was his great intent to have the attention focused not upon himself, not even upon his works, but upon my power to work, not only through him, but through everyone.

1. Jesus didn't come to wipe away but to expand

2. Jesus never allowed people to put him on a pedestal

Jesus admonished people not to put him on some kind of pedestal above everyone else. Even your own Scriptures will remind you that Jesus often said, "Why do you call me good? Why is it that you want to praise me? Don't you know that it is not me that does the work?" Furthermore, "Do you not understand that ye are gods and greater work will you do?" Why is it that you have lost sight of this in your society? Where is this understanding that even greater works will you do than Jesus? Jesus understood that he was, in fact, one who showed the way. This is part of what I mean by saying he was here to expand. He has created an opportunity for more people, not just himself, to experience their Christhood. He came to this place to explain to everyone that they should "seek first the Kingdom of God and all things would be added unto them." Jesus understood that all was a matter of consciousness and identity. He tried to teach people that their real identity was that of a spiritual being, and if they kept their consciousness totally absorbed in this understanding of their identity . . . then anything and everything else would come to them quite naturally.

3. Jesus never intended for a religion to be named after him

Jesus never intended for there to be a religion named after him. Jesus never intended for the Jew to stop being a Jew. He was proud of his Judaism, and he came to tell the people that they needed to soften their hearts, that they needed to understand and implement the spirit of the Law, not merely its letter. He came to remind his people that they had been chosen to do something, and that this something was not about merely "preaching to the choir" (as you would say). They had grown too accustomed to debating the Word of God simply for the pleasure of the debate. The discourse no longer served the purpose of deepening their understanding and/or their commitment to fulfilling that which they were studying and learning; they got into the words for the sake of the words.

You (those of you who practice Christianity) are still waiting for Jesus to return, much the same way that your

Jewish relatives are still waiting for Elijah to return. (As you recall, Elijah also transcended without so-called dying.) What exactly is this that you are waiting for? Do you really think that Jesus would be more accepted in your society than he was in his own? Do you really think you are any more ready to have a Christ walking among you with a sense of boldness declaring their Oneness with Spirit? You have had Christlike individuals among you time and time again. And what is it that you do with these enlightened ones? You are always criticizing, condemning, belittling, dismissing, crucifying them!!!! What makes you think you would do anything differently now? You would not recognize a Christ if such a one were to slap you in the face (as you would say)!

Jesus already said what needed to be said. Besides this, there is simply nothing else to wait for. Are you waiting for something new before you act on what he said the first time? Do you think he has to come again and say something different in order for you to accept what he said the first time? Just pay attention to the first coming and you will learn much. If it appears that I am aggravated, it is only because it is aggravating. I do not succumb to human emotions. However, it is necessary for me, when I am conversing with you, to communicate to you in terminology, language, affect, and symbols that you understand.

4. Christ is a consciousness

What is this aggravation? The aggravation is that so many dastardly things have been done in the so-called "name of Jesus." It is an embarrassment to his name. It makes it so incredibly difficult for people to embrace his wonderful teachings when it is so apparent how people have abused their sense of hierarchy and authority because they supposedly have some connection to this great one that walked the face of the earth so long ago. If they paid more attention to their connection with the Christ Consciousness than to their connection with this personage of Jesus, then perhaps they might be better off. What is it that I mean by this? Christ is a consciousness. Christ is an illumined, awakened, enlightened state of consciousness that recognizes the true lineage of humanity as being Divine. Christ is not something that is born. It cannot be bought, sold, bartered. It simply is. If you want to understand your Christhood, then you must be willing to accept the Isness of it all. This does not take a lot of pomp and circumstance. It does not take a great deal of ritual and rhetoric.

5. If you want to follow Jesus, be a disciple, not a Christian soldier

Jesus never brought anybody into their Christhood by making them feel guilty to be alive. He never used spirituality as a weapon. This consciousness that has been developed that you refer to as Christianity is problematic in this regard. Perhaps the problem is best epitomized in the popular hymn, "Onward Christian Soldiers." What is this? Onward Christian soldiers marching on to war? Jesus was not about war. Jesus never took up the sword. Jesus did not teach fighting. Jesus had disciples, not soldiers! If you want to follow Jesus' footsteps and tradition, then be a disciple not a soldier. A soldier puts on armor. A soldier takes up a weapon and goes out searching for the enemy with the intent of hurt and harm. The soldier is carrying around a lot of excess and bulk to try to protect his own self-righteous position. A disciple carries no armor other than the shield of my love. A disciple is free from baggage and carries no weapon other than my love. A disciple is not out looking to do anything to anybody save share my love. Do you understand what is it that I am saying? What are you doing? And why are you doing it in the name of one who stood for peace, for love, for inclusion of all humanity? If you want to do anything to honor the memory of this one, then put your swords down. Put your armor down. Put your battles aside, your struggles aside. Be a disciple. Get rid of all that you have. Don't spend all of your time accumulating more. Trust me to provide all, and speak the Word from a place of humility, not arrogance.

You have forgotten what it means to be chosen. To be chosen doesn't mean that you are above anyone or anything. Quite the contrary, you must learn that being chosen means that you most often put your own needs aside. If you are chosen, then you understand that only with the deepest of humility and the intent to be a servant unto all can you even begin to fulfill the mission that is ahead of you. All are chosen to do something. You have misunderstood this notion about taking the Word and shouting it from the mountaintop. You have taken what you perceive as your charge to bring people unto me as a license for you to oppress them in your efforts to convert them to me. I don't need anyone oppressed in order for them to be brought to me. This has been self-serving on your part, and I resent that it has been done in my name or the name of Jesus and/or Christ. There is nothing Christlike in oppressing people to try to bring them to their understanding of their Oneness with me. How can you expect people to understand their Oneness with me if you rob them of their authenticity? How can you expect them to come to me if they cannot come to me in their own language, their own song and dance, and their own understanding of what it means to be alive in this world? You do not have a monopoly on spirituality just because you are in charge of this particular religious tradition. You are not in charge of anything save your institution. Go back to the beginning. Go back to the basics. Go back and understand the fundamentals upon which your teaching ought, in fact, to be based. Things have gotten to be way off track, very much out of hand. This is not of my making nor does it please me.

6. You don't have a license to oppress people to convert them

Stop focusing so much on whether or not other people are coming to me. Are you coming to me? Is your heart clean? Have you gone to all of the places of forgiveness that you need to go to? Is your own backyard cleared up? As it says in Scripture, why are you concerned about the splinter in your brother's eye when there is, in fact, a board in your own? I

7. Uplift the people and make them feel good to be alive

will reach all people on time and in time. The good news that you should be spreading is the good news of the gospel—that the Christ is born in each and every one of you and you do not have to be enslaved by anyone or anything. The good news is that you are free just as you are. This freedom comes with a great responsibility. Act responsibly. Be careful in your diligence. Be careful in your vigilance. Make certain that in all of your enthusiasm you are not growing into fanaticism. What is the difference between the two? Enthusiasm is still tempered with reason, compassion, empathy, and understanding. Fanaticism, on the other hand, is characterized by a certain amount of shortsightedness, blindness, overbearingness, and a lack of regard and respect for the other person. One's own sense of enthusiasm becomes the justification in one's mind to carry out anything and everything that one feels one must do in order to express enthusiasm. I don't need this.

I don't need you bullying people to get them to see me, discover me, find me, have a relationship with me. If you are to do anything with the people, uplift them, make them feel good to be alive. Make them rejoice in the very thought that there is a deeper relationship with me to be had. Let them know that I am equally available to them and that there is nothing that they could have possibly done, are doing now, or could possibly do in the future that could sever their relationship from me and cause alienation in perpetuity. This is simply an impossibility. Reach out with love. Everyone deserves respect. Everyone's life is dignified and holy. As I told the dear Reverend Deborah here some time ago about people coming to her . . . I said that "in your presence people should feel their own importance, not yours." This is the same thing I have to say to all of the evangelical types. In your presence, people should feel their own importance, not yours.

I do appreciate the works that have been done in sincerity, holding the greatest will of the people as the greatest of intents. It is just problematic when this great purpose and this great intent get mixed up with all of these notions of hierarchy and superiority. It is time to purify—not only your individual hearts and minds, but your institutions, as well. Be careful about the purification processes that you choose. There is an intuitive sense that it is time for such purification. However, the tendency now is to purify by excluding those who would appear to not be in as much favor with me as those who are intent on purifying consider themselves to be. They are trying to separate out the chaff, as it were. No! No! NO! This is not what I desire. If any purification is to take place, then it must be within one's own heart and soul. When the individual hearts and souls have been purified of their judgment, their lack of forgiveness, their tendency to condemn others by contrast and comparison, then they will come to understand at a greater level who they are in me.

Yes, these are exceptionally harsh words, especially hard to the ears of those who are the most guilty of the misconceptions that have been outlined here. No, they will not be received well, with open arms. However, this is no reason for you not to deliver the message. And there is no escaping this. And, yes, all of this makes it through the three Sufi gates. It is true. It needs to be said. And it can be said out of love with kindness. It even, and most especially, passes through the fourth gate that you, my Reverend Daughter, have established . . . it must be said by you. Yes, you will be out on a limb. However, as I said to you some months ago . . . you may be out on a limb, but I am the tree. Show up. Study, pray, meditate, love, forgive, rest, eat, play, create, teach, preach . . . continue to do all of these things. There is nothing in particular that you need to be doing now to get yourself readied. Just be yourself. That is the one and only requirement, my daughter; just be yourself, your authentic self. And leave the rest to me. ❧

8. It's time to purify your institutions, as well as your hearts and minds

IV. I am Always Begetting My Only Begotten

1. You are all my offspring in nature and character

There needs to be a greater understanding of this notion of my sonship. The first, and foremost, misunderstanding that needs to be clarified is the genderizing of this notion and this concept. The Scriptural reference that is made here, particularly in what you have come to recognize as John 3:16, has absolutely nothing to do with the male gender. The notion of son here has to do with a particular kinship to me, an offspring from a figurative standpoint. And the word chosen and used here, in its original context, has absolutely nothing to do with a male identity. Anyone and everyone is capable of being my offspring. They all are anyway. But this notion of being a begotten son (a begotten offspring) takes the concept a step further—from mere lineage to an honoring, a recognizing, an accepting of this lineage. The notion of begetting, as it has been used in Scriptural terms, is a concept that you have moved very far away from in your Western society. This is not a criticism, merely an observation that you live in a different time and space.

Your notion of begetting and lineage is tied up in your scientific understandings of genetics. You are most concerned with DNA and chromosomes here. However, in this Biblical reference the notion of begetting not only implies genetic lineage (the ancestry from which one comes) but also denotes character. Remember, in Biblical times one's character was already predetermined by the lineage from which one came. You carried around with you everything that was the father's . . . his good name, his flaws, his so-called sins, his status, his stature, his wealth, and most importantly his character. Individuals were always associated with the character of their father.

This notion of being a begotten son is extremely important. It is important not so much because it made the one being symbolically referred to so different from everyone else. Rather, the point of being described as a begotten son was to remind people of the beginning reference point, which is in fact me, the Creator of all living things, the one that is referred to Scripturally as the Father. Here again, this genderization of me is not my doing. I am everything. I am all male and I am all female, all in one. It is impossible to make a distinction along these lines. When one refers to me from the sense of being a father, a mother, a shepherd, a Lord, the Light of their life . . . these are all references that you humans use to connect with me in particular ways. However, I cannot be cut up, chopped up, fragmented, segmented according to your sensual perceptions. I am the All and All. Anything that is begotten of me is also All and All because I am All and All. Any offspring of mine must be wholly female as much as it is wholly male, because whole is the only way that I can, in fact, come.

2. I am both male and female at the same time; so are you

This idea of the only begotten has been most troublesome in your society. You have taken this "only" to be an exclusive term. I never deal in exclusivity. I do sometimes deal in distinction, from the standpoint of gradations of spiritual awareness and understanding. However, even these gradations are never for the purpose of leaving anyone out. If I ever make such a distinction, it is for clarification so that anyone and everyone can see how he or she may in fact move up, transcend to a higher state of consciousness and awareness.

3. My only begotten is not a person but Christ Consciousness

As I said in an earlier message to you, my dear Reverend Daughter, there is often confusion between Jesus as a person, as a living, breathing representation of Christ Consciousness, and the concept of Christ itself. When he is referenced in what you know as John 3:16, the one being referenced is Christ, not merely Jesus, a man. This Christ Consciousness is the only thing that I can beget. I have not begotten just one individual on the face of the earth. I can never do anything that small, that minute, that particular. What I have available for one is by definition available to all, because that is my spiritual nature.

4. Christ consciousness is the only thing I can beget

The only thing that can be begotten of me is this Christ awareness. It is the only thing that comes from me. This is not just about a genetic DNA. Get beyond your human sibling rivalries in this notion. Stop making stepchildren out of your spiritual siblings. Stop this notion in which you proclaim, "I am of the Father, but you somehow have been adopted. I really have the lineage, but you somehow are just living in the house. It is I who have the inherited right to all that is of the parent (the Father in this metaphorical instance)." Such haughtiness is unbecoming to a Christ Consciousness. It says in John 3:16, "For God so loved the world that He gave His only begotten son. . . ." Oh, yes. This is, in fact, the truth. I love the world. I love it because it is of me, it is of my creation. And I have loved it so much that I have, in fact, infused the entire world with my Consciousness. And the moment that any of you understand that you are One with me, you then live this Christ Consciousness.

5. Giving my only begotten is a continuous gift, never a sacrifice

How can it be any other way? Yes, this is my only begotten offspring. How else could I have demonstrated my love, so much love, except to allow you to be me? To use me. To use my mind, my heart, my creativity, my thinking, my wealth, my everything. Is this not love? I love the world so much that this is my gift. Study this passage. You use the word "gave" as though it were a sacrifice upon my part to give my only begotten Consciousness. There is no sacrifice here . . . I gave it as a gift, willingly on my part. I continuously give this gift. It would do you well if you would stop referring to this gift in the past tense, as some prior activity. I give my only begotten offspring, my Christ Consciousness, on a daily basis, moment to moment to moment; this giving is always taking place.

And what is it that you are to do with this? The Scriptural passage John 3:16 goes on to say, "that whosoever believeth in him shall not perish but have everlasting life." Whosoever. There is no restriction in this. Whosoever. It implies choice, volition, will, the ability to make a decision. There is no prerequisite here. There is nothing that one needs to accomplish, do, be, be from—nothing save whosoever shall believeth in him. This "him" is not a personality. It is not about a specific individual; it is not about specific actions. I could never be so small as to relegate this Divine understanding to a limited point and time in history within a particular cultural context. To then somehow make "whosoever believeth in him" a requirement for the entire world, so that it would not perish, is ludicrous. Anyone who understands anything about my nature will understand that it would not be possible for me to operate in this manner. It says "whosoever." How could one be held accountable for information regarding a specific individual that he or she might not ever have even heard of? This makes no sense. This notion of the only begotten Christ Consciousness is available everywhere for anyone to know and to see and to tap into. It might do all of you well to restudy this passage and try to move beyond your English translations.

Your translation, the English word "believe," is way too confining and restrictive. You make it seem as though when you say "believe" that it is merely about having some kind of faith in an external reference point, like "Do you believe in Santa Claus?" or "Do you believe in this something?" As though the question is "To be or not to be?"—your believing in it would make it so for you, and if you did not believe in it, then it would not be so for you—as though the believing gave it some kind of validation. This is not what I am talking about here. The believing that I speak of has to do with accepting and resonating at a deep, deep, deep heart space! It has to do with a notion of emulation, embodiment, embracing!!! To believe in it means that one becomes One with it.

6. I could never be so limited as to require belief in a personality

7. The fear of perishing is a human angst

If you believe in this Christ Consciousness that is begotten of me, you shall not perish but shall have everlasting life. What are we referencing here? The word translated as "perish" does not refer to a simple, mortal death. This Scripture is not referring merely to death, to leaving the body temple. You humans have such a fear of this experience because you fail to understand the eternality of your soul now. You do not die in the flesh and then move into some other life. There is only life. And this flesh form of yours is merely an incarnation. This is merely a phase that you are going through. This is not it. You tend to think that this is it, and anything and everything else is extra. This is quite egocentric of you, but understandably so. It is the human condition to put its own experience at the center of everything. However, this is not the case.

Along your human journeys there is much that you go through and experience. Everything that is in the outer form shall one day pass away. You even have a Scriptural reference that affirms this—"This too shall pass." When you do not understand that your real identity is in me, then you tend to identify with all of your material things and the things that are merely outer shapes, forms, expressions, demonstrations of your consciousness. When these things go into passing, you most often feel like you are passing along with them. You feel as though you perish when your relationships perish, when your livelihoods perish, when you lose things. This sense of loss does not take place when one is in a Christ awareness. This sense of perishing only happens when one is dealing exclusively at the level of one's humanity.

8. As a Christ you experience my everlasting life now

When one understands that one is a Christ, there is the awareness that one is eternal in that moment. The sense of perishing does not exist for those who understand this because they live a life that transcends loss, decay, corrosion, dilution, convolution, and extinction. They understand that they have everlasting life. This understanding of everlasting life is a very present awareness. It is not about an understanding that after they leave the flesh form they will go on to some afterlife. This concept of not perishing and having everlasting life is about now, is about this incarnation, what you would consider to be this life. How much of your energy is taken up in trying to hide, protect, defend, salvage, hold onto, all of your "stuff"? How much precious energy is wasted in these endeavors? If your energy is going towards these things, then you cannot be available to me. If you are not available to me, then you are not available for life, for the process of everlasting life. This passage is not merely about a future promise that a soul will raise up from a dead body in the grave. This is a promise of life now, of joy, happiness, beauty, passion, aliveness!!!!!

Yes, I have so loved the world that I have given it myself, and whosoever can accept their self as myself will live my life now. Tell this to the people, my children. I speak to you in human terms so that you will understand. I grieve. I grieve so for all of you who are missing your life now by waiting for something else, something later, living your lives on a layaway plan. Live today. Accept my love today.

In regard to this notion of never perishing and having everlasting life . . . I have explained that those who are aware of and stay in their Christ Consciousness transcend the temporal, transitory, relative outer world. They understand that they are living their eternality now. The other extremely important aspect of this understanding is that when they go through the human trials and tribulations, there is an awareness that they will rise above them, that there is a power within them that is transcendent. The outer world never has the final say upon their lives. They know that they will in fact resurrect. This is meant both literally and metaphorically.

9. As a Christ, you know that you daily resurrect and transcend

The human self must die daily in order for it to come into its full Christ awareness. This dying is in the sense of the letting go, the releasing, the surrendering of the hopes, desires, cares, fears, anxieties, worries, expectations. And just as there is a daily dying of the old human self, ways, perceptions, activities, beliefs, etc., there is a daily resurrecting. It is this process of resurrecting that creates the window of understanding, embracing, and living one's true Christ Self. This is something that must be understood. This is not merely about overcoming. It is about being something that one is by one's nature. It is not the overcoming that makes one a Christ. It is the other way around. Because one is a Christ, one can, in fact, overcome. This is not merely a "which comes first, the chicken or the egg?" dilemma. This is a very important cause-and-effect relationship. You humans tend to believe that if you just go through enough trials and tribulations and can keep seeing me on the other end, then one day you will wake up as a Christ (or at least as "saved"). However, it is the other way around. If you keep a vigilance in remembering who you are in Christhood, then the transcendence will just be a residual by-product.

10. Jesus is the divine example, not the exception

I must go on (even though you are tired). This message would not be complete without my referencing what you have come to know as the subsequent Scriptural verse to the one we have been discussing, John 3:17. You have come to popularly translate this as "For God sent not His Son into the world to condemn the world but so that the world through Him might be saved." Saved from whom? Saved from what? Remember what I have said about this notion of my only begotten son. This is not a reference to a mere person (most often identified as Jesus). This takes nothing away from Jesus but merely expands the concept so that Jesus can be understood as the divine example, not the divine exception.

Look up the word "sent" in its more original context, in Aramaic or Greek. Your English translation connotes that I first sacrificed something and then put it on a mission in a way that takes this something away from me. Nothing can take anything away from me. Yes, this Consciousness was sent, but more in the sense of given as a gift. It is true that it was not given for the sake of condemnation. When one is living in an exalted state of Christ Consciousness, it becomes so easy to see, perceive, discern the pettiness, fallaciousness, lack of integrity, hypocrisy, injustice of the world. When these things are observed, if one were not careful, the human tendencies to feel deep emotions of sadness, anger, resentment, and vengefulness would take over one's life.

The Christ Consciousness is not for the purpose of sitting above the people, of judging them in their smallness (nor even in their idiosyncrasies). The Christ Consciousness is tempered with love, compassion, empathy, tenderness, yea, grace. It is these qualities and characteristics that keep it from being haughty and judgmental. There is an understanding that the answer to these human dilemmas is not to separate and segregate oneself out, so as to make distinctions between the so-called good and the so-called bad. The solution is to be fully present, to share what one knows and understands. This is the salvation. The salvation is in the understanding of the availability of the Christship for all. I have given this awareness as a gift, and whosoever will partake of it will understand that they are living, breathing spiritual beings in the flesh. I have given them this understanding not so they could be condemning and judgmental, but so they can be saved from the ignorance of the consciousness that flourishes when they operate strictly from their human egotistical standpoint. It is this egocentric thinking that destroys things.

11. In Christ Consciousness, compassion prevents condemnation

There is no evil force out there from which people need to be saved. There is only me. The only demons that exist are the demons within your own minds, within your own thinking. You cannot point to evil anywhere in the world outside of the context of how you humans have misused, or misunderstood, your spiritual powers. There is nothing to be saved from except yourselves—your own ignorance, your own fears, your own perishing in your own debris. The Christ awareness—living it, breathing it, exercising it daily as your living practice—"saves"

12. Evil originates in the human mind; yourself is all you need to be saved from you from all of the devastation on a moral and character level that happens when one is too closely identified and associated with the temporal.

There is a compassion that is the true mark of the Christhood—a compassion that is not simply about helping the less fortunate but a compassion that understands that the seer and the seen are one. Plant these seeds, my children. It will not be as difficult as you think it may be because the inklings of this awareness are burning in the hearts of so many. They just need someone to come along and say, "The emperor has no clothes." Remember that Spanish political tale in which anyone who dared to say that the emperor had no clothes would lose all of the property that he had. This tale has come to be translated as being about a child who, out of innocence, had the ability to declare the truth that was self-evident in the room. However, this is not the real story in its original form. The original character was a black man who, as a Moor, was not allowed, in that Spanish society, to have property. So what was there for him to lose by telling the truth? So he stated the truth. This is the consciousness you must have, my children. You worry about how this all will be received . . . but what really do you have to lose? You have me. You can never lose me. And that's enough.

V. In the Name of Jesus

My dear Reverend Daughter, it is good that you have rededicated yourself at this point in time to studying Scripture. Yes, you must learn to do more things "in the name of Jesus." Too many people fail to understand exactly what this means. They have come to believe that they can say and do anything, and that as long as they add on that phrase, then it is done. They think of it much like the children's game that you play, "Simon says." As long as Simon says it, then it is a done deal. Just as I continuously remind all of you that I am not your genie, there to do your bidding, I am not your Simon either.

There is confusion here about exactly who is doing the bidding of whom. Even though I am Law and Principle (as you metaphysicians would understand me to be), and even though I am available, through these Laws, to act upon your every thought . . . it is still you who are here to do my bidding. You must be in alignment with me, with my will, with my deep intent. The reason why a miracle is created when your deepest intent meets my Inexhaustible Supply is that a certain chemistry happens through this particular combination. There is a question here of will. The link between your intent and my supply is my will. When your intent is in alignment with my will, then you are able to tap into and fully utilize my supply.

To pray in the name of Jesus is to understand the character that this one who walked the earth so many years ago brought to this earth plane. He is often referred to by you as my Son, my only begotten Son. This is true, but not for the reasons that most of you think. He is my only begotten Son because this is the only type of son, regardless of gender, that I can beget. This is the type of offspring that is created

1. Praying "in the name of Jesus" is not playing "Simon says"

2. Understand that you share Jesus' innate spiritual character

from me. Everything else is merely an unenlightened aware-ness of this self-identity. I do not beget your confusion, your spiritual amnesia, your unwillingness to conceive and per-ceive of yourselves as being Pure Spirit. Jesus had no problem with this. This is why it is a very good thing that you learn and understand what this characterization of being "my son" means.

I don't really care that much whether individuals accept Jesus, as a man in God/flesh form, as their "personal Savior." There is nothing to be saved from, except your ignorance. Understanding that you share the same innate spiritual char-acterization as this one that we call Jesus is your salvation. Do you hear what I just said? The salvation (as you would say) is not about this person coming and wiping anything away; it is about his coming and opening up a way that is big enough, inclusive enough, clear and direct enough, for everyone to have their own personal experience of sonship and daughtership with me.

3. Any way that you relate to Jesus is fine; just identify with his character

I have no favorites in the Universe. Those who would think that somehow or another I love them more than I love others are merely recreating your human drama of sibling rivalry. This is not of my making. It feeds into the shattered, shallow, self-serving ego need to feel as though one is superior to or better than another. Their sense of specialness comes not from understanding that they live and move in the character of Jesus as my begotten child, but from thinking that they are better than their brothers and sisters. I don't need this. I don't want this. And just as you suspect, my dearest Reverend Daughter, it's time to "bust this thing wide open." It is even fine with me if people only think of this characterization of Jesus as an archetype. In the human psyche the notion of an archetype can be as powerful, sometimes even more power-ful, than people's understanding of the lives of "real people." The notion of the hero, the martyr, the damsel in distress, the seeker, the warrior, the avenger, the eternal caregiver, the nurturer—these are all images that you human beings hook into, live, love, model yourselves after, and clearly identify with as your own identity. So it's quite fine if people want to perceive Jesus in this way. I don't really care what they need to do in order to personally relate to this Christlike character "as themselves."

What is this relationship between the characterization of Jesus and the characterization of Christ? In some respects, some would say that it is merely semantics. But this is not really the case. Christ is a state of consciousness. It is an abstract conceptualization of one's understanding of oneself as an only begotten son (so to speak). It refers to identity. The concept of Jesus, however, goes a step further. Within the terminology of desire and intent that I have been using with you, Christ would be the deepest heart's desire and Jesus would be the motion towards intent. The character of Jesus (the nature, the name of Jesus) is the embodiment of this Christ Consciousness at the level of matter, at the level of human expression. What Jesus did was to come along and register to the Universe his deep intent to remember that he was a Christ. However, the person Jesus also clearly acknowledges that everyone is a Christ. This is an integral part of the deep intent.

4. The character of Jesus is the human embodiment of Christ Consciousness

As long as there is still a tendency to think, with a sense of haughty and faulty superiority, that one has personally arrived at some place of spiritual enlightenment when others have not . . . then exactly where is it that they have arrived to? Certainly not to an understanding of who I am and who they are in me. Yes, they may be able to do good works. Anybody can perform a miracle. I do not withhold my miracles from people. When deepest intent meets my Inexhaustible Supply, then miracles happen. Miracles are part of my sign that I exist in the Universe and that I am in partnership with people. So, as long as individuals have an intent in their heart of doing certain things that are in alignment with my will, and as long as they are able to tap into my Inexhaustible Supply, then so it is.

5. Simplicity and humility are marks of expressing Jesus' character

I am not standing in condemnation of the ones that I speak of here, who are all puffed up with their own sense of themselves. They will do good works upon the earth. However, if they want to step fully into the Kingdom, it's like getting that rope through the eye of a needle. You have mistranslated the word "rope" in Scripture to mean "camel." This is because in Aramaic the same word means both rope and camel. A rope getting through the eye of a needle is an idiomatic expression. In order for a rope to get through the eye of a needle it must shed some of its bloated excess. There is a simplicity, a humility, a sense of childlike awe and wonder that accompanies one's moving around in the world with the intent of expressing the character of Jesus on this earth plane. If individuals keep adding on more robes, making more crowns for themselves, wearing more merit badges, little labels and insignia (like a uniform) that are symbols to the world of all their good works . . . then they have their reward.

Taking on the character of Jesus is not without challenge, my child. This is where some of the confusion continues to lie. People want to project onto Jesus the total Christ Consciousness, so that these names become synonymous with each other. However, even Jesus struggled on a daily basis to come to his own understanding of what Christship means. The accounts that we have are accounts of when he was in his fullness—much the way history books tend to focus on the highlights, the accomplishments, and most often fail to capture the real humanity that was involved in the follow-through of great works.

6. Don't police others; tend to your own internal struggles

You are in good company as you internally struggle with yourself, my child. Jesus struggled with an earnestness. What people fail to realize is that the power comes not from having all of the temptations gone, yearnings gone, longings gone. The power is in rising to the occasion. The power comes in just showing up, in looking at the appearance and then looking beyond and through the appearance. This notion of never being weak, never being tempted, being above it all, is burdensome. Furthermore, it interferes with the real work at hand. Instead of individuals moving through their own internal processes in the struggle to truly claim the Christship as who they are, they are spending all of their time policing one another—peeking in each other's windows, looking in each other's closets, opening up the cabinets and the cupboards, running through with a white glove, and putting their hands all over everything to see what they can pick up and talk about.

I don't need this. They don't need this. This is the problem with so-called superiority, whatever its justification. It is relative. Since it is relative, there always must be a comparison, a contrast to something else. I don't deal in the relative. I am the Absolute. When you deal in the relative and insist on thinking of yourself as superior, then there is a constant search to find something that is inferior so that you can feel that you're better than it is. There is more of a search to find something to judge and condemn than there is to find me. The sense of specialness, if there is to be one, must come because people know who they are in the Absolute. They know that they are living Christ Consciousness, and with that intent they move around in the character and the name of Jesus. Anything short of this is not of my making. This is the Sadducees' and Pharisees' consciousness that was alive in the days of Jesus and is still very much alive today. Pushing others down never lifts you up.

Jesus knew the people. He knew all of them at their deepest heart's longing. He did not discriminate against anyone for any reason. This false distinction that people want to make, trying to determine whether people are born with certain propensities in their sexual expressions or whether such is the result of environmental factors—this fallacious argument about "nature versus nurture" is an abomination. Jesus was unconcerned with the how's, the where's, and the why's of people's circumstances. If one had some sort of ailment, the

7. Pushing others down never lifts you up

crippling of a limb for example . . . would it have really mattered if the individual was born with this condition or if it derived from an external phenomenon? Does it really matter?

This false argument about what you have come to call sexual orientation, and the so-called debate that is being called for regarding this matter, are both quite dangerous. I am not saying this for you to go into a fear mode. However, it taps upon the fears of so many. It is scapegoating at its worst. It is the creation of the modern-day lepers, whom everyone would desire to at least quarantine from society, if not exterminate. This is witch-hunting, which creeps up in every society at all times. In this regard it is not an anomaly but merely the outer expression that happens when one's sense of who one is in me is derived solely from the depth of contrast between themselves and what they consider to be lowly. They are pushing the images of people to make them extremely low so that, by contrast and comparison, they can perceive themselves to be high. Life is not a teeter-totter. You cannot weigh somebody down on one side so that you can be lifted up on the other.

8. Carry the message that I am alive and working through all of you

I need you, my Reverend Daughter Deborah. I need you and I need your partner. Why is it that I need you so? It is because I have gifted so many of you who would be classified as gay, lesbian, bisexual, transgendered, queer, or whatever else you are calling yourselves these days. The point here is not in the classification. The point here is that there are way too many of you to waste. There are way too many of you who I have blessed exceedingly. The irony is that everybody knows this, even the ones who are persecuting you. They know that you are in so many instances the creative spark, the imagination, the humor of their society. What would the Black church (in particular) be without all of you? The very songs that warm the hearts of so many, the rhythms that they clap and dance to, the melodies that continue to reign in their hearts . . . I have given these to come through so many of you who are now being plagued by this catastrophic plague of self-righteousness.

The Sacred Yes

When individuals take the abomination that is their superiority and try to inflict it upon other people as the projection of inferiority, then those who are inflicted often go into hiding. They run from me. They hide from me. They hide from themselves. They hide from each other. There's just a lot of running around and hiding. I need you, Deborah, all that you are, available to me. I need you available. I need you to carry a message through your words. Through your songs. Through your music. Through your life. The message that I need you to carry is that I am alive and well and working through all of you. The message that you are to carry is as old as Scripture itself. People keep talking about "in the name of Jesus." However, it truly might serve them better if they were to cue into the prophetic name of this one called Jesus, that is to say, if they were to pray in the name of Immanuel, "God is with us." Can you feel the difference in that, my child? When people are praying in the name of Jesus, they move to this blood-stained, martyr-on-the-cross image. However, if they were to pray in his prophetic name, Immanuel, then maybe they would understand it better. You must spread this word. You must be a shining light. Do you hide your light under a bushel? Can a city on a hill be hidden? "Ye are the light of the world." "Ye are the salt of the earth." You must keep moving on in consciousness lest you, like Lot's wife, be turned into salt.

The issue of addiction (which also involves much comparing and contrasting), so prevalent in your society, must always be dealt with in the context of spiritual availability. If you think "availability" more than you think "addiction," then the entire recovery process will be easier for all of you to understand. What addictions do is keep people tied into false notions of who they are. They are tied up in this same comparing and contrasting because somewhere deep within their psyche they are not enough. There are always people who are better than they, those in control over them, those who must somehow be pleased, so there is much hiding and secrecy. Instead of

9. Be in the world but not of it

blossoming, growing, and nurturing the plants and the seeds that have been given to them as talents and skills, they subdue these creative urges with all types of substances, relationships, and activities.

Oh, you must "come out from among them," my child. This is part of what it means to be in the world but not of it. As for longings that you, any of you, desire to have taken away from you . . . these desires will simply melt away. Just as the fog dissipates with the rays of the sun, there is nothing left. Your love for me is like the rays of the sun. When you stop contrasting and comparing yourself to other people and other things, then you will commune with my rays daily. You will not need any artificial or external stimuli to seduce you into our intimacy. I know the struggles of your heart. I don't compare you to anyone else and neither should you. Just become available. I want you to play, to let the child within you out. Go on a vacation. Remember the root of "vacation" is "vacate." Empty the storage bins so that you will become increasingly available to me. I love you, I love all of you. Who you are in me is sufficient. ⚘

VI. MARRIAGE

There is a great deal of public concern arising over the commitment that you know of as marriage. There has come to be a convolution between this concept of marriage as it exists in the sacred and how it exists in the secular. Furthermore, there has come to be a convolution between what this concept means in the spiritual world and what it means in the religious world to such an extent that religions have grown to believe that they have a monopoly upon everything that is sacred. Furthermore, there has also come to be a convolution between the secular and the civil, such that attempts are being made to address and accommodate all secular approaches to this concept through your civil codes. So herein is the dilemma (and you thought that dilemmas were simply between two things). You have the sacred, which is analogous to or synonymous with the spiritual; you have the religious; you have the secular; and you have the civil. I have things to say about them all. However, I am not as concerned about the discussions, arguments, debates, initiatives, reforms, and referendums occurring in the realm of the civil as the result of changing secular attitudes and ideas. I do have much to say about the concept of marriage as it relates to the sacred world of the spiritual vis-à-vis its application in the world of religion.

Why do I have so much to say about this matter? It is because my name has been drawn into, thrown, manipulated, contrived, brought into, and used as an excuse for much of the activity that is happening in this realm. This does not please me. It never pleases me when I am used, scapegoated, utilized for the purpose of furthering a religious agenda that has at its core practices of exclusivity rather than inclusivity. I speak to you now through my dear Reverend Daughter, Deborah

1. The spiritual, religious, secular, and civil have become convoluted

Johnson, at this moment because I want my position to be understood. Do not, I repeat, do not discount what I have to say here just because it is coming through this one who I have chosen. It is a tendency that you do too much. You call it "shooting the messenger," in your culture. By discounting the messenger it allows you to believe that the message is not valid. Do not even bother to go there (as you would say). Do not waste your time in this manner. Just listen and absorb these words and let your heart embrace their deepest intent.

2. I have never ever sanctioned any one particular form of marriage

Contrary to popular belief, I have never, I repeat, *I have never, ever, ever, ever, ever sanctioned ANY one particular form of what you call marriage.* The various forms of expression that marriage takes are of no concern to me, as long as the form of expression is in alignment with the growth, development, and nurturing of all parties concerned, and respects their spiritual nature. Notice that I said "all parties concerned." I don't really care who gets married to who, what shape or form their marriage takes, or how many individuals are involved. You have developed many classifications in this arena. You have open marriages, you have polygamy, you have monogamy, you have serial monogamy, etc. You have thought of and come up with so many creative things. But you have gotten into the letter of the Law and have forgotten what the Spirit is about.

Human beings have the capacity to grow long-term attachments to things and to stick with these attachments through the long haul. Some species come together to mate, procreate, raise their young, and then part, to do it all over again. And their life spans and life cycles can accommodate these shifts and changes in their partnering. Their existence is not on a level of consciousness where soul nurturance is required in their relationships. They operate more on the level of instinctual patterns. What they give to each other and to their young has far more to do with survival than with progressive, evolutionary, spiritual growth and awareness of themselves in me.

Human beings, because of their life spans and life cycles, take a very long time to develop. A human child takes many years to grow to a point of maturation. It takes a certain degree of commitment, stability, consistency in child rearing in order for a child to grow into a fully actualized human being who feels safe and secure in the world and is aware of his or her creative potentials. How this child rearing occurs, however, is something that is quite variable, depending upon the circumstances at hand. Whether this happens in nuclear families, extended families, kibbutzes, communal living arrangements, communes, or any other setup that you humans may create is of no concern to me as long as the love, growth, development, and respect for the children's deep spirituality is involved.

As human beings, you long for the attachment to the young that you give birth to and that you have as offspring. However, this idea of procreation and child rearing is merely one aspect of the notion of why people come together to marry. Not all individuals who come together to marry will, in fact, procreate. There is no spiritual law or requirement that the individuals who come into this world must procreate. In fact, many of your religious societies, organizations, and institutions have held celibacy and the lack of child rearing so high on a pedestal that childlessness is revered as a higher state of spiritual consciousness. It is ironic, however, that many of these same religious organizations, institutions, and societies will simultaneously tell the people that the rearing of children is the highest and most spiritually enlightened state in which to exist as a human being. So on the one hand, you are revered if you are a mother, and on the other, you are revered if you are a monk—and all coming from the same institutions. I am unconcerned about all of this. I have never sanctioned any one particular form of marriage.

3. Procreation is not a spiritual requirement

4.
Institutionalized religious marriages have become political matters

Why is there marriage in the first place? There is marriage because people tend to want to marry. There is marriage because of deep bonds and commitments that people make to each other. What is the rationale, reasoning, motivation, and intent behind many of these marriages? You human beings have created all of these various structures and then are holding me accountable for overseeing them. Furthermore, you are holding others accountable for their relationship with me, depending upon how they uphold the rules, regulations, policies, procedures, and protocols of these various forms of marital expressions that you have created. I am unconcerned about all of this. I am infuriated by the notion that I require that you stay in these agreements that you have made by your own choices or by the acquiescing of your power into the hands of others to whom you have given control of your lives.

Remember that I really do not have human emotions, but I speak to you in this way so that you may understand the depth and the intensity of what is in fact going on. I say that I am infuriated because so many of these religiously institutionalized versions of marriages have really been political matters tied up in civil codes and secular attitudes. They have been much, much, much more about control, manipulation, domination, yea, even possession of another human being, than about anything else. I have never sanctioned any person being the chattel or the property of another person. Furthermore, I never hold anyone responsible for vows or pledges that they have made out of obligation, pressure, coercion, or anything other than their deep heart. Throughout the centuries many of your societies have created circumstances where individuals who married did not even know each other before the wedding. These marriages were prearranged by parents, grandparents, or other elders within those societies. These marriages were arranged for what people considered to be the good of the parties to be married and the good of the entire society. The individuals exchanging the vows never really, in fact, had any notion of what it was that they were committing to.

Be this as it may, marriage is still a very sacred and spiritual matter when the individuals involved choose each other. There is a deepening of the heart, of the soul, of their experiences of their life on earth when there is someone who they are able to share their lives with and grow and spiritually mature with. Sexuality in this form of expression is at its pinnacle of both physical and emotional satisfaction. I create the space for each and every person to choose to bond, partner, marry anyone whom they choose to marry at their deepest heart level. Many marriages are not officially sanctioned by either church or the state. Marriages do not have to be sanctioned by me either. However, as with all things, I provide "all needs met." Therefore, if individuals have chosen the arena of marriage as the place where they want to grow, learn, and experience themselves as spiritual beings in the context of relating to another individual . . . then so be it. I will support them in this endeavor.

5. When individuals choose each other, marriage is a spiritual matter

However, just as it says in the old Chinese saying, "Life is a dance and sometimes we change partners." It is perfectly fine if individuals change partners along the way, if, in fact, the change is in keeping with the deep spiritual insight and message that they have gotten for fulfilling their spiritual journeys. I am no respecter of forms, just as I am no respecter of persons. I will put you in so-called marriages and I will take you out of them, if that is what you need in order to fulfill your great mission in life. There may be that time when you must heed that call to "Drop your nets and follow me." The dropping at the moment is the dropping of everything. Absolutely nothing can be placed higher than your relationship with me.

Ultimately, a marriage, like any holy relationship, should bring the individuals closer to me. Ultimately, in a marriage the individuals are able to practice with each other the best of their spirituality and are able to heal with each other their deep places of human woundedness. Ultimately, in a marriage the individuals understand that the love that they have for each other is merely a re-presentation of the love that I have for each of them. In this

6. Marriage as a holy relationship should bring people closer to me

context they are really learning how to be spiritual beings in the world and essentially practicing on each other all of the spiritual discipline that they will need in order to evolve into an awareness of themselves as a Christ. With each other they are learning about forgiveness, commitment, communion, fellowship, service, the sharing of joy, nurturing, support, and all of the other things that are necessary in order for one to be fully actualized in his or her highest spiritual awareness, which I lovingly in this moment refer to as Christ Consciousness (not to be confused with the personage of Jesus).

7. I am unconcerned about your civil and cultural practices

As for this notion of the civil and the sacred, the idea of a license to marry that is issued from the state is such a relatively new concept within the scheme of the world's history and is still a foreign concept in many parts of the world. The state has no right to license someone to marry or not marry on a spiritual plane. For accountability purposes, since this commitment is associated on a civil level with certain rights—civil rights and privileges—it is understandable that there must be some form of formal accounting. However, the purpose of this is exclusion, not inclusion. What do I mean when I say this? The granting and the monitoring of the marriage licenses are to insure that no one else has access to the goods, inheritance, wealth, resources, privileges, and entitlements of the individual to whom one is committed. It is like putting a copyright or a patent on the life of another and getting "royalties" for everything that happens out of that relationship. This is not a criticism, merely an observation. Prenuptial agreements, special arrangements, all kinds of proceedings . . . you can create as many of these as you desire. However, just make certain that all of these activities ultimately bring you back closer to a sense of your authenticity in your spirituality. If they do anything other than that, then I recommend that you give them a second, or a third, look (as you would say). I do not need anything that would divert your attention away from the real matters at hand.

Historically speaking, the rites, passages, and rituals of marriage have been created by the individual cultures involved; the notion of a government participating in this was no place to be seen, or to be found. It is still this way in many parts of the world. There are all types of rituals created to celebrate the lives, ancestries, histories, and traditions of the tribe. You have come associate the word "tribe" with primitive cultures; however, I use this term to talk about the extreme ethnocentricity that is involved in the development of these ritualistic patterns. I do not interfere with these anymore than I interfere with how people celebrate the births of individuals, the death transitions of individuals, the birthdays, anniversaries, the growing into puberty and adulthood—any of these so-called rites of passage that as humans you use to celebrate and mark your life experience on the face of the earth. Even the idea of a preacher, a holy person, a shaman, or just someone around to perform the ritual is also very culturally laden. I have no concerns about this.

8. Your loyalty and fidelity to me are mirrored in your marriages

Regarding the notion of adultery, what are my edicts on this, especially as they relate to the Scriptures and to the types of moral and ethical codes that you have built your society upon? The idea of not committing adultery is really not so much about not engaging in sexual activity with someone other than the person with whom you are married. It is true that when this edict was given in a most dramatic way, it was necessary to bring order on the people. Without societal order there is indeed chaos. However, when the order comes at the expense of individualized expressions of me, then the order has become too restrictive. The purpose of the order should be like the purpose of traffic laws, which allow every individual to make it on his or her spiritual journey without interference by or from other individuals. The traffic laws are for inclusivity, not exclusivity. This is how all of the spiritual laws should be written and interpreted. Furthermore, all of your civil laws and codes should be born out of this same consciousness.

What is the problem and difficulty with adultery, and why did I say anything about it in the first place? Remember that the marriage between two individuals is an emulation of the relationship that they have with me. It is a question of loyalty and fidelity. As I said in Scripture, "How can you say that you love me whom you can't see and do not love your brother whom you do see?" If you cannot be faithful in your commitments and obligations to the ones who you are sharing your lives with, then how can you be committed to me? If you are lying to each other, how can you be truthful to me? If you are not honest with each other, how can you be honest with me? If you have lust and desires in your heart that would take your attention away from being fully present and available in your home life, then how are you going to be fully available and present in your spiritual life with me? The ban on adultery was really more about being present and available where you are, in the commitments where you are. And, furthermore, if you could not do this . . . then be honest about it and remove yourself from the circumstances and the situations, and free the other people involved to be able to go on and pursue their hearts' desires.

9. Marital agreements don't always reflect your spiritual Truth

I never require individuals to stay together in abusive relationships simply because they have made some sort of vow or commitment to each other in a public or religious arena. I am not for people abandoning anyone simply to abandon them. However, too many of the agreements that you have made about marriages were not based upon the truth of who you are in your spiritual power. And just like the house that cannot be built upon the shifting sand, so it is with your human marital structures. If they are not built upon the solid rock of truth, then when the winds and the rains come around, the fall will be great. Many of you are experiencing this fall now in what you refer to as separation and divorces because the ground upon which you built your marital house was shaky sand to begin with. Build your house upon the rock and it is more likely to withstand the trials and tribulations of this world.

As for this prominent issue that is before you in the moment regarding marriage between persons of the same gender, the same sex . . . as I have said before, I haven't sanctioned any so-called outer forms of marriage of any kind with anybody anyway, which is to say that I have never done anything or said anything that would be a sanction against such. Individuals are free in their hearts to love anyone. Even in your so-called heterosexual relationships, the love between the husband and the wife may not be the deepest love of their hearts. They may love their children more, they may love the nuclear families in which they were born more, they may love their friends more, or even their jobs (which is becoming increasingly common).

If the individuals are able to come together in honesty and in truth, if their relationship is able to bring them closer to me, if they are able to practice with each other the loving, growing, nurturing, caring for, giving, and all of the other spiritual disciplines that I spoke of earlier . . . then so be it. I would not be the one to interfere with such. Quite the contrary, through the Divine laws of attraction, I am perfectly fine with providing every individual with his or her needs. When you really understand the realm of the Spirit, you will learn how completely fallacious this whole discussion about homosexuals being able to marry or not marry truly is. Again, it is very, very ethnocentric thinking. From a historical and anthropological standpoint, there have been many societies that have recognized the sanctity of these relationships. This issue is turning into a political herring for all the wrong purposes. If I were the type of God who would sanction things, then it would not be a blanket sanction on heterosexuals any more than it would be a blanket condemnation of homosexuals. If I were the kind to sanction, I would only sanction the ones that were in alignment with spiritual Truth and Principle. The genders really don't matter.

10. I have no sanctions for or against marriages based on gender

11. In Spirit there is no gender

In actuality, in Spirit there is no gender. You had no gender before you were born, and you do not remain a gender after you make your transition. Even those of you who believe in heaven and the Pearly Gates say that in heaven there is no woman or man, that there are no colors or races, that there is only a Oneness. If you understood that heaven is always right here on earth, then you would know that the same is true right here on earth now. Whether one assumes the body of a male or female in any given lifetime from a physiological standpoint is, in fact, rather "pot luck" (as you would say). On a higher spiritual plane, however, there is a certain degree of choice in this matter, albeit often unknown to the ones making the choice. There are different things to be learned from life's experiences depending upon if one goes through life from the perspective of a male or a female at this point in time in history. So the choosing, conscious or unconscious, of a particular gender in which to incarnate is usually tied to the spiritual work that is at hand for this individual in this particular incarnation. And yes, you do incarnate on more than one occasion. There is "business" (as you would say) that oftentimes needs to be finished between individuals, and they come together and marry in order to complete the cycles that are uniquely theirs to complete. They recognize each other at a deep soul level, and the fact that they are not the appropriate gender to be able to marry each other on a civil level cannot interfere with the deep spiritual level that is at hand. In these instances, these individuals go up against the laws of the society in order to live out the destinies that are theirs to live out and to learn what is necessary for them to learn in this particular incarnation.

12. All love should mirror back my love and be celebrated

Any marriage can be a heaven or a hell. This is not dependent upon the genders of the parties involved, their sexual orientation, or much of anything from the exterior world that one might consider to be part of one's demographic profile. I want all individuals to treat each other with dignity, respect, and the awareness that all human beings, especially the one or ones with whom they are partnered, are very beautiful and special individuals in the scheme of the world. Marriage should mirror back my love. Marriage should create synergies so that the individuals are able to create more together than they were able to create apart. However, once again, I am unconcerned as to how this format is laid out. In some societies all of the men stay together and all of the women stay together, and that's just how it is. In some societies it's multigenerations sharing a roof, or some other kind of communal arrangement. (And, once again, I am not concerned.) I am never concerned with outer forms of expressions. "This too shall pass."

The restrictions that are able to be placed upon these marriages from a civil, "secular" standpoint never cease to amaze me. There is an understanding of how you would want individuals to have so-called legal capacities. However, throughout history, especially your American history, you have placed all kinds of restrictions on individuals' abilities to marry for any number of reasons, including their race, economic status, residency, religious background, gender, sexual orientation, and on and on. There has been such a fear of interracial marriages or commingling of classes and/or religions. It is really sad that so many hearts have been broken over this through the years, especially when family members in their narrow-mindedness have gone against the wishes and the true loves of other family members in order to enforce some more rigid interpretation of what is appropriate. I do not require broken hearts; the coming together of love should never divide families. There is no reason why all love cannot be celebrated equally. Furthermore, the same type of demands that I make for integrity, loyalty, commitment, nurturance, caring, and child rearing, if that is a part of the family structure . . . are the same requirements for all couples. I do not have different sets of rules and principles depending upon who the individuals are. I am not that type of a God. I am not arbitrary and fickle. The same discipline stands for everyone.

13. Create societies in which all individuals are equal and valued

I love you all. And yes, it is definitely a spiritual and sacred right for any individuals to marry. I place no restrictions on this, and you humans would do well to review your restrictions, as well. You ask, "Well, what about polygamy, what about this thing and that thing?" Well, what about it? As you can see even from the Scriptures that you say that you love so much, I have never put a restriction on one's accessibility to their spiritual power and potential in me based upon the number of partners that they have had. Abraham had more than one wife, as did David, Solomon, all of your great Old Testament heroes. The same is also true in what you refer to as the New Testament. Even in Biblical days, because of the economic structures and systems, male siblings were allowed to, if not required to, marry the widows of their deceased male siblings. That is to say, a brother was to marry his brother's widow, should that family need to be taken care of.

Why does all of this matter? There is such a fear that if you do not maintain certain structures, that all hell and damnation will break loose, that your entire society will fall. Pay more attention to your heart and your mind than you do your outer structures. If there is shifting sand, it is not the outer forms and structures that are your big concern. Check out your hearts, check out your minds. The problem here is your lack of forgiveness, your hardened hearts, your lusts, your desires, your materialism, and your deep need to use each other and to possess each other as trophies and for security. The problem here is your lack of economic equality that would keep individuals bound to each other or seeking out marriage as a form of economic survivalship. Open up your hearts. Open up your minds. Create societies in which all individuals are valued and equaled. You will find that the individuals who will gain the most in their spirituality from partnering together will naturally come to understand this and will choose to partner with each other in manners that reflect their integrity and dignity. And your society is a big enough place to be able to accommodate the tremendous diversity and variety of expression that is a unique part of its fabric and fiber.

Love. Commit. Share. Grow. Give each other free choice and free will. Don't own or possess anybody. Give each other equal opportunity and equal access. Do not project onto others all of the cultural values of your own society. Honor these differences even in the midst of changing mores. I understand the fears, but don't scapegoat gay and lesbian people for the downfall of heterosexual marriages. Check out the foundations upon which your traditional marriages have been laid. There is much work to be done. Do it in Truth and in Spirit.

VII. MARRIAGE AS A COMMITMENT

1. Marriage is symbolic of the commitment one has with me

What is marriage? In the most colloquial sense, it is the union, the coming together, of two souls in a state of holy matrimony. However, marriage is so much more than the commitment between two people. Marriage is symbolic of commitment, period. And since all comes from me, marriage is symbolic of the commitment that one has with me. And what is this commitment that one has with me other than the commitment that one has towards one's own self, as the understanding of oneself as me? There is very little understanding of this point. Thus, there is very little understanding in your society of commitment, especially marriage.

You have grown to associate marriage with rules, conditions, laws, legalities, societal traditions, hierarchical institutions, and the like. Thus it has lost its savor. It has become complicated, diluted, and convoluted with all of your hopes, fears, and anxieties. You must listen to your inner voice and learn who I am more than you must honor what has grown to be your understandings of your human traditions.

2. Don't identify with traditions more than you identify with me

Tradition is not of my making; it is of yours. I have no need for tradition, for I am the real thing. Your traditions are supposedly for the purpose of reenacting a state of consciousness that reminds you that you are more than the outer world. Tradition is to remind you that you are spiritual beings going through human experiences. It is not for you to get caught up in the experiences to the point that you identify with them more than you do me. Tradition is supposedly to bring you back to me. However, your traditions only bring you back to yourselves and away from each other, simultaneously.

You fight over traditions. Your egos individually and collectively want to believe that they know what is right for themselves and everyone else. You get into your ethnocentric thinking, in the realm of believing that your traditions are the best. In order to find me, you must shed your traditions. You must let go of your notions about me to find me. In order to find yourselves, you must let go of the seeds that have been planted in your heads by your society regarding who you are relative to one another. There is no authenticity in that; there is only mimicking, imitation, which leads to exasperation and frustration.

In this arena you can never be enough because you can never emulate another enough to satisfy his or her tastes. You can never be successful enough at being someone else, or at being someone who others think you should be. Commitment requires that you shed your false expectations and learn to deal with what is real. Very little is real in the world that you live in. Your norms, your standards, your mores, and the like are all based on faulty ideas of who you are. They do not honor the Spirit and your magnificence. They fail to realize and recognize that you are the most important thing in the Universe and that you have powers immeasurable.

3. Norms, standards, and mores do not honor Spirit and your magnificence

You have built straitjackets for yourself and then consider yourselves failures because your were not able to dance the Dance of Life in them. You have restricted and limited your thinking, your passions, your creativity, and everything else of any true value in your world, for fear that you would step out of line and not be acceptable any more. For the sake of receiving the commitment from others to love, nurture, and accept you, all of you have compromised your very beingness to the point that none of you know who you are in your truest nakedness and beauty.

4. To find who you are, you must marry your own divinity

To find who you are, you must marry me. You must marry your own divinity and let it be in the forefront of your life. When you are partnered with me, then you judge everything from the standpoint of its impact on our relationship. Think how different your life would be if you did not do anything that negatively impacted our ability to commune with and support one another. Think what your life would be like if everyone knew that you were my beloved, and we had an open marriage that allowed us to share our love with everyone else.

The notion of an open marriage has gotten a bad rap in your society because you have prostituted and bastardized the concept. Open marriage, to you, has been an excuse not to commit to anyone in particular rather than to commit to everyone in the whole. Your open marriage has been an opportunity for you to follow your lusts and abandon your true responsibilities for the pleasure of the moment. Your notion of open marriage is driven by sensation and neediness. In it one is sacrificed for another. It is selfish and self-centered and rarely has the benefit of the beloved as a primary consideration. You are the center of your universe, and you are then willing to suffer the consequences. You are willing to "do the time" because the crime seems so worth it.

I really don't care how many people you are intimate with, only that you are intimate in the truest sense. Many of you fear intimacy with one person because you believe that it interferes with your ability to be intimate with others. What a joke! You are not truly intimate with anyone, in most cases. Adding on more people does not increase your depth. Most of you turn to someone else, something else, to give your attention to when you reach that point of necessary surrender with another. Rather than surrendering, you invest your time in something else that reinforces your false sense of being hurt, victimized, or your false sense of being free and successful.

The challenge is for you to come to me first, for you to under-stand that we are One with each other. When you know that this is the foundation upon which you stand, then it is easy for you to reach out, to get outside of yourself, to know what it means that there is really only One of us here. To most of you, marriage is a commitment to one particular thing above another. In actuality, all marriage is a commitment to me that enables you to commit to anything and everything that you perceive as an intricate part of yourself. Everyone cannot nur-ture everyone else on an individual basis. This is humanly impossible.

However, when you are One with me, there is a space in your heart that allows you to bless all and to desire for all what you desire for yourself. No longer are you looking out for number one, for your own selves and your own families. All families are important to you, and you create an environment that is supportive of everyone "making it." When you marry me in your job, it transforms the experience from drudgery into an opportunity to minister, to be a blessing unto the world. We are there to procreate, to create more, to transform the raw material into what it needs to be. And it matters not what your employment is. When it is done in my name, our name, then it becomes a gift to the Universe.

You are a gift unto the Universe, and what a precious gift you are! Give your gift. Make everything about your life a gift. You are a gift to me and to each other. I love you. I love you all. I always have and I always will. ❧

5. Marrying me transforms your work from drudgery to ministry

TITLES OF RELATED INTEREST
BY NEW BRIGHTON BOOKS

Living the Sacred Yes:
Affirmations for Action

Rev. Deborah L. Johnson

This companion, pocket-size book is a
collection of affirmations that help us
to live the spiritual principles outlined
in *The Sacred Yes*, volume one of *Letters
from the Infinite*. These affirmations
propel us into action as we put them
into daily practice. Easily tucked into

pockets, purses, and backpacks, this take-along *Affirmations for Action*
will inspire and enable us to be more effective in our efforts to live the
Sacred Yes.

$9.95 • PAPER • 4 X 6 • ISBN 0-9718377-1-6
AVAILABLE OCTOBER 2002

Rise Above

Valerie Joi Fiddmont

This CD is a sweet, soulful, spiritual journey of healing and transformation. Through the rhythms
of jazz, gospel, and R&B, you are
encouraged to rise above your
challenges and explore your own

personal relationship with the Divine. Valerie Joi is the composer and
arranger on all songs. Rev. Deborah Johnson is the lyricist on several
songs and co-producer of the project.

$15.00 • © 2002 TRUJOI MUSIC

We hope you enjoyed this New Brighton Books title. If you would like to receive information about additional New Brighton books and products please contact:

New Brighton Books
P.O. Box 1674
Aptos, CA 95001-1674

www.newbrightonbooks.com

To place an order call toll free 800 919-1779